Community
of
Citizens

Community of Citizens

On the Modern Idea of Nationality

Dominique Schnapper

With a preface by Daniel Bell
Translated from the French
by Séverine Rosée

Routledge
Taylor & Francis Group
LONDON AND NEW YORK

Originally published in French by Editions Gallimard, © Editions Gallimard, Paris, 1994.

Published 1998 by Transaction Publishers

Published 2017 by Routledge
2 Park Square, Milton Park, Abingdon, Oxon OX14 4RN
711 Third Avenue, New York, NY 10017

First issued in paperback 2017

Routledge is an imprint of the Taylor and Francis Group, an informa business

Copyright © 1998 by Dominique Schnapper.

All rights reserved. No part of this book may be reprinted or reproduced or utilised in any form or by any electronic, mechanical, or other means, now known or hereafter invented, including photocopying and recording, or in any information storage or retrieval system, without permission in writing from the publishers.

Notice:
Product or corporate names may be trademarks or registered trademarks, and are used only for identification and explanation without intent to infringe.

Library of Congress Catalog Number: 97-40882

Library of Congress Cataloging-in-Publication Data

Schnapper, Dominique.
  [Communauté des citoyens. English]
  Community of citizens : on the modern idea of nationality / Dominique Schnapper ; preface by Daniel Bell ; translated from the French by Séverine Rosée.
    p. cm.
  ISBN 1-56000-351-0 (alk. paper)
  1. Nationalism. 2. Nation state. I. Title.
JC311.S2913   1997
320.54—dc21   97-40882
                                                                              CIP

ISBN 13: 978-1-138-50834-7 (pbk)
ISBN 13: 978-1-56000-351-9 (hbk)

Contents

	Preface *Daniel Bell*	vii
	Introduction	1
1.	Definitions	15
2.	The Political and the National	35
3.	Transcendence by Citizenship	65
4.	The Institution of National Uniqueness	95
5.	Conceiving the Nation	131
	Conclusion	155
	Works Cited	171
	Index of Names	177
	Index of Places and Themes	181

Preface

Daniel Bell

Dominique Schnapper, née Aron, is one of the leaders of the third generation of French post-World War II sociology.

French sociology before World War II was dominated by the intellectual legacy of Émile Durkheim, who died in 1917. The major figures were Maurice Halbwachs, Paul Fauconnet, and Celestin Bouglé in sociology, Marcel Mauss (Durkheim's nephew) in anthropology, Georges Davy (who was director of the École Normale Supérieure) in law, and Marcel Granet in Chinese civilization. The famous *Annales* group, founded by Marc Bloch and Lucien Febvre, showed Durkheim's influence in their emphases on *mentalités* and social structure.

Yet, despite Durkheim's work on suicide, little empirical investigation was undertaken in this period. The reasons were varied. There was, in large part, the traditional philosophical distrust of empiricism as wayward and contingent, as against *la logique*, the underlying structure of knowledge. (As Claude Lévi-Strauss describes the classical method in his *Tristes Tropiques*: "there are two choices; take one.") And there was a paucity of chairs of sociology: one at the Sorbonne occupied by Fauconnet, one at Strasbourg (where Durkheim had taught) occupied by Halbwachs, one at Bordeaux. Research funds were almost nil; only after World War II was sociological research introduced into L'Ecole Pratique des Hautes Études (where graduate seminars are held), with the support of the Rockefeller Foundation, and the CNRS.

More important for sociology, however, was the decline of the Durkheim legacy itself. Durkheim had espoused a rational secularism and in his image of the moral order had proposed, in effect, a civil religion identical with the Third Republic and humanism. But in the years of the Depression, of heightened class conflict, the rise and success of fascism and a looming war, the Durkheimian view of society comprising a moral center seemed anachronistic, if not irrelevant.

The first generation of post-World War II sociologists—Jean Stoetzal, Georges Friedmann, and Raymond Aron—had been members of Celestin Bouglé's Centre de Documentation at the École Normale Supérieure—one still needed to be a *normalien* as the path to teaching positions. Though Bouglé had been a Durkheimian, his students rejected the inheritance. Aron, who had gone off to Germany to study, in the early 1930s, became influenced by Max Weber (who had been entirely ignored by Durkheim and never mentioned in his magazine *L'Année Sociologique*) and brought Weber to France. Friedmann (originally a philosopher and a student of Leibniz) was influenced by Le Play (though that was not acknowledged) and undertook studies of work and the rationalization of work by the machine process. Stoetzel, a social psychologist, became interested in public opinion, polling, and survey research. The three were joined by Georges Gurvitch, a Russian émigré who had spent the war years in the United States, and who constructed his own system of phenomenology.

But, again, institutional positions were few. In 1952, the teaching positions in sociology in the faculty of letters were hardly more numerous than in 1910. Davy and Gurvitch held the two chairs at the Sorbonne. Stoetzel taught in Bordeaux. Friedmann had a chair at the Conservatoire National des Arts et Métiers (originally an evening school for workingmen who sought technical training). These men became the *patrons* for those who desired advancement in sociology and they dominated the juries of the grand examinations, in particular, the doctorat d'Etat, the major sign of achievement and recognition. Aron taught part-time at "Sciences Po," while concentrating on journalism. Recognition came relatively late in his academic life, first with a chair at the Sorbonne and at École Pratique des Hautes Études, and then to a chair at the Collège de France, the most prestigious institution in French academic life.

Gurvitch had few students. (At the examination of Michel Crozier for the doctorat d'Etat, on his book the *Bureaucratic Phenomenon*—these were celebrated events and were reported in *Le Monde*—Gurvitch accused Crozier of subverting French intellectual life with American methods of research, and thus abetting "American imperialism." Crozier was defended by Aron). Stoetzel and Friedmann were the patrons of the younger *normaliens*, Boudon and Touraine. Aron, who stood aside from academic politics was the major intellectual influence, though the Centre de Sociologie Européene, which he headed with support from the Ford Foundation, sponsored the work of Michel Crozier, Jacques Lautmann, and Pierre Bourdieu, who broke with Aron after 1968.

Claude Lévi-Strauss once remarked that sociology was not a discipline with a specific field, but an attitude: "therefore one does not need to be a sociologist to do sociology." In the postwar years, in effect, there were two sociologies: the sociology of Saint-Germain des Prés, and the academic sociology that expanded with the growth of research groups.

The sociology of Saint-Germain des Prés had its roots in the existentialism of Jean-Paul Sartre, the Marxism of Louis Althusser, the radical Nietzscheanism of Michel Foucault, the subliminal psychoanalysis of Jacques Lacan, the literary ethnography of Roland Barthes and Edgar Morin (whose patron, initially, was Georges Friedmann), the deconstructionism of Jacques Derrida, the postmodernism of Jean-François Lyotard, and the pop sociology (frothing like instant coffee) of Jean Baudrillard. There is an old observation that intellectual fashions, like couture, originate in France and sell in the United States. (I leave aside the structural anthropology of Claude Lévi-Strauss, with his heroic, if overweening, effort to find a rational underlying structure of the human mind which would encompass all levels of social exchange from economics to communication to kinship.)

Sociology as an academic discipline was established by the second generation, and largely by four men who gained international reputations—Raymond Boudon, Pierre Bourdieu, Alain Touraine, and Michel Crozier. To these one can add the late François Bourricaud, Georges Balandier, Henri Mendras, Jean-Daniel Reynaud, and Eric de Dampierre.

What is crucial about these men, particularly the first four, is that they established research groups which acted as a training center for students, and their extraordinary productivity (each of the four has published more than a dozen books, growing out of their research). Boudon runs the Groupe d'Étude des Methodes de l'Analyse Sociologique; Touraine, the Centre d'Étude des Mouvement Sociaux; Crozier, the Centre de Sociologie des Organizations; and Bourdieu, the Centre de Sociologie de l'Education et de la Culture and is the director of *Actes de la recherche en sciences sociales*, a journal he founded in 1975 as the outlet for his studies.

The fields that have covered are vast. Boudon has written on social mobility, the unintended consequences of planned actions, methodological individualism, and more recently on Simmel. Touraine has focused on social movements, tracking each new one with alacrity, and on postindustrial society.*

---

* His conception, understandably, differs from mine. As he has written: "Despite my personal efforts, the idea of postindustrial society, introduced by Daniel Bell, has

Bourdieu has charted the social reproduction of society through cultural mechanisms as against the older Marxist emphasis on economic property relations. Crozier has studied organizations and bureaucracies and the way they inhibit change. Each has given rise to new vocabularies: Bourdieu, *habitus* (durable systems of dispositions which condition the collective responses of social groups); Crozier, *la société bloquée*; Boudon, *effets pervers*; Touraine, *action sociology*.

All have achieved prominent positions in French academic and intellectual life. Boudon, a professor at the Sorbonne, was elected to the Academie des Sciences Morales et Politiques. Bourdieu is at the Collège de France. Crozier has been given the Prix Tocqueville. They direct publishing programs at major houses: Boudon at the Presses Universitaires de France, Bourdieu at Editions de Minuit, Touraine at Le Seuil.

What is striking about these men (and some of the others I have cited), is their deep involvement with American academic life. Boudon spent considerable time at Colombia, working with Paul Lazarsfeld at the Bureau of Applied Social Research, learning mathematical sociology, as well as teaching at Harvard. Bourdieu for a number of years has spent a quarter teaching at the University of Chicago, and working for a period with James Coleman. Crozier has taught at Harvard and regularly at several California universities. Touraine has written a major assessment of American higher education for the Carnegie Endowment.

As against the fashionable sociology of Saint-Germain des Prés, which has attracted followers among the literary intelligentsia, but rarely understood American society, the academic sociologists have gained a deep understanding of American life even when, as in the instances of Bourdieu and Touraine, they have been critical of American society. But what has been important is that the problems they study, and the methods they use, are part of the common coin of sociology as an international discipline.**

---

maintained the meaning which he gave it. It is seen as a society guided by knowledge, capable of continual adjustments and freedom from fundamental conflict." Except for the last phrase, Touraine is correct in his acknowledgement and characterization. See, Alain Touraine, "The New Social Conflicts," in *French Sociology*, edited by Charles C. Lemert (New York: Columbia University Press, 1981), p. 315.

** To note briefly, the achievements of the others I have cited: François Bourricaud, who died a few years ago, was a specialist in Latin America, an appreciative exponent of Parsonian sociology, and a collaborator with Boudon in his research group. A gentle and beloved figure, he was respected widely in French sociology. Georges Balandier, a transitional figure between the first and second generations, held a chair at the Sorbonne and was the leading specialist on Africa. Jean-Daniel Reynaud, who

And yet. All four have been "established" for more than thirty years each, and have now retired (e.g., Crozier and Touraine) or are on the verge of doing so. The routinization of charisma, to invoke a tired phrase, may be at work, for in the course of its trajectory many hard-working but specialized sociologists have been produced, but few have matched their path-breaking achievements. Much of the strength of French sociology depends upon the third generation that is now coming into its own.

Dominique Schnapper is probably the outstanding person of the third generation of sociologists. She is married to Antoine Schnapper, a leading art historian and professor at the Sorbonne, and mother of three children. She has been extraordinarily productive intellectually, writing to date about a dozen books and over a hundred scholarly articles in a period of less than thirty years. She is surely the major female figure in French sociology. Schnapper took her undergraduate degrees (Diplôme and Licence) in politics, history, and political science at the Institut d'Études Politiques (popularly known as "Sciences Po") and the Sorbonne in 1957 and 1958, and wrote a Doctorat-ès-Lettres (the famous doctorat d'Etat, the magisterial degree), which is rarely taken any longer by sociologists, who are content with the lesser Ph.D. (The doctorat was abolished twice in the intervening years as being too difficult, time-consuming, and unnecessary, though it is now formerly restored.) Since 1981, she has been director of studies at L'École des Hautes Études en Sciences Sociales, the school of graduate studies located on Boulevard Raspail, the central building for history and social studies in Paris. She has served on six government commissions. She is president of the Société Française de Sociologie in the current term, 1995–1999.

Her field, which she has made uniquely her own, has been the study of nationality and minorities in France (though she has also written

---

succeeded Georges Friedmann at the Conservatoire des Arts et Métiers, continued the tradition of research on work. Henri Mendras became the leading authority on French peasants (his doctorat d'Etat was on the *fin de paysan*), but in recent years he has headed a research group on social indicators (the Observatoire Français des Conjonctures Economiques) which publishes its studies under the collective *nom de plume* of Louis Dirn; Mendras also edits *The Tocqueville Review*. Eric de Dampierre, an anthropologist at Nanterre, and head of a research group on linguistics and central Africa, has been the cultural eminence of French social science, in particular because of his publishing role in introducing such varied figures as Leo Strauss and Max Weber through extensive translation, and his direction of the *European Journal of Sociology*.

A representative compilation of essays, by members of this generation, can be found in the aforementioned book edited by Charles C. Lemert, *French Sociology*.

extensively on fields as widely distant as aesthetics and unemployment). Her book, *La France de l'intérgration*, published by Gallimard in 1991, won the prizes of several French academies. A previous book, *Juifs et Israelites*, published by Gallimard in 1980, was published by the University of Chicago Press in 1983, as *Jewish Identities in France*. In addition, she has written about fifty scholarly articles on Jewish life in France, on nationalities and immigration, as well as a prize-winning book on immigration.

The present book, *Community of Citizens: On the Modern Idea of Nationality,* published by Gallimard in 1994, is her masterwork. It was widely reviewed and praised in France on its publication by, among others, François Furet, the great historian, who died a tragic death in July 1997, and Philippe Seguin, the Gaullist political leader. It won the prize of the National Assembly in 1994.

In the last decade, the study of nationalism (along with gender and race) has become the major focus of sociological studies (Gellner, Anderson, Hobsbawm, Liah Greenfeld) as the interest in class has receded. Yet as Professor Schnapper points out, the very term nationalism conflates the political and the ethnic, though the two, she argues, are not the same. It is, in fact, this very difference that is the signal contribution of her book. What she has sought to do is clarify the term *nation*, as an idea and a social fact, and bind the idea of the nation to the integration of society through the community of citizens.

For the sociologist, the central problem of inquiry is the nature of the social bond, the ties of cohesion of individuals in collective entities. Here the central contribution of Professor Schnapper is a set of rigorous definitions and distinctions, and their exemplification in the history of Western societies. Her argument is that what defines a nation is the *political* form, as against the religious and the social, and by the fact of citizenship, individuals are integrated into the society. She contrasts the political bond with the ethnic group—here she employs a neologism, the *ethnie* as the counterpart to the *polity*.

The ethnie are members of a historical and cultural community, often tied by common descent, who emphasize their *particularity*, even when they seek to become a political entity. The polity is multicultural, with the nation as a supra-bond.

It is this emphasis on the political which is essential to Professor Schnapper's argument. The political cannot be reduced to the religious, though this is attempted in theocratic societies, for then other groups in the nation are excluded. And the political differs from the social bond, because of its specificity as a juridical and legal concept. Here Schnapper directly confronts Durkheim, who made the social and moral bond the central ties of a society, for the social tie cannot account for the character of rights and of citizenship, the nature of sovereignty, that defines the political. And against the Marxian tradition which emphasizes conflict as inherent in the political, she argues that the nation integrates the people as a common community of citizens. (This is a way of explaining the fact that despite the claims of internationalism as the basis of solidarity, the French and German working classes, the two most advanced in Europe, fought each other as Frenchman and Germans in two world wars.)

Professor Schnapper's subtle exploration of the nature of the political bond lends her to some startling and convincing statements. Thus, many conservatives claim that secularism undermines a society and call for a "return" to religion. Yet as Schnapper points out, "Secularism in particular is an essential attribute of the modern state, because it allows one to transcend the diversity of religious belongings, to consecrate the privatization of beliefs and practices, and to make the public domain into a religiously neutral place shared in common by all citizens."

The nation has been one of the major sociological developments of the past one hundred years, though most sociologists, as Schnapper points out, Durkheimian and Marxist, have shied away from the subject. Today, however, the major problems are the threats of the decomposition of the nation. Within the nation, she points out, the intensified hedonistic drive for wealth emphasizes individual interests as against common, national allegiances. Multi-ethnic states, not only in the former conglomerates such as the U.S.S.R. and Yugoslavia, but in nations such as Canada, Belgium, and Lebanon are on the verge of flying apart. Religious fundamentalism, as in the Middle East and North Africa, seek to subordinate the political to religious orthodoxy. And with globalization, the defensive steps by nations to create wider economic and political entities, such as the move to the European Community, create dilemmas of national allegiance and identity. In short Professor Schnapper's work forces us to think about the fundamental question of what holds a society together, and the fate of the nation, as we enter the twenty-first century.

Dominique Schnapper, as one knows, is the daughter of Raymond Aron, the leading sociologist of the generation after Max Weber and Émile Durkheim. In recent years, she has spent considerable time and energy in the project of the Friends of the Society of Raymond Aron, to bring together a full collection of his oeuvre and develop his work. Her own work is one of the best testimonials to his character and intellect. The field she has carved out is her own. But she also shows the stamp of the father in the splendid nature of her achievements.

Daniel Bell is the Henry Ford II Professor of Social Science Emeritus of Harvard University and Scholar in Residence of the American Academy of Arts and Sciences. He is also the president of La Société Tocqueville, a French-American organization devoted to carrying out work in the spirit of Tocqueville.

Introduction

The Conceptual Nation and Democracy

We are witnessing today a weakening of public spirit and political bonds. In fact, nothing assures us that in the future the modern democratic nation will retain the capacity to ensure the social ties. Today the globalization of economic exchanges and relations between political units limits political and economic independence and the sovereignty of each nation. Moreover, the internal evolution of democracies, where collective life seems to be concentrated on the means of wealth production and its redistribution, tends to undermine the very political idea which founded the nation. This process has reached a point at which it seems impossible for democracies to demand that their citizens protect themselves with the price of their lives. In a democracy there is no longer any sense of the supreme sacrifice: the individual and his interests have replaced the citizen and his principles. This leads to a retrospective reflection on what was once the presiding logic of the construction and functioning of the nation. It is not, then, a matter of discussing ideas, in the sense of representations that men have made of the nation: *it is the internal logic, or the idea—in the Kantian sense of the term—of the nation that I will attempt to analyze here.*

The Political and Social Tie

This universally observed decline of the nation most often arouses satisfaction and, perhaps, even hope. Many people would agree with the expression proposed by Mario Vargas Llosa at a conference entitled "Democracy Today." Both tyrannical and inefficient, the political fiction of the nation, for him, has served as an excuse for the worse excesses of the twentieth century: "If we consider the blood it made run through history, the way with which it contributed to fomenting prejudices, racism, xenophobia and the lack of understanding between peoples and cultures, the apology it has lent to authoritarianism, totalitarianism, and colonialism, to religious and ethnic genocide, the nation seems to me the privileged example of a malicious imagination."[1]

The national is condemned by its accusers for having given rise to the collective passions, conflicts, and horrors of the twentieth century. It is regrettable that an important South American writer, a democrat, made himself the spokesman for these analyses in all their simplistic allure. Obviously, my task is not to apologize for or to justify convictions or actions as reprehensible as those, which have culminated in the slaughter of human beings and the effacing of civilizations. But at the same time, were great empires, and dynastic and theocratic regimes tolerant and pacific? History has known wars, tyrannies, xenophobia, and genocide before the birth of modern political nations. The Thirty Years War in the seventeenth century was no less costly for Germany than the wars of the twentieth century. It took more time to rebuild its ruins and to repair the misfortunes of the population. In this respect, the uniqueness of the twentieth century owes less to the existence of nations than to the technical efficiency of its instruments of destruction, and specifically, to the fact that it methodically and bureaucratically applied the rational spirit of man toward the ambitious goal of physically eliminating certain peoples in their totality, and formulating and organizing such efforts by means of a State. Once the political order is organized into nations, wars and other constraints of collective life due to the centralization of political life are inevitably national. This does not mean, however, that the national is *in and of itself* responsible for the provocation of conflicts. When the political order is organized into nations, wars are national; when it was founded on dynastic, religious or imperial principles, wars were dynastic, religious or imperial. Merely suppressing nations—"alibis for authoritarianism, totalitarianism, colonialism"—would not be enough for the world to enjoy the global democracy, whose vision Mario Vargas Llosa evoked, founded on peaceful economic exchange and the preservation of small authentic cultures. Nor does it signify that one can conflate all national forms—democratic, authoritarian, or totalitarian—and equally condemn them *without taking into account their political regime*.

Modern democracy arose from a national form. The modern nation, whose democratic ideal was born in England during the sixteenth century, appeared since the American and French Revolutions as the sole legitimate and universal political organization. In all Eastern European nationalist movements of the nineteenth and twentieth centuries, and subsequently in the rest of the world, the claims of national independence and national sovereignty were inseparable from democratic aspirations and the hope of human emancipation. Until World War I, the nation appeared to be the sole means of respecting the truly human in man, that is to say, his autonomy, symbolized by the values of equality and liberty. In this sense, "the nation holds as its principle and final end the participation of all the governed in the State. It is in order to participate in the state that all minorities demand the recognition of their language.... To deny the modern nation is to reject the political advent of the eternal claims of equality."[2]

From that point onward, political legitimacy was no longer founded on dynastic and religious traditions, but instead on the principle of the sovereignty of peoples. Despite their obvious differences, both Fichte in his *Rede an der Deutschen Nation,* written after the Prussian collapse in Jena in 1806, and Renan, in his famous essay, *Qu'est-ce qu'une nation?* written in 1882 after the defeat of France during the war of 1870, respectively pondered this newfound legitimacy. As a source of sovereignty, the nation was not born of nothing, with Sieyès and article 3 of the Declaration of the Rights of Man, asserting that "the principle of all sovereignty resides essentially in the nation. No body, no individual can exercise any authority which is not expressly issued by it." Proclaiming itself in 1789, the nation as a new historical actor inherited the legacy of political centralization and the development of the central State that the monarchy had cultivated for centuries. But the Revolution, by situating political legitimacy hereafter in the will of peoples, symbolically represented a fundamental rupture throughout Europe, one with which we still live.

Beyond the very principle of political legitimacy, the foundation of the social bond itself was called into question. In the age of nations, the political principle replaced the religious or dynastic as the unifier of men. In all democratic nations, the political institutes the social.[3] In a society where, to borrow the language of Tocqueville, hereditary differences of rank were eliminated and the equality of conditions was established, the primary social value ceased being honor—defined by the place an individual occupies within a particular familial or statutory group in a fundamentally unequal and hierarchical society—and became instead the equal dignity of all human beings as ends in themselves. The French Revolution highlighted the principle of radical social and political individualism, when unequal status and ties of dependency between men were abolished on the night of 4 August 1789. Each citizen, invested with a fraction of political legitimacy, would heretofore regard himself as possessed of the same abstractly defined rights and duties consigned and consecrated by the law. Citizenship was not only a juridical and political attribute in the narrow sense of the term. It was a certain means of acquiring social status, the necessary—even if not always the sufficient condition—for the individual to be fully recognized as an actor in collective life.

But the democratic nation nourished a productivist society, one in which individuals progressively became more concerned with material interests and self-satisfaction than with their civic duties. Modern Westerners were unique in forging economic realities into a distinct system. The aristocratic ethos of honor was replaced by a bourgeois work ethic. Today, this productivist-hedonist logic, intimately linked both to the goal of democracy and efficient production, tends to overshadow strictly political values. Employment establishes the position of the individual, organizes his relation both to society and to others, and defines his social and personal identity. Participation in economic life progressively became the essential source of social status. Democracy is justified less by the political values underlying the political goals of major Western democracies—that is, liberty and equality—than by the fact that democracy allows all its members to partake of the benefits of collective wealth. All this demonstrates the predominance of the economic and social dimensions of collective life at the expense of the previously dominant political dimensions. The welfare state, which is the direct fruit of democratic ambitions, tends to transform an ever-increasing segment of the population into producer-consumers, benefactor-beneficiaries of social services, rather than into citizens. But these ties and exchanges brought about by participation in economic activity, the transfer of resources, and State intervention in the social order, are qualitatively different than the essentially political national tie. What if the social tie had been reduced solely to the collaboration imposed by collective work, merely to the objective solidarity created by the redistributive system and the integration of marginal groups by the politics of social intervention? Does this not attenuate the principle and practice of citizenship, which lay at the very foundation of the idea of nation, to the point of endangering what Durkheim called *social cohesion*? Does not this weakening of the political nation risk leading to the erosion of the very fabric of society?

The Reticence of Sociologists

Regardless of their sensibilities, sociologists have underestimated the fact that in modern society, the social tie was from here on essentially political, that is to say national. This curious neglect bespeaks an almost professional reluctance to consider the political. This is not surprising. For in the nineteenth century, sociological thought was in fact founded by overthrowing the idea, inherited from the philosophical tradition, of the primacy of the political regime over economic and social organization and by analyzing the place of the social *in and of itself*. However, it is primarily in political terms that the nation must first be analyzed. That is, by according their deserved place to the symbols and institutions by which the nation is established and maintained.

Émile Durkheim, Max Weber, and Marcel Mauss experienced more profoundly their national identity than their social origin. A fervent patriot, Durkheim analyzed patriotism in moral terms: "All societies in which man takes part or can take part do not have an equal moral value. But, there is one which enjoys over all the others a true primacy, and this is political society. It is the homeland, on the condition, however, that it is not conceived of as an eagerly selfish personality, preoccupied only with extending and expanding itself to the detriment of similar personalities, but instead like one of several organs in which participation is necessary for the progressive realization of the idea of humanity."[4] Nevertheless, even if he apparently took seriously the distinction between political society and the State, Durkheim moved away from his reflections on the nation in his early texts of 1885 and subsequently analyzed society "as a system of norms." He implicitly admitted that society coincided with the nation. In so doing, Durkheim fell victim to Norbert Elias's criticism of the majority of sociologists who exempt themselves "from the rather unpleasant obligation of recognizing that the limits of one society in comparison with another coincided most often with state borders or perhaps with ethnic borders."[5] In other words, Durkheim refused to take into account one of the unique characteristics of modern society: namely, the fact that the social tie is primarily national.

The texts of Mauss and Weber devoted to the nation remain incomplete. Yet we must not draw too many conclusions from this fact: this is the case with a large part of their work. Even so, today their analyses are approached with a willful arrogance. Mauss would apparently have been blinded by the devotion that French Jews gave to France since the Emancipation, in refusing to see ambiguities of the politics of assimilation; Weber, forgetting his admiration of the balanced neutrality of the scholar, would have participated with enthusiasm in the hypertrophic nationalism of the Wilhelmian empire: "I have never considered politics except from the national point of view, not only foreign politics, but any politics in general."⁶ Both would therefore be responsible for the weakening of sociological reflection on the nation. However, if one merely takes care to abstract from a style linked to a period of conflict between European nations, their analyses are far from negligible. Although the texts of the nationalist Max Weber are most numerous, the thought of the scholar is nevertheless irreducible to a simple contribution to the ideology of Wilhelmian imperialism. As for the uncompleted text of Mauss, it contains all the elements of a theory of the nation.

Under the direct or indirect domination of the Marxist cult of productive forces, paradoxically fused with the liberal "economism" of development theorists like Walt Whitman Rostow, sociological thought since World War II has virtually abandoned the study of the political dimension. Researchers in the social sciences strove to interpret the birth of nations in terms of technical and economic conditions: the organization of ever-expanding, ultimately global market industrialization, the means of communication, capitalist relations of production, and the need to train men for an industrial culture.⁷ The theoretical effort to conceive of the nation for its own sake has scarcely been undertaken since that time. Only Norbert Elias has proposed an analysis of the progressive integration of men by the great national monarchies, describing the secular process by which men internalized the necessity of controlling their natural and emotional urges, particularly under the influence of court society. But his work was recognized only lately; his influence began only recently with the interest in his work among historians and sociologists.

The romantic criticism of rationalistic and abstract "modernity," which often inspires sociologists, is in effect willingly transposed to the nation, the specifically "modern" form of political order, whose abstraction and rationalistic ambitions are condemned as inhumane. Since the 1970s, most researchers have either implicitly or explicitly denounced the politics of national assimilation as both tyrannical and impractical. Vargas Llosa states: "The extraordinary thing is that in spite of the fabulous energy invested by the most ancient nations in creating this common denominator, this protective and insular 'we', which is everyday more obvious, it is the irresistible movement of centrifugal forces which calls this myth into question."⁸ In the name of the authenticity and intrinsic value of any particularism, they especially attacked French Jacobinism as the destroyer of particular identities. But the "internal colonialism" of Great Britain was also judged with no more indulgence.⁹ For Anthony Smith, who has given this point of view its most serious and erudite expression, the true social reality remains those ties and ethnic belongings based in community and rooted in emotion. The nation remains an abstract society, one which at best serves only to prolong myths, memories, values, and symbols of preexistent ethnies and which has never managed to transcend them.[10]

The majority of scholars in the social sciences, given their sympathy for the intimate over the grand, for the natural rather than the artificial, evoke the ethnie with warmth while condemning the nation. This attitude illustrates the "sociological tradition" as characterized by Robert Nisbet: the majority of sociologists have a fundamentally critical attitude toward modern society—even if, among the vast majority, they make "progressive" political choices.[11] A kind of "anarcho-Marxism" leads them to willingly denounce the constraints of collective life and to refuse to appreciate the present conditions of democratic life. Sociologists, on the one hand, are eagerly assimilated to their object of study: those who study divisions, conflicts, fractures, and social revolts are characterized as progressives. On the other hand, to analyze the particular form of political integration which constitutes the nation means to study the forms of "consensus" and hence to think as a conservative would. Because he was troubled over the social cohesion of modern society, Durkheim was for a long time condemned in these terms. Recent scholarship on the social bond focuses primarily on relations between individuals and groups, thereby continuing to neglect the political and national tie. However, it is important also to consider the symbolic, the abstract Idea or the ideal—such as democratic equality—without being content to render it the simple product of social conditions.

The theoretical reflection on the nation to which Continental, German, Italian, or French thinkers devoted themselves during the triumphant epoch of the nation (from Fichte to Mazzini, Renan, Weber, or Mauss) has been virtually ignored by British and American political science, despite the studies of Clifford Geertz and his collaborators.[12] Perhaps dismissed as ideological or pre-scientific, it has also been neglected in European countries since the end of World War I.[13] During an age when one celebrates—that is, unless one deplores—the globalization of exchanges and communication, and when one willingly extols the intellectual fruitfulness of interdisciplinarity, intellectual undertakings in different countries often expand in parallel ways unbeknownst to one another.

Such is the case with the study of the nation and nationalisms. The French pride themselves on having invented the modern nation, a point of view that French historians and sociologists willingly accept even with some reservations. Still, they might nonetheless benefit from the study of various judgments formulated by renowned American anthropologists or sociologists: "There are states *manqués* just as there are *manqués* artists, as France perhaps demonstrates."[14] "Without such consensus political authority remains the most sensitive political problem in the new nations. Some older countries have never been able to overcome these difficulties. France never institutionalized her constitutional order sufficiently. Primordial loyalties still flourish. Political authority, never fully integrated within the framework of law, demeaned the framework itself in spite of the very elaborate legal structure of France as a modern state."[15] "[In] France today the rule of law has not been institutionalized to nearly the same degree, and populism remains a principal source of, and threat to, the legitimacy that is granted to agents of authority.... France sought to adopt the same syndrome of values which the United States developed: achievement, egalitarianism, universalism.... The French failure stems from the fact that, in contrast to America, the forces of the Revolution were not strong enough to sustain value consensus among the key social groupings."[16] "The American War of Independence eventually facilitated the identification of radicalism with nationalism in France and strengthened the appeal of the collectivist (statist)—and undemocratic—reinterpretation of the values of liberty, equality, and nation."[17] French criticisms of the United States, in particular the exclusion from public life of blacks and Native Americans until the 1960s or the discriminations to which Chinese, Japanese, and other minorities were for a long time victims, were no less numerous. Only English democracy, since the time when Montesquieu and Voltaire expressed their admiration, has partially escaped, at least until recently, the severe judgment that all nationals apply to neighboring nations.

Today, as in the time of Mauss, sociologists have "neglected to do their part to the individualities, especially national, and above all in modern times."[18] Likewise Durkheim, founder of the French school of sociology, wrote only a few years prior to Mauss's observation: "most certainly the concept of nation is a mystical, obscure idea." In our time one willingly invokes a "complexity" so large that it legitimates our laziness in analyzing it. But why should the nation not recede from rational knowledge, when it is no longer, to repeat the phrase of *La Marseillaise*, the object of a "sacred love?"

Internal Logic or "Systematic Coherence"[19]

One must not conclude that the "point of view"[20] of sociology is inherently fruitless. Instead, the task of the sociologist lies between the historian, who tells the story of the destiny of a particular nation, and the philosopher, who carries on with Hegel's ambition of elaborating the Idea of nationhood, or, more modestly, of tracing the history of the Idea of nationhood through the work of venerable philosophers neglecting the specifics of any given nation. From an analysis of historical experience, the sociologist can distinguish between the order of realities and those of ideas and ideologies; can formulate generally valid propositions with respect to the social and political determinants at the origin of the formation of nations; on the social conditions which permit the functioning of that particular political society; on the regular relations which are established among the subsystems of every national entity; and on the manner in which the Idea and values unique to the nation are effectively incarnated in historical societies.

I will study ideas and their relations with social realities, for "Ideas interest us only as facts or corresponding to facts."[21] The following analysis focuses on specific national experiences. Some examples are used throughout the volume as particularly significant and illustrative. These include not only the countries of Western and Eastern Europe, and Switzerland, but also "new" nations such as Israel and Turkey. Although the arguement of this work has its basis in historical studies, it does not aim at describing a particular nation—past or contemporary—nor at writing the history of its institutions or ideas. Likewise, this volume does not intend to analyze nationalist ideas or show their diffusion *within* a country or *from* one country to another. Instead, rooted in the observation and analysis of social realities, and using the best research available, this volume seeks to furnish intellectual instruments by which to understand the nature and the evolution of historical nations and clarify the logic of the idea of the nation.

In Europe, the birthplace of the national idea, the intellectuals—historians in particular—served as the high priests of national and nationalist ideologies. The intimate relationship between intellectual debates and conflicts linked to nations and nationalisms is hardly a new development. For instance, Renan's lecture might never have become so famous if it had not surfaced during a period of rivalries and oppositions between Germany and France. Intellectuals, often militants themselves, formulated—then celebrated—the very values that nationalists invoked in their demands that their *ethnie* be recognized as a nation. Through their texts, one can study national and nationalist ideologies, but not the social realities of the nation—just as the sermons of priests allow us to understand the Christian ideal which they attempt to diffuse, but do not allow us to judge the nature of the religious practices and beliefs of their disciples. One can say of these nationalist writings precisely what Marcel Mauss wrote of contemporary works devoted to religious phenomena: "They reflect more or less adequately the religious feelings of their authors, but they do not clarify for us the objective nature of these feelings."[22]

The following chapters are not intended to celebrate, justify, or denounce the national idea. By proposing a theory of the nation, founded on the sociological point of view and on empirical knowledge of society—one which leaves room at the same time for social ideas, values *and* institutions—that is to say, the concrete forms assumed by collective life—I will try insofar as possible to escape the ideological discourses commonly aroused by nations and nationalisms. Since the dawn of nationalisms, the national idea has been proclaimed, demanded, and exalted as the political *ideal*. In 1919, the victorious powers strove to rebuild political Europe on the so-called principle of nationalities invoked throughout the nineteenth century: namely, the coincidence of *ethnie* or "nationality" and political organization. It was believed that the nation was *the* political form which conformed to human nature. It was, as a result, destined to herald the reign of universal peace. Conversely, since World War II, there have been numerous denunciations of the misdeeds of the nation-state, of which the polemic of Mario Vargas Llosa is a brilliant example. Since then, any exposition of the national idea risks being read not as an analytical argument, but rather as a normative injunction.

In the following volume, then, when one writes that the citizen "must" respect the law, this is not be taken as advice or as an order in the name of civic and political morality—as was the case in our grandparents' books of civic instruction during the age of the triumphant nation—but in showing that this attitude is inscribed in the very *logic* of the functioning of the democratic nation. Revealing the objective meaning of the nation and articulating the values which undergird it does not mean that one exalts the nation or defends it against its political or intellectual detractors. In order to avoid a new misunderstanding, even easier since the subject remains loaded with values linked to political legitimacy and to the specific ethnic identities of modern societies, I want to underscore again that I do not intend to propose a model for political action, but to analyze the idea of nation, in the sense of an ideal-type. It is obvious that the goal of objectivity can never be fully realized; it can be nothing more than a governing idea. But to renounce the effort towards objectivity in the analysis of social and political life is to renounce the scientific undertaking itself. The sociological analysis of the nation is not to be confused with the political discourse of nationalists.

In distinguishing two orders—on the one hand, that of principles, values, or ideas and, on the other, that of concrete realities—I avoid explicitly or implicitly condemning the gaps between the former and the latter. Like democracy the nation is at the same time an ideology and a political system. One must consider one and the other—insofar as symbols are part and parcel of objective reality—but it is important not to confuse them. By distinguishing practices and ideas, we avoid surrendering to the intellectual simplification and comfort that moral denunciations bring, even if these are made in the name of science. It is only in objective, and not in moral or partisan terms that one can analyze the nation's inherent tension between the principled universal aspiration of democratic citizenship and the singularities of each national society: between the universal values to which democratic nations refer and the particular national interests for which their leaders inevitably stand up.

If I am unable to pretend, more than others, to have escaped the influence of my national identity, whether as a matter of historical experience or of intellectual formation, I nevertheless hope to elucidate an interpretation which reconciles the attention that contemporary scholars devote to empirical realities and the theoretical ambition of classical sociologists. One must recognize that theorizing about the nation was not born in the past few years, after decolonization, the collapse of the Soviet empire, or the renaissance of extreme-right social movements. Rather, by recalling the thought of Weber, Mauss, and, more recently, Elias, I will propose a theory of the nation as a unique form of political organization, born between the sixteenth and the nineteenth century in Western Europe and in North America, and hereafter diffused throughout the world. Here again, it is a matter of applying to the nation that which Marcel Mauss wrote of religion when he sought to establish a sociology of religious facts: "There is not, in fact, one thing, an essence, called Religion; there are only religious phenomena, more or less incorporated in systems that one calls religions and that have a definite historical existence, in groups of men and in determinate times."[23]

The passions which still surround national and nationalist phenomena, so often confused, require that in my first chapter, whose austerity I do not disguise, one must distinguish the terms—nations, ethnies, nationalisms, state—which are both the instruments and the objects of political or even scientific debate. Although most political actors tend to avoid giving precise definitions to the words they employ, it is our role, as social scientists, to make such clarifications, at least, as far as we entertain the hope of contributing to rational knowledge. Only after one rigourously distinguishes the nation as a community of citizens from other forms of historical or cultural collectivities (ethnies) and from the state, can one analyze the tension, constitutive of the idea of the nation, between the universal ambition of transcendence by the political and the concrete forms of the process of particularization in each historical nation (chapter 2). I explicitly describe the origin and the working principles of the political domain as the site for transcendence of all particularisms by means of citizenship (chapter 3). Here it is not a matter of describing national reality, but of formulating a governing principle: specifically, the national state works to institute and reinforce national differences, by which the community of citizens, which is an abstract notion, becomes a concrete reality, inscribed in time and space and capable of mobilizing populations (chapter 4).

If one accepts these analyses, it is clear (chapter 5) that there are not two ideas of the nation, as has been mistakenly repeated in Europe since the French Revolution and the great conflicts between France and Germany, opposing in a ritualistic way the civic or political nation as in the French case, to the *Volk*, i.e., to the ethnic or cultural nation, as in the German. The very notion of the "ethnic nation" marks a contradiction in terms. For it is the effort of effacing these putatively "natural" identities and belongings by means of the abstraction of citizenship which properly characterizes the national project. *There exists only one idea of the nation.*

In the conclusion I will attempt to show how, after having clarified the internal logic, or the systematic coherence of this idea, one can more easily understand both the transformation of the social tie in modern democracies and, more generally, the present weakening of historical nations in Western Europe. It is in light of this ideal-typical analysis, presented throughout the work, that I have formulated some general discussion about the liberal democratic nations of today and their destiny.

Like its predecessors, this book was written in the context of my course of research at the École des Hautes Études en Sciences Sociales.

It has benefited from the discussions and criticisms of faculty members, students, and colleagues. Philippe Besnard, Jacqueline Costa-Lascoux, Pierre Hassner, and Antoine Schnapper kindly read the manuscript and gave me invaluable advice. Philippe Gauthier made me generously benefit by his science. My exchanges with Serge Paugam are constant, and they nourished this work as well. Pierre Manent, by his decisive criticism, allowed me to better understand my intentions: my debt to him is immense. Inspired publisher Eric Vigne's insightful criticism forced me to improve much more than just my writing style. They all deserve to be thanked here.

Notes

1. This lecture, the seventh Patocka Memorial Lecture, delivered in Vienna, 3 June 1993, (from which the extracts were published in the *Newsletter* volume 40 of the *Institut für Wissenschaften vom Menschen* of Vienna), expressed with conviction many of the generally accepted ideas. It will be referenced several times in the following text.
2. Aron, 1962, p. 299.
3. Rosanvallon, 1990; Shklar, 1991; Schnapper, 1991.
4. Durkheim, 1925 (1899), p. 89.
5. Elias, 1991 (1986/1987), p. 216.
6. Quoted in Mommsen, 1985 (1959), p. 75.
7. For the development of these analyses see chapter 5, part 2.
8. Lecture of Mario Vargas Llosa.
9. Hechter, 1975.
10. Smith, 1981; Smith, 1986.
11. Nisbet, 1984 (1963).
12. Geertz (ed.), 1963. Greenfeld, 1992, takes up this perspective.
13. Only exceptions in Europe: Bibo, 1946; Aron, 1962; Szücs, 1986 (1981); Dumont, 1983 and 1991; Elias, 1991.
14. C. Geertz in Geertz (ed.), 1963, p. 129.
15. D. Apter in Geertz (ed.), 1963, pp. 80–81.
16. Lipset, 1963, pp. 11, 224–225.
17. Greenfeld, 1992, p. 182.
18. Mauss, 1969, (1920?), p. 594. The text of Mauss, recently published, was probably written in 1920.
19. This expression is borrowed from Louis Dumont in Dumont, 1991, p. 25.
20. In the meaning where Saussure could write that "the point of view creates science."
21. Mauss, 1969 (1920?), p. 605.
22. Mauss, 1968 (1904), p. 93.
23. Mauss, 1968 (1904), pp. 93–94.

1

Definitions

Because these terms are so heavily laden with values and emotions, it is common to speak of the necessity of clarifying the terms of the debate over ethnies, ethnicity, state, nations, and nationalisms. Still, one rarely succeeds in doing so. In everyday life, as well as in the social scientific literature, it is common to use the terms "ethnic" and "national" interchangeably. Nor is it unusual to make contradictory reproaches to the nation because, on the one hand, it is a matter of the nation and, on the other hand, of the ethnic group. To overcome these difficulties, the sociologist must make explicit the vocabulary used in the controversies of everyday life. He must eliminate semantic quarrels, especially since the latter are not only the instruments of political and scientific discussions, but also their object. It is important to distinguish the nation from other terms with which it is confused and to criticize the political, ideological, and scientific ambiguities of the word. Indeed, there is a tie between the concepts used and the theoretical presuppositions of an author: a definition of the nation is in itself already an implicit theory of the nation.

I do not pretend that the following definitions are valid once and for all. I do not believe that they may be imposed at the expense of all those that preceded them and all of those that will follow. It is not a matter of choosing sides among innumerable definitions, some juridical-political, and others cultural, which have already been proposed. My only goal is to make my remarks clear and to put forward an analysis which may be submitted to rational discussion and would prove, to repeat Popper's term, falsifiable, that is to say, susceptible of being either invalidated or confirmed. These definitions will eventually be justified a posteriori. That is, if they prove fruitful and if the analysis that they allow permits a better consideration of historical realities—such as the long history of the formation of democratic nations, the strength of nationalisms after the collapse of communism, or recent breaks between Czechs and Slovaks, who had been organized in the Czechoslovakian nation since 1919, or between Flemish and Walloons, who had been so organized since 1830.

These definitions are founded on a nominalist conception, according to which concepts are instruments of comprehension, but not concrete realities. Accordingly, these definitions take issue with those nationalist thinkers who presume, on the contrary, an essentialist mode of thinking and who strive to demonstrate the immateriality and the eternity of their "nation" (that is to say, their ethnie), in order to justify that it be recognized as a political nation. Nations, Mazzini said, are the product of a divine project. It is difficult for nationalists to concede that the same populations are defined, according to historical periods, in terms of ethnie or nation. Contrary to these nationalists, one must be reminded both of the historical character of the nation, as of any political organization, and the instrumental character of the concepts which permit us to analyze it.

Between the Ethnie and the State

Nation and Ethnie

The nation is a particular form of political unit, whose uniqueness should be analyzed in terms of rigorous definitions—without forgetting that every definition is a theory. *Like any political unit, the nation is defined by its sovereignty, exercised internally to integrate the populations that it includes and, externally, to assert itself as an historical subject in a global order founded on the existence and relations between politically constituted nations. But its uniqueness is that it integrates populations in a community of citizens, whose existence legitimates the internal and external action of the state.*[1]

The nation is to be distinguished from ethnic groups, which are not themselves politically organized. I will therefore designate as *ethnies* those groups of men who live as heirs of an historical and cultural community (often expressed in terms of common descent) and who share the desire to maintain it. In other words, the ethnie is defined by two dimensions: the historical community and cultural specificity.[2]

The ethnie is often called nation. One of the sources of the confusion owes to the fact that from the thirteenth century to the birth of the modern political nation, contemporaries have designated as "nation" what we today term the ethnie. The term itself appeared in England around

1250; two decades after, the "French nation" designated the whole group of French. Historiography was hereafter narrative released from the shackles of the church and the flat narrative of annals; the genre of the *gesta* found a new object, the people. In the whole of Western Europe, as in Hungary, historiography became national and contributed developing the consciousness of that which one termed nations.[3] Authors competed to find a prestigious inheritance for their people, preferably in antiquity: the English, the Celts of Wales and of Brittany, the French, and the Germans pretended alike to be descended from Trojans. Hereafter, in French or in German, "nations" designated groups of origin: students of the University of Paris, for instance, were gathered in four nations, "the honorable nation of France, the faithful nation of Picardy, the venerable nation of Normandy and the constant nation of Germany."

But if modern political nations have been the inheritors of, if not the borders, then at least, the feelings and initial statist institutions of these "nations" of the Middle Ages, they nonetheless constitute a different historical and political reality. They must be distinguished from ethnies, or whatever the name given by contemporaries and historians to ethnies: nations before the Revolution; nationalities of the nineteenth century; protonationalisms, defined as "certain variants of feelings of collective belonging which already existed and which could operate, as it were, potentially on the macro-political scale which would fit in with modern states and nations";[4] "prepolitical matrix of institutions, beliefs and solidarities";[5] or even "subnations."[6]

These definitions effectively demonstrate that ethnies are as varied in their forms as the organization of humans in society. But, in any case, the ethnie has two characteristics: it is a group of belonging; and it does not necessarily have a political expression.

Ethnies are not more "natural" than nations. In both cases, there are historical forms, that should not be reified or substantiated. Contrary to that which has been put forward by some sociologists, John Armstrong for instance, ethnic identity is not necessarily more fundamental, solid, or durable than the national reality and sentiment.[7] Ethnies are not essences but are also products of a political situation, in the widest sense of the term. The rivalry between Yorubas and Ibos is often mentioned as an example of ethnic rivalries within the Nigerian nation. But the very term of Yorubas to designate various peoples of Western Nigeria was invented by Anglican missionaries who came to Abeokuta in the nineteenth century. They unified the languages of the region and organized these peoples as an entity recognized by the colonial administration: the Yuroba ethnie is hardly more ancient than the Nigerian nation.[8] More generally, African ethnies have often been created in and of themselves by the policies of the colonizer. Similarly, in 1968 Tito invented the united "Muslim" ethnie of Bosnia-Herzegovina to reinforce his power. That is to say, he constituted populations which shared the same religion into an entity which was endowed with specific rights, thereby reinforcing and even arousing feelings of ethnic identity. Ethnies can be divided, gathered and reorganized by defining new social "borders,"[9] by processes of "amalgamation," of "incorporation," of "division," or of "proliferation," depending on economic or political circumstances.[10] But if ethnies are, like nations, historical constructions, individuals nonetheless experience ethnic belonging as a natural given, even if the ethnie does not have a proper political organization. Ethnies are distinguished from the modern or political nation, which was born in England, precisely by the fact that ethnies do not possess an autonomous political organization. The modern or political nation had already been conceived by the classic authors of the eighteenth century (Montesquieu or Rousseau), but it symbolically arrived as political actor with the American and French revolutions. Since then, it is not the size, or any other objective characteristics which distinguish the ethnie from the nation, but rather the nature of the tie which unites humans.

Even the scientific literature, however, does not always retain this distinction. Walker Connor, for instance, holds that the nation is the ethnie which has consciousness of itself. "An ethnic group may be readily discerned by an anthropologist or other outside observer, but until the members are themselves aware of the group's uniqueness, it is merely an ethnic group and not a nation."[11] He adopts Hugh Seton-Watson's conception, who, after having observed: "Thus I am driven to the conclusion that no 'scientific definition' of the nation can be devised; yet the phenomenon has existed and exists," adopts the definition according to which "a nation exists when a significant number of people in a community consider themselves to form a nation, or behave as if they formed one."[12] Neither John Armstrong in *Nations Before Nationalism*,[13] nor Suzanne Berger, in treating the *Bretons, Basques, Scots and other European nations*,[14] distinguishes between ethnies and nations, since both designate by nations those subpolitical collectivities without proper political expression and without a state. But isn't this an implicit justification of eventual claims for the transformation of ethnies into nations, leading us to think that the nature of one is as legitimate as that of the other?

The rebirth of the concept of ethnicity, which has become the key term of contemporary social scientific literature, particularly in the United States,[15] has contributed to maintaining this equivocation. By discovering within the United States the strength of belongings in particular communities and by assigning the term "ethnic groups" to mean at once blacks, Irish-Americans, Italian-Americans, Jews and Native Americans, sociologists could avoid pursuing the potentially emotional theorizing on the nature of the individual's belonging to the collective: racial in the case of blacks and Native Americans? National in the case of Irish and Italians? National and/or religious for Jews? In that way, one could avoid raising the question, now taboo, of race—even if one affirms that it is a socially constructed concept—or one of culture—which has commonly become the socially accepted way to designate what one once called race—to define groups. In particular, Jewish sociologists, prominent among theoreticians of ethnicity in the United States, could refrain from formulating the issue of Jewish identity made heated by secularization and the construction of nations in the modern epoch. That is, when the political order is organized by nations, can Jews constitute a simple religious or cultural group within non-Jewish nations by renouncing their possession of specific political rights, or do they remain a people with an essentially national vocation, hence destined to build their own sovereign nation?[16]

The classic argument between the two schools of thought—the "primordialist," which holds that nations, as natural units of human association, have existed for eternity, and the latter, termed "modernist," which insists on the essentially modern character of national construction—has always appeared to me to be based on the fact that its terms were not clearly defined. If one designates by "nation" any form of historical collectivity instead of speaking of the ethnie, then it is clear that humans have always belonged in collectives, even if its form has varied considerably throughout the ages. In that sense, nations, that is to say ethnies, have always existed. On the other hand, if one calls "nation," as I do, the political form of the contemporary democratic age, it is a recent construction, even if it was not born from nothing, and if it perpetuates, even while transcending them, various preexisting ethnic feelings and institutions. Sentiments of belonging in a historical collectivity might very well have existed for centuries, but it is only in contemporary times that they founded and justified a particular form of political organization.

Nation and Political Unit

Nations are also commonly confused with political entities or states. The term "nation" designates political units whose sovereignty is recognized by the international order. Recent scholars neglect in this respect an analytical distinction that the original theorists of the nation clearly appreciated. In particular, marked by the memory of the revolutionary experience and the proclamation by the Third Estate of the nation as new source of political legitimacy, French authors clearly distinguished political unit and civic nation. Some texts of Max Weber, on the other hand, remain ambiguous at that level.

Renan thus distinguished between "nations like France, England and the majority of modern European countries" and the other "forms of human society," that is to say, "large agglomerations of humans such as China, Egypt, and the most ancient, Babylonia; the tribe like Hebrews or Arabs; the city like Athens and Sparta; gatherings of various countries as in the Carolingian Empire; communities without homeland, maintained by the religious tie, like that of the Israelites, Parsees; confederations such as Switzerland, America; relationships like one of race, or rather language, established between different branches of Germans or Slavs."[17] By means of distinction, he is able to discern that "nations, *understood in this manner* (italics added), are something quite new in history."[18]

Mauss also explains how he came to distinguish nation from political unit. He classifies human societies in four large groups according to their increasing "rank of integration," that is to say, of their degree of political integration: from polysegmented, clannish, and tribal societies; finally to societies integrated, in increasing degrees, by "the presence, strength and the consistency of a central power." "To that type of society one proposed to give the name of nation, and I must say that Durkheim and I, for our part, employed this nomenclature until only recently."[19] Yet this was, as he observes, to confuse any political unit with the nation: "These countries are in fact integrated and administrated, but they are not directly administrated by the concerned people themselves. The law was not the work of citizens."[20] Mauss adds then to the criterion of political integration, characteristic of any political unit organized by a stable central power, the additional criterion of citizenship, which permits one to distinguish the modern nation from other political units—and which in turn leads him to notice that "an enormous number of societies and states still exist in the world which do not merit in any way the title of nation."[21]

By adopting the same distinction in the introduction of *Paix et guerre entre les nations*, Raymond Aron specifies that the nation, in this case, "is equivalent to any kind of political collectivity, territorially organized," and that international relations "are relations between *political units*, this last concept covering Greek cities, the Roman or Egyptian empire as well as European monarchies, bourgeois republics or popular democracies."[22] This was also the sense that Adam Smith gave to nations in his work, *The Wealth of Nations*.

It is also in this sense that the term is used in the intellectual discipline called "the study of inter*national* relations": nations there designate political units.[23] It was this same assimilation between the nation and political unit which led the winners of 1919—at a time when the democratic nation seemed to be accepted as a universal model of political organization—to create the League of *Nations* and to reorganize the political order into nations which were, in some Eastern European countries, nothing more than political units. The multiplication of the number of new nations since World War II, recognized by the Organization of United *Nations*, illustrates the existence of new states or new politically constituted nations, not necessarily new democratic nations. Iran or Saudi Arabia, for instance, do not constitute a nation in that sense of the term. Mauss had already observed that jurists tended to confuse state and nation.

This is sometimes the case with Weber, when the nationalist thinker overrides the scholar, especially since the latter did not complete his theoretical texts. Obviously Weber did not ignore the distinction between State and nation: "In ordinary language 'nation' is, first of all, not identical with the 'people of a state,' that is, with the membership of a given polity. Numerous polities comprise groups who emphatically assert the independence of their 'nation' in the face of other groups: or they comprise merely *parts* of a group whose members declare themselves to be one homogenous 'nation' (Austria is an example of both)."[24] Moreover, he accorded a particular value to small nations, concerning their democratic quality and the culture. "We too have every reason to thank destiny that there exists a Germanness (*Deutschtum*) outside the borders of the German national state (*Machtstaat*). Not only the simple bourgeois virtues and authentic democracy, which has never yet been realized in a large state, but also much more intimate and yet eternal values can flourish only on the soil of communities which renounce public power. This is also true with artistic values: as authentic a German as Gottfried Keller was, he would never have become such a prominent and unique figure within the military camp that is inevitably our state."[25] In his incomplete text on the nation, one finds another note of the same inspiration, in which he underlines the difference between the *Machtpolitik* and the value of culture: "Pure art and literature of a specifically German character do *not* develop in the political *center* of Germany."[26] Max Weber clearly distinguished the order of the state and power (*Staatpolitisch*) from that of the nation and culture (*Kulturpolitisch*).

But he did not make this distinction the center of his reflection, which was founded on two essential ideas: (1) the state is the instrument of the nation, the nation cannot exist without a state; and (2) there is a necessary tie between the internal properties of the nation and its external action. From this point, the incomplete character of his texts has led to controversies on the proper interpretation of his thought. Developing a conception which accorded primacy to external action, did Weber render the internal organization the mere instrument of the will to power of the state, acting to affirm its will in relation to other states, as Wolfgang Mommsen seeks to demonstrate?[27] Since his reflection was developed from his own historical experience—the construction of a unitary German state and the conflicts between major European powers—and since he could not imagine a political world organized in a form other than that of nations "naturally" in conflict, and given his Nietzschean conception of the will to power and the primacy which he gave to external politics, is it then true that the nation and the national State became for him two sides of the same thing?[28] Despite the ambiguity of his texts—one can find some in which the parliamentary regime is appreciated for its own sake and not as a mere instrument of the will to power—it seems clear that the more Max Weber defined the nation in terms of *Machtpolitik,* the more the instrument of that will, i.e., the state, risked becoming confused with the nation itself. The nationalist Weber tended to marginalize the distinction between political unit and the nation and to assimilate the true nation—or the ideal-type of the nation—to the "great power," since, for him, according to the often quoted formula: "The reason of State is for us the ultimate standard of values..."

As an assembly of institutions and of the means of control and coercion, the state has as its goal the creation and the maintenance of the internal cohesion of political units, permitting them to exercise their action externally. This state is at once the expression and the instrument of any modern political unit. It is the state which distinguishes all politically constituted nations from other forms of collectivities or ethnies. In the case of the democratic nation, the state, as Hegel says, is both the rational support of the nation, without which the nation would have no authentic existence, as well as the objective, political expression of the collective identity. But this necessary bond must not for that reason lead us to assimilate one to the other. To the contrary, it is the existence of a community of citizens, distinct from the state, which makes the democratic nation unique among political units.

Nation and Nationalism

The nation, as historical reality, must finally be distinguished from nationalism. Nationalism designates claims of ethnies to be recognized as nations, that is, to make the historico-cultural community (or ethnie) coincide with the political organization; or the will to power of extant nations to affirm themselves at the expense of others. Very often, criticisms made against nations really concern nationalisms. Conflicts occurring right now in the Balkans, for instance, are not national conflicts, but ethnic or nationalist: they demonstrate the weakening of the strictly national tradition of the former Yugoslavia, which attempted to constitute a nation in 1919 from Serbian, Croatian, Slovenian, Bosnian, Hungarian, Albanian, and other ethnies. Despite its title, Ernest Gellner's book, *Nations and Nationalism*[29] and, more generally, much recent Anglo-American political science literature, has as its focus nationalisms—in the sense of claims to create nations—but not nations in their own right.

The confusion of terms in social life—such as between nations, ethnies, nationalisms—is rarely just a matter of chance. I have already observed that words are as much the objects as the instruments of ideological and political conflicts. This is the reason why they are, consciously or unconsciously, used in such an equivocal way. Since the nineteenth century, one designates the ethnie in social and political life by the term "people." To call the ethnie (scientific concept) a people (political term) means implicitly or explicitly to give it the right to demand political independence, the right to become a politically constituted nation. If, even in the scientific literature, one willingly confuses the nation with the ethnie, this is because, in the age of nationalisms, all ethnies can claim, in the name of the rights of a people, to be able to dispose of themselves and to be recognized as politically constituted nations. Renan well understood that the nation was a matter of a revolutionary principle. If one often assimilates the nation to the State, it is because all States pretend to be the expression of a democratic nation. The ambiguity of the term nation in social life adheres in the fact that it is necessarily linked to the modern principle of political legitimacy and to the foundation of the social bond.

This is also the reason why the democratic nation remains an implicit model today, to which all political units refer, even if only symbolically. In the communist countries of Europe, where a single party reigned alone, the leaders nonetheless organized elections and pretended to represent a democratic nation. Leaders of the Islamic Republic of Iran, as soon as they attained power, organized a constitutional referendum followed by the election of members to parliament. In December 1992, Cuban leaders carried out the first general elections since they assumed power. During the Persian Gulf war, Saddam Hussein submitted each of his major decisions to the preliminary vote of the Parliament. He transmitted to Western societies the image of a popular mobilization apparently in conformity with the wishes of political representation. All the governments of politically constituted nations possess some kind of constitution and gather an elected assembly.

Even if ethnic sentiments and passions continue to exist in civic nations, as Anthony Smith has for some time argued, we must not conclude from this that there is no difference between the ethnie and the nation. The nation must not be confused with the ethnie or the State. Indeed, the nation is defined in a dualistic or dialectic relationship with the former and the latter, according to which the nation is incarnated in the social reality. The political recognition of ethnies, integrated in the nation, leads to disintegration and to impotence; the State, when it becomes too powerful, tyrannical, or totalitarian, absorbs the nation and destroys the community of citizens. Between the ethnie and the State, the nation must find its place.

The Meaning of Integration

As we have seen, the nation integrates populations into a community of citizens, whose existence legitimates the internal and external actions of the state. This latter, as instrument of the nation, functions both to integrate populations by citizenship as well as to act in the world of politically constituted nations.

The Process of Internal Integration

The nation is not given once and for all. Rather, it is the fruit of a dynamic process of integration. It was in that sense of an *integrative revolution* that Clifford Geertz analyzed the building of new nations stemming from the dissolution of French and English colonial empires.

Integration is one of those general concepts of sociology that one must adopt, as Claude Lévi-Strauss said of identity, as a concept-horizon: "a sort of virtual home to which it is essential for us to refer in order to explain a certain amount of things, but without it ever having a real existence."[30] The term integration is used here not in the current sense of political life in France, as applied to immigrants, but in the sense of the sociological tradition. This last meaning was fundamentally inspired by an examination of how the social tie—or integration—was preserved in modern societies now founded on the fact and value of individual autonomy.

Whatever the ambiguities of the concept, it refers to two principal meanings. It can characterize the unity of a system or of a society—what one can call the integration *of* society or systemic integration. It is in this meaning a property of a group in its unity. But it can also characterize the relation of individuals or a subsystem *to* a bigger system—what one can call integration *to* society, or tropic integration. In this sense, it is the property of the individual or a particular group within a wider unity. One can analyze in sociological terms the nation as a process of integration *of* society by the political—or "systemic" integration—which by definition is ongoing. The integration of this or that group of populations (for instance, populations of foreign origin in countries of immigration) *to* the society already constituted—or tropic integration—is only a particular dimension of the integration *of* political society in its unity, or systemic integration.

To define the process of internal integration in these terms implies, if one liberally follows Durkheim's analysis, that the common goals of collective undertaking should be defined and accepted, that individuals share a certain number of common practices and beliefs, and that there are interactions between members of the group. In the case of the nation, it is a matter of goals, practices, and political beliefs, but they cannot be independent of social reality. The community of citizens cannot be constituted from just any kind of social and economic conditions.

Because it is a matter of process, one has to take into account every collection of objective conditions and their internalization by individuals. One often notices that nationality—the juridical tie between the individual and the national State—is an exception to the Parsonsian idea that achieved status increase at the expense of ascribed status in modern societies. The vast majority of individuals hold their nationality from birth; it is neither the product of their will nor of their merit. It is a given which is imposed on them. But the example of nationality is, after all, only a particular example of the general fact that the socialization of individuals in modern society occurs within extant national societies.

When Rousseau wishes to rediscover man previous to any social convention, while man develops his qualities within the very development of society, he designates man as being "a kind of animal endowed with *perfectibility*, that is to say the capacity of becoming a human."[31] Alain Renaut similarly extends an insight of Fichte who, following Rousseau, insists on the importance of the role of education. Concerned with overcoming the simplistic opposition of the nation-by-choice and the nation-by-birth in founding the new national contract of the democratic age, Renaut proposes the concept of *educability* as the foundation of the idea of the nation. This is true insofar as "the visible sign of the inscription of liberty within a culture and a tradition consists in the capacity of being educated, in the *educability* to the values of this liberty and this tradition."[32] I have myself made recourse to the traditional sociological concept of *socialization*.[33] In any case, it is a matter of designating the process by which the individual, born in a particular society, internalizes its demands, acquires its common values, and adopts the norms of behavior by which the collectivity maintains itself. These concepts permit one to analyze the socially constituted capacity of men to acquire by education—in the broadest sense of the term—the means to participate in the common, national life.

The introduction of these concepts calls attention to the contribution of the social sciences. Indeed, the social sciences underscore not the absence of human liberty but rather the constraints and concrete conditions within which it can effectively be exercised. They remind us that the liberty of man is a historically situated liberty. The dialectic of liberty and of determinism that the social sciences make evident can be reconciled thanks to these concepts—perfectibility, educability, socialization. By means of these concepts one can give an account of the process by which the individual becomes a member of the collectivity into which he is, by chance, born. Education doubtless permits individuals to take part in a technical society, one which requires a high level of competency, as Gellner has argued. However, the fact that all theoreticians of the nation—Rousseau, Kant, Fichte, and Mauss—insisted the role of the school is not only for reasons of technical apprenticeship. It is primarily because the school forms the citizen. In its role of socialization (to adopt the most general concept), the school is an essential instrument in modern societies. Socialization is the means by which one becomes a member of the national collectivity. National belonging and feeling are born out of this internalization of knowledge, norms and common values. Whatever concept one adopts, it is a matter of recalling that man is susceptible of learning to know and respect the practices of public life and, even more precisely, to internalize the idea that there exists a public domain. In this manner the determinism of birth becomes liberty. It is not a matter of a mere transformation of words: national belonging and feeling are effectively born from the internalization of a group of cultural models and specific values, which define a personal identity indissolubly linked to a collective identity. From then on, the individual finds his nation within himself.

The term integration must not lead to misunderstanding: it is not a matter of an irenic process. On the contrary, it is normally by means of internal violence—by reducing political and cultural particularisms—and external violence—by wars—that the processes of national integration have occurred. But no political entity is maintained solely by violence. What makes the state of the democratic nation unique is that its action is legitimated by the community of citizens.

One saw earlier that Weber, as nationalist, assimilated the civic nation and the politically constituted nation in a number of his texts. He wished at the same time both to build German democracy and to see its power affirmed. He personally favored parliamentary government as one of the primary conditions which, by encouraging the adhesion of individuals to their nation, reinforced its capacities of external action. He saw in parliamentary practices the best organization of public life, allowing citizens to participate more actively in the national ambition and thereby increasing the power of the nation. Weber admired the fact that the English had once dominated one-fourth of all humanity, and he emphasized that liberty reinforced the will of ambitious peoples. However, insofar as he accorded primacy to external politics, he did not make a clear distinction between the democratic nation and the politically constituted nation; nor did he formulate the idea of citizenship as foundation of the national idea—which explains the passions that his nationalism aroused among modern West German intellectuals who were searching for a great German theorist of democracy.

Mauss and Aron, on the other hand, both begin with the idea of citizenship. Mauss evokes the "assembly of citizens of a State, an assembly distinct from the State,"[34] and Aron this "particular species of political community, one where individuals have, in large degree, a consciousness of citizenship and where the State appears the expression of a preexistent nationality."[35] Moreover, both add to this first definition the idea of the coincidence between cultural unit and political unit, between ethnie and nation. "A complete nation is a society sufficiently integrated, with some degree of central democratic power, with at least the notion of national sovereignty and which, in general, the borders are those of a race, civilization, language, and morality: in a word a national character.... In completed nations, all of this coincides. These coincidences are rare, so they are even more noticeable, and, if one permits us to judge, more beautiful. Because it is possible to judge societies, even without political prejudices, just as one would animals or plants."[36] "The nation as an ideal-type of political unit has three characteristics: the participation of all governed in the State by the double means of military service and universal suffrage; the coincidence of this political will with a community of culture; and the total independence of the national State toward the external."[37] The idea of citizenship remains expressed, in Mauss, by "the central democratic power" and, in Aron, by "the participation of all governed in the State," but the coincidence between cultural unit and territorial political organization—inspired by the experience and the ideal of the French nation-state—becomes essential.

It is generally accepted that the principle of the nation-state is based on the right of each ethnie to become a political unit.[38] However, this is less the precondition than the *consequence* of the nationalization of populations. "A certain number of persons, united in a political body, speaking the same language, and which for reasons of common security, trade or government gathers together almost daily, can not fail to conform themselves one to the other, and to assume the resemblance which adds national character to the unique personal character of each individual."[39] It is political hegemony which progressively gave peoples a unique language. Since the thirteenth century in Europe, intellectuals have contributed to creating this linguistic community, by translating the Bible and writing literary and historical works in the vernacular. Nationalist militants subsequently invoked the argument of cultural homogeneity to demand that ethnies be recognized as political nations, even if necessary by arousing this homogeneity by their actions. Nations pretended to be heirs of an ethnie. Once established, they worked to increase the vitality of the nation by reinforcing the cultural homogeneity of populations or, to recall Mauss, the uniqueness of their "race," their "civilization," their "language," their "morality," or their "national character." The cultural uniqueness and homogeneity of various ethnies and nations were therefore at the heart of *political* debates over nations and nationalities. But it is not for that reason either the cause or the precondition of the nation's existence. One can apply to all objective characteristics—race, language, religion or culture—that which Max Weber wrote of race or "the blood relationship": "All history shows how easily political action can give rise to the belief in blood relationship, unless gross differences of anthropological type impede it."[40] The coincidence between the political unit and the cultural community was the political ideal of the nation, but it is not the "ideal-type" of the nation, in the analytical sense of the term.

In principle, the community of citizens can be culturally heterogeneous, as demonstrated by the usual example of Switzerland; the cultural homogeneity of populations is but a single factor tending toward the constitution of a political society. Cultural homogeneity has never been sufficient to constitute a nation. Conversely, political loyalty toward the nation can be combined with various forms of attachment to preexistent ethnies, more or less recognized by the political organization (see chapter 3). On the other hand, the existence of the nation depends on the fact that citizens commonly accept that there is a political domain independent of particular interests and that they respect the rules of its functioning. "What the civic sense more than anything else seems to involve is a definite concept of the public as a separate and distinct body and an attendant notion of a genuine public interest, which though not necessarily superior to, is independent of and at times even in conflict with, both private and other sorts of collective interest."[41]

Internal and External Dimensions

It is necessary to link the processes of internal integration and of external action for reasons at the same time logical and historical. Insofar as the democratic nation is a political unit, it is defined in comparison with other politically constituted nations. This action, on the other hand, has an effect on the process of internal integration. "Any political success which ends up imposing the will of one country on another reinforces the internal prestige, power, and influence of the classes, status groups and political parties under whose authority the success was obtained."[42] The process of internal integration would be unintelligible without taking into account the will of the nation to act externally, either by imposing its will on other nations or preventing them from imposing theirs. Definitive of the nation, this sovereignty is expressed at the same time in the constraints which it exercises over the populations it includes as well as in its intervention in the "concert of nations," that is, in relations between political units.

This relationship was at the heart of Weber's thought, which posited the primacy of external action: "Superior peoples alone possess the vocation to advance the development of the world."[43] Internal integration was, first and foremost, one of the conditions requisite to the "development of the world." Parliamentarism, which permitted the selection of real political leaders and struggled against the routinization of bureaucrats, became for him an instrument of national power. Similarly, Mauss formulates no less clearly the same idea of the necessary tie between internal integration and external action: "It is in fact an abstraction to believe that the internal politics of a nation is not deeply shaped by external politics, and vice versa."[44]

Politically constituted nations are usually born in the collision of wars. The number of political units in Europe went from some 500 in the year 1500 to some dozens by the beginning of the nineteenth century : most of them disappeared through war, absorbed in greater units. The Europe of nations was drawn by the treaties of Westphalia in 1648, which concluded the Thirty Years War; by the Congress of Vienna in 1815 after wars of the Revolution and of the Empire; and by treaties which sanctioned the end of World War I. The nations of Central and Eastern Europe acquired their independence in 1919 and 1920, after the military defeat of the Austro-Hungarian and Turkish Empires and their subsequent dissolution. At the end of the eighteenth century, the United States; at the beginning of the nineteenth century, the nations of Latin America; and in the twentieth, those of Africa or Asia were created in and by wars of independence against imperial European powers. Most states owe their existence to the direct action of other states. Conflicts sometimes aroused a new entity which engulfed, totally or partially, the belligerent units or, conversely, resulted in the division of vast political units into smaller entities.

The goal and function of the first statist institutions were to supply European sovereigns with the means of waging war against their neighbors.[45] In all politically constituted nations, wars develop and transform the organization of the state and its modes of action. Bismarck used the German victory of 1870 as an instrument for the construction of the Wilhelmian *Reich*. In democratic nations after World War I, the number of civil servants and the intervention of the State in economic and social life violently increased in all the European countries. The construction of a welfare state in the countries of Western Europe was a direct consequence of World War II. The famous Beveridge report was written in 1942 while battles were occurring.

On the other hand, wars awaken or arouse the consciousness of ethnies or of extant political units. Whether it is a matter of resisting danger or of spreading its power, the common battle against the external gives birth to a self-conscious community. Wars of conquest led by Western European nations—Spain, Portugal, France, the Netherlands, or England—to dominate faraway foreign peoples and to control global commerce contributed to the integration and the pride of peoples. National feelings were born in Europe from the rivalries and conflicts between major countries. Only after the wars of the Republic and the Empire, did the majority of the French confuse the national idea with revolutionary principles. The nations of central and Eastern Europe became "completely aware of themselves...under the pressure of the foreign," according to Renan's formulation. That is, by fighting against the French *Grande nation* and Napoleonic imperialism. In order to compete with the West on equal terms and to preserve their collective identity, Japan and Turkey adopted the forms of the democratic nation.

Wars revive the feelings which link individuals to their ethnic or national collectivity. Their consciousness of particularisms is attenuated by the feeling of solidarity born of common danger. This weakening of particular ties is reinforced by the rigor of collective organization and the temporary militarization of the social organization. During the war of 1914–1918, Polish immigrants whose children were killed as French citizens justified this sacrifice by dedicating a passionate attachment to their new homeland. After World War I, German-Americans became American patriots and ceased demanding that the German community be recognized in and of itself in the public life of the United States. Blood spilled on the battlefield unites combatants.

Wars reinforce the democratic nation, like all political units, when its norms and values are deeply internalized by citizens; the feeling of public devotion, revived by the war, is confused with adhesion to the democratic nation. One finds himself in the situation Durkheim implicitly invoked when he wrote: "The image of the threatened homeland occupies in consciousnesses a status that it does not occupy in the time of peace; the ties which reattach the individual to his society are reinforced."[46] The victories of Western democracies in 1919 and 1945 probably increased their citizens's trust in the value and efficiency of their regime. During the years of battle against Hitler's Germany, the government of Winston Churchill imposed—in the name of the defense of democracy—a quite authoritarian regime upon British populations; but, after the war, the reversion to the practices of democratic life was almost immediate, even if the organization of governmental institutions remained heavier and more complex than before 1939. On the other hand, the Germans of the 1920s attributed to the idea of democracy their military defeat and their humiliation.

Can one speak of the political nation if it does not possess a fully sovereign state? Or, put differently, can one define the state only by its ability to integrate populations in a community of citizens, even if it does not have external autonomy of action? In this regard Anthony Smith advances the idea that the Catalans form a nation, because they possess a territory, language, educational system, specific economy, and the right to levy taxes.[47] He recognizes that the Catalan state is not sovereign because it has no externally independent politics outside of the Spanish state, but for him the nation exists insofar as there is a community of Catalan citizens. This is to reduce the nation only to the single dimension of internal integration. I did so myself in my earlier work, when I defined the nation as a political form which transcended differences between populations—whether objective differences of social, religious, regional or national (in countries of immigration) origin, or differences of collective identity—and which integrated these populations in an entity organized by a common political project.[48] But this definition is not sufficient: the nation is not only a community of citizens, it is also a political unit. The ideal-type of the nation implies not only that the State, in its concrete forms, is the instrument of internal integration, but also that it autonomously acts within an international system founded on the idea of sovereignty of politically constituted nations.

Raymond Aron, as we saw earlier, held "the total independence of the national state toward the external" as one of the three elements of the ideal-type of the democratic nation. If this is in effect one characteristic of the state of the democratic nation, it is by no means exclusively linked to it: rather, it is a requirement of any state acting in the concert of politically constituted nations. In any political unit, the state is historically and logically linked to war. Insofar as the democratic nation is *also* a politically constituted nation, it is true that the "independence of the national state toward the external" describes reality. But the definition of the *democratic* nation, in terms of its ideal-type, consists in the fact that it is the community of citizens which legitimates the action of the state, in its double dimension of internal integration and external action. From that primary characteristic one can understand the internal logic of the idea of the democratic nation.

Notes

1. I will speak, then, without distinguishing among the civic nation, political nation, democratic nation, or nation as community of citizens.
2. Is it necessary to underline that the terms *ethnie* and *ethnic group* have no pejorative meanings, and that they are not used in the meaning of political life, where some condemn with disdain the "ethnies" or "tribes" of Eastern Europe?
3. Szücs, 1986 (1981).
4. Hobsbawm, 1990, p. 47.
5. E. Shils in Geertz (ed.), 1963, pp. 21–22.
6. W. Petersen in Glazer-Moynihan (ed.), 1975, pp. 177 and passim.
7. Armstrong, 1982.
8. Wallertstein, 1960, p. 132.
9. Barth, 1969.
10. D. L. Horowitz in Glazer-Moynihan (ed.), 1975.
11. Connor, 1978, p. 589.
12. Seton-Watson, 1977, p. 5.
13. Armstrong, 1982.
14. Berger, 1972. The literature of essays has not obviously been outdone. One has seen flourish since the collapse of the Berlin Wall the essays on the "return of the nations" or the "glory of nations," that is to say, of ethnies.
15. J. Crowley in Delannoi-Taguieff (ed.), 1991, p. 187.
16. D. Schnapper in Birnbaum (ed.), 1991, pp. 296–310.
17. Renan, 1947 (1882), p. 887.
18. Renan, 1947 (1882), p. 888.
19. Mauss, 1969 (1920?), p. 581.
20. Mauss, 1969 (1920?), p. 583.
21. Mauss, 1969 (1920?), pp. 584–585.
22. Aron, 1962, p. 17.
23. I will utilize in this case the term "politically constituted nation."
24. Weber, 1947, p. 627. "'Nation' im üblichen Sprachgebrauch ist zunächst nicht identisch mit 'Staatsvolk,' d.h. der jeweiligen Zugehörigkeit (zu) einer politischen Gemeinschaft. Denn zahlreiche politische Gemeinschaften (so Österreich- vor 1918-) umfassen Menschengruppen, aus deren Kreisen emphatisch die Selbständigkeit ihrer 'Nation' den anderen Gruppen gegenüber betont wird, oder anderseits Teile einer von den Beteiligen als einheitliche 'Nation' hingestellten Menschengruppe (so ebenfalls Österreich)." (*Economy and Society*, vol. 2, p. 922)
25. Weber, *Politische Schriften*, cited in Aron, 1967 (1964), p. 646.
26. Weber, 1947, p. 630. "Reine Kunst und Literatur von deutscher *Eigenart* sind nicht im politischen *Zemtrum* Deutschland enstanden." (*Economy and Society*, vol. 2, p.926n.)
27. Mommsen, 1985 (1959).
28. Mommsen, 1985 (1959), p. 79.
29. Gellner, 1983.

30. Lévi-Strauss, 1977, p. 332.
31. Manent, 1987, p. 161.
32. A. Renaut in Fichte, 1992 (1806), p. 42.
33. Schnapper, 1991, p. 27.
34. Mauss, 1969 (1920?), P. 574.
35. Aron, 1962, p. 297.
36. Mauss, 1969 (1920?), p. 604.
37. Aron, 1962, p. 297.
38. For example, Gellner, 1983, p. 11; Ferry, 1991, v. 2, p. 181.
39. Hume, 1972 (1748), pp. 291–292.
40. Weber, 1971 (1913) (trad.), p. 421; 1947, p. 222. "Wie auszerordentlich leicht speziell politisches Gemeinschaftshandeln die Vorstellung der 'Blutgemeinschaft' erzeugt—falls nicht allzudrastische Unterschiede des anthropologischen Typus im Wege stehen—zeigt der ganze Verlauf der Geschichte." (*Economy and Society,* vol. 1, p. 393)
41. C. Geertz in Geertz (ed.), 1963, p. 156.
42. Weber, cited in Mommsen, 1974, p. 44.
43. Cited in Aron, 1967 (1964), p. 643.
44. Mauss, 1969 (1920?), p. 608.
45. Tilly (ed.), 1975.
46. Durkheim, 1925 (1899), p. 78.
47. Smith, 1986, p. 166.
48. Schnapper, 1991, p. 71.

2

The Political and the National

The uniqueness of the modern nation lies in the integration of all populations into one community of citizens and in the legitimation the action of the state, which is its instrument, by this community; it therefore implies the principle of universal suffrage—the participation of *all* citizens[1] in choosing their governors and judging their methods of exercising power—as well as conscription—the participation of *all* citizens in foreign affairs. This double participation is undoubtedly real, but it primarily symbolizes the principle of political legitimacy. It constitutes at once both the logic and the ideal of the democratic nation.

The nation is defined by its ambition of *transcending particular belongings by means of citizenship* and of defining the citizen as an abstract individual, without particular identification and qualification, over and above all concrete determinations. These particular belongings might include the biological (such at least as they are perceived), historical, economic, social, religious, or cultural. Secularism, in particular, is an essential attribute of the modern state, because it allows one to transcend the diversity of religious belongings, to consecrate the privatization of beliefs and practices, and to make the public domain into a religiously neutral place shared in common by all citizens, whatever the church to which they belong (which does not preclude, of course, as we will see in chapter 4, various forms of recognition and of collaboration between the state, religious groups, and the churches).

This secularism is indicative of the essential fact that the social bond is no longer religious but national, and hence political. The national project is universal, not only because it is fated to all who are gathered in the same nation, but also because this principle of overcoming particularisms by means of the political is easily adopted in any society. The ideology of liberty and the postulated equality of individuals which lies at the heart of the idea of the democratic nation has a universal horizon.

36   Community of Citizens

The universalism of the republican idea, or the "civic nation" in Kant's words, combined with the particularism of the ethnies from which the nation is constituted and which are perpetuated in more or less recognizable forms, explains the tension between universalism and particularism which is constitutive of the nation. The multiplicity of cultural or ideological references is implied by the very definition of the nation. Nations are historically constructed from one or several preexistent ethnies. To the degree that the nation transcends, according to circumstances and specific political traditions, the ethnies—the "protonationalisms," that is nationalities or religions which preceded it—each nation is unique.

On the other hand, the actions of the state, whose institutions and ideology work to assimilate various populations to the national culture, reinforce this singularity. Merely to affirm the principle of citizenship would not alone be sufficient to constitute a community of citizens. Sovereignty and citizenship are fictions. Individuals are not mobilized by ideas of such abstraction. They effectively integrated only in the name of a certain number of concrete realities, values, and interests, which justify the inevitable constraints of collective life and their adherence to the external actions of the nation—which may even require them to sacrifice their life. One is able to integrate them only by the continual action of common institutions, in the broad sense that Durkheim gives to this term: established forms of practices by which the generations transmit the shared habits of common life characteristic of a particular historical collectivity.

The Political Project

Some theorists have focused on the subjective or spiritual dimension of the nation; others on the objective characteristics and the economic or technological conditions which are at the origin of nationalisms. But we must overcome these often simplistic distinctions in order to take into account the ideas, values, and at the same time, the concrete conditions for the existence of the nation.

Renan demonstrated that race, language, religion, mere interests, and the objective givens of geography are insufficient to define a nation. "The truth is that there is no pure race, and to base politics upon ethnographic analyses is to rest them upon a chimera. The noblest countries—England, France, Italy—are those where the blood is most mixed." "What we have just said of race, we must also say of language. Language invites us together; it does not force us." "Each believes and practices at his will, what he can, as he likes. There is no longer a state religion; one can be French, English, German, and be Catholic, Protestant, Israelite, without practicing a cult." "The community of interests makes treaties of commerce. There is within nationality an aspect of sentiment." "No, it is not the land more than race which makes a nation... A nation is a spiritual principle, resulting from profound complications of history, a spiritual family, not a group determined by the configuration of the soil."[2] From this critique, Renan defined the nation in a "subjective" way, he spoke of "soul," of "spiritual principle," of "solidarity," of "moral consciousness." More recently, John Armstrong, Hugh Seton-Watson, and Walker Connor have also distinguished the nation from the ethnie merely by the consciousness of self, without reference to Renan. But the subjective dimension alone does not distinguish the nation from other social groups. The idea of human will and of "the plebiscite of everyday life," in which this will would commonly be manifested in the quotidian, according to Renan, might apply equally well to "clubs, conspiracies, gangs, teams, parties, not to mention the many numerous communities and associations of the preindustrial age,"[3] and "the national states do not have the monopoly on consent."[4] The nation, as any political unit, is not only a "spiritual principle" (Renan). It also consists of an element of constraint. It allocates power. It is incarnated in institutions.

Weber and Mauss went further than Renan in their criticism of the "objective" definition of the nation. Against nationalist militants, who invoked the objective character of ethnies in order to have them recognized as nations, they restored the meaning of their arguments: common characteristics—race, language, culture—of nationals are not the cause, but the *effect* of national construction. "Race creates nationality in a good number of spirits...But all these paradoxes and these paralogisms and these sophisms of political interest are produced by a fundamental fact that they reflect; new races are formed within modern nations...it is because the nation creates the race that one has believed that race creates the nation."[5] Max Weber made the same remark (see above, p. 29). More generally, "if nationalities created that way languages, it is also true that, in modern times, the language creates if not the nation, then at least nationality...Whereas it is the nation which makes tradition, one looks to reconstitute this latter around tradition."[6] In his unfinished text, Max Weber also observed that the nation was not "identical to the linguistic community," that it was founded neither "upon common blood" nor on "a common anthropological type," nor on religion, "the other great culture value of the masses." In a general way, "it certainly cannot be stated in terms of empirical qualities common to those who count as members of the nation."[7] It is true that "objective" characteristics allow one to define the ethnie as well as the nation. National sentiment is not qualitatively different from ethnic feeling: internalization, passion, and the will to participate in a collective founded on interests and feelings. But, contrary to Renan, neither Weber nor Mauss appealed to the "soul." They essentially proposed a political definition of the nation. "The sovereign political body: it is the totality of citizens."[8] "It is evident, then, that so long as 'national' signifies something which is unitary, it also would be a kind of specific passion (*pathos*). In a group of men united by the community of language, religious confession, mores or destiny, this passion will be linked to the idea of an organization of political power, preexistent or ardently desired, which is fitting to them. It will become even more specific as the emphasis will have been placed more on 'power.'"[9] No characteristic of populations is either necessary or sufficient to form a nation. Rather, it is the political organization which creates the nation and which lends meaning to characteristics termed objective.

If Weber tended to assimilate the nation to the state, and this latter to the will to power, contemporary thinkers, on the contrary, underestimate the role of political institutions. Some privilege the effect of technical and economic conditions on the building of nations, neglecting ideas and political institutions: this is the case, for instance, with Deutsch, Gellner, or Wallerstein (see below, chapter 5). Others like Lipset, Kedourie, or Anderson argue with good reason that the existence of the nation necessarily implies that men previously elaborated the idea of it. They tend, however, to neglect the concrete and institutional dimension of national construction. The former and the latter groups are embedded in a political culture which tends to underestimate the role of the state, and to postulate, based on the experience of England, the priority of the individual over the collectivity and of society over the state.

For Lipset, key events which were at the origin of nations generate "values and predispositions" which in turn "determine the continuation of events"; they become more established when "they come into interaction with material conditions."[10] Contrary to this cultural interpretation, "material conditions" are not only the means to reinforce values and predispositions born from the historical origin of the nation: material conditions are, as much as values and predispositions, the very precondition for the existence of the nation. One has to distinguish analytically the nation from the state, and even if there is no direct correspondence between the two terms, it remains true that a nation exists only if it is incarnated in objective social forms. From the moment one defines the nation as the source of legitimacy, the privileged object of collective loyalty and the foundation of political solidarity,[11] one must have institutions in place so that the power which is founded on this legitimacy can be effectively exercised, and so that this loyalty and this solidarity are supported and maintained. The very idea of the nation as political community, formed by free and equal citizens, was progressively born in modern times in sixteenth-century England. But this idea would not have given birth to the English nation in the subsequent centuries if citizens did not possess the House of Commons and independent courts to limit the king's powers and to anchor this idea in concrete reality. Only insofar as they are institutionalized do collective values become a part of common life. Today, most democratic nations invoke identical values of equality and efficiency; but in each national unit they are incarnated differently in the objective institutions of collective life. The social world is formed not only of individuals, but also of organized and permanent entities or institutions, which exist independent of the concrete individuals who compose them. These individuals inevitably act within these systems of predictable relations the constraints that they imposed on individual action. It is therefore important neither to neglect the existence and the efficiency of ideas, nor the concrete realities contained in the form of social institutions.

The concept of *political project* seems to me capable of overcoming the facile contrast between an objective and a subjective definition, as well as of giving some account of the tension between the universalist project of citizenship and the concrete reality of national particularity. It allows one to extend the essentially political analysis of Weber and Mauss. The elaboration of a political society is not a "soul" (Renan). Philosophers and historical experience have demonstrated for some time that no social organization is perpetuated if it is not sustained by the desire of individuals to live together, to respect a certain number of values and common norms, and to act collectively. This consent can be obtained by fear and faith in tyrannical and totalitarian regimes. In the modern democratic nation, it is the community of citizens which must bear this will, although it has a meaningful and effectual truth only if it is incarnated in institutionalized forms of social life.

The political project can correspond to the *Machtpolitik* of Max Weber, where "time and time again we find that the concept 'nation' directs us to political power."[12] But this is not necessarily the case. For Weber himself, even before he formulated the relation between "nation" and "power," observed: "On the other hand, the pride of the Swiss in their own distinctiveness, and their willingness to defend it vigorously, is neither qualitatively different nor less widespread than the same attitudes in any 'great' and 'powerful' nation."[13]

To define the political project in these terms does not imply that one has eliminated the "spiritual"—the elaboration of the very idea of the nation, the myths of origin, the beliefs of the nationals in their uniqueness, and the values by which democratic nations are asserted. On the contrary, ideas and symbols form an integral part of this project. Objectivity is located in the values and symbols unique to each society. One does not succumb to the allure of the nationalist ideology by merely observing that men have beliefs and wills—aroused and maintained by collective authorities—which are part of the objective reality which the sociologist must take into account. The political project designates at the same time ideas—values and ideologies—and objective realities—social practices and institutions—in a process of continuous interaction by which the process of national integration comes into being.

In each nation, the political project was born from a unique history, most of the time after violent events, wars and revolutions, in a given territory. It was formulated, then made use of by one or several particular social groups. In England, with the old feudal noblesse destroyed by the War of the Roses, the national idea was developed by a commercial aristocracy, open to new intellectual talents and to the merchant bourgeoisie. By its origin and its system of values, this class was the bearer of the liberal and parliamentary project. The British colonists of American society, filled with biblical culture and nourished by a spirit of political independence, left their imprimatur on the history of the United States. The State of Israel extends the project of Zionist Jews, inspired from the beginning of the century by their experience with the nationalisms of Central and Eastern Europe. The political project is perpetuated by political actors and institutions, in particular by the state, which gives form to the abstraction that is the civic nation. Afterwards, it is progressively internalized by a majority of citizens.

National activity is not completely determined by their political project. Rather, this project is continuously reinterpreted by populations, until its élan is eventually exhausted. Because any charismatic power is threatened by "routinization" (Weber), it always risks being attenuated until it dissolves, particularly if citizens cease to participate in the values, practices, and institutions which established it. Even weakened, however, it remains a source of common values.

Nations created as "fragments" of European nations seem especially marked by the conditions of their birth. In the United States, Australia, Canada, South Africa, and Latin America, these fragments, once separated from the European motherland, apparently ceased to evolve.[14] For two centuries, Australia remained "radical," according to Cobbett and the Chartists. The United States, founded as a "bourgeois fragment" of seventeenth-century British society, continued to maintain the values which lay at the origin of their birth as independent nations. The comparison between the United States and Canada is in this respect enlightening. English liberalism was the culture common to all British colonists settled on lands which would later form Canada and the United States. But after the War of Independence, British loyalists who intended to remain faithful to the British Crown took refuge in Canada, where they imported a more conservative political culture whose remnants are evident even today. In comparing the political culture of Americans and Canadians, Seymour Martin Lipset observed that the former continue to maintain ideas of equality of opportunity and achievement, and other values of "revolutionary" or "left" inspiration. By celebrating their own nation in essentially political terms, they prolong their original ambition of building a society liberated from the ballast of old Europe. Canadians, on the other hand, remain marked by their original political project, more conservators, continuing to accord a more prominent place to the values of solidarity and social protection.[15]

The comparison between the two peoples within Canada suggests another interpretation along the same lines. All colonists of British origin in North America, even those who had affirmed their faithfulness to the Crown by taking refuge in Canada after the American Revolution, were liberal and heterodox, nourished by a spirit of dissidence. Conversely, French colonists wanted nothing more than to be the docile subjects of the King of France. The treaty of 1759, in creating British Canada, consecrated the existence of two distinct political projects. For British Canadians, it was that of building on the American model, while at the same time maintaining a certain distance from their neighbors, and by remaining faithful to the British Crown. For French Canadians, it was the task of *surviving*—as a religious, linguistic, and cultural minority—their immersion in the world of English origin and English culture. Arising from two distinct political projects, two different societies were maintained within the federation until the 1960s.

Democratic nations are distinguished from one another by the manner in which a political project strives to overcome objective differences between populations and to create a community of citizens, the source of the legitimacy of the politically constituted nation. This uniqueness occurs both in the dual dimension of ideas—for example, the values of English liberalism, the abstract rationalist universalism of France, or Swiss pluralism—and of concrete and abstract institutions—for instance, the practices of parliamentarism, concrete forms of state organization and public services, nationality law, national emblems, the School, the teaching of history, and markers of identity. Ideas and values are uniquely incarnated in social life. What one can call the integrative capacity of the nation is defined by the relationship between the *political project* and the ethnic and social characteristics of populations organized into nationhood by the state.

Historical Projects[16]

"An autonomous local unit becomes a nation only if its autonomy is accompanied by notable and lasting political events, capable of communicating to it the feeling of its singularity and of commanding the respect of its external circle."[17] In each of the great Western democracies—in England, the United States, and France—there was a sense of uniqueness, and hence the "grandeur" of its political project: to have "invented" a new political regime truly constitutes one of these "notable and lasting political events," evoked with nostalgia by the Hungarian historian Istvan Bibo, when he reflected on the "misery of the small states of Eastern Europe."

Political Invention
Great Britain; or, the Invention of Liberty and Parliamentarism

This feeling is strongly internalized in England where, in fact, the national idea and the parliamentary regime were born and where, for centuries, foreigners admired the supreme example of political liberty in a modern nation. Since the eighteenth century, the British have developed a pride in the fact that they enjoy a freedom of the press and individual liberty unique in the world. Indissolubly myth and reality, the conviction of having deliberately invented parliamentary institutions, the guarantors of these liberties, is nevertheless at the heart of the English political project.

Traces of this national sentiment may be found since the Hundred Years War. In the following century, the thinkers and poets of the Elizabethan age formulated the idea that man realized what was properly human in himself by political participation in liberty—the first glimpse of the modern idea of nationhood, as a community of free and equal individuals, and as a political organization founded on the Reason of man.[18] Patriotism became not only a virtue, but a right, necessarily linked to the essential dignity of each individual. Since the Glorious Revolution of 1688, the English could pride themselves on being the only nation born of an endogenous process, one which invented modern political freedom and parliamentarism. It was a nation which had no model and which was born before the democratic idea and the principle of the right of peoples to self-possession were diffused throughout Europe and the world. The conviction that other nations could only study and attempt to emulate this properly British creation attained the status of national myth.

The English also took pride in being the only nation founded on the meaning and the value of tradition and of empiricism, on the safe respect of historical reality and the recognition of the fragility of social ties. Alone among all nations, England was not born from a revolutionary project. It was not born of the ambition, foolish as well as dangerous, if not also criminal, of creating a New Man. Throughout the centuries, it alone knew how to forge by practice the political form transformed in the twentieth century into parliamentary democracy; it singularly knew how to remain founded on the Common law and jurisprudence; it alone knew how to make precedent into the equivalent of the Constitution and to adapt itself delicately but efficiently to the changing necessities of each age. It alone could escape the populist element which inevitably marked the birth of other nations. Against the metaphysical abstraction of revolutionary ambitions on the European continent, England assured the true liberties, that is to say concrete liberties—not the abstract Liberty. These were progressively wrenched away from royal power by the installation of counterpowers, in particular that of Parliament. England could thereby avoid brutalizing men and consciences; it respected entities, bodies and real groups. In cultivating this national myth, even to the point of underestimating the violence which marked English history until the revolutions of the seventeenth century, and even until the middle of the last century, the English wrote their national history just as T. B. Macaulay described the "Glorious Revolution" of 1688. That is, by opposing it at least implicitly to the revolutions of the European Continent: in light of which it appeared "moderate, conservative, responsible and humane."

Historians have for some time focused on the cautious reforms which permitted the establishment of parliamentary institutions and practices during the seventeenth and eighteenth century—in successive stages without destroying the social fabric—and later, the extension of political democracy by successive reforms of the right to vote and of the coordination of powers between the King, Lords, and the Commons. They demonstrated how parliamentarism was progressively established with a cabinet, responsible and filled with solidarity, led by a prime minister, dependent on the vote of the majority of the Houses of Commons, of which the ministers were themselves members; how the parliamentary and liberal regime was later democratized by extending the right to vote and allowing by degrees the participation of the various social stratums in political life; and how these measures, completed by the reform of 1911, which limited the powers of the House of Lords, finally assured an effectively equal representation of the people to the Commons. The British Parliament, which was first the instrument of the control and limitation of royal power by the aristocracy and the place where liberties were founded and expressed, became the site for the political elaboration and the practice of democracy without any need for revolution.

The idea of checks and balances was praised by English historians as much as by foreign admirers of the British tradition. Many celebrated the balance between the power of the king and that of Parliament, between the king and the people—what Hume called "the right balance between the monarchical and republican part of our constitution"..."Its government is at the same time monarchy, aristocracy, and democracy: the nation is half noble, half merchant: all sects are tolerated in it; and the great liberty which one enjoys, allows each to give free rein to his humor and to his tendencies."[19] Montesquieu's theory of what he calls "the distribution of powers" remained even in England the classic interpretation of English politics.

Hume and Burke were the great thinkers of a political project founded on the idea that only time lends solidity to rights and that political legitimacy is born of tradition. "Little by little time overcomes these obstacles and accustoms the nation to regarding as its legitimate sovereign the one whom it first took for a stranger and a usurper." This is moreover why "we owe obedience to the prince who is on the throne, and who is directly descended from a series of ancestors, who for several centuries have reigned over us." It is necessary to modify the goals of politics and to adapt ourselves to changes, but only with caution and moderation. Politics must take its lessons from historical experience and respect the continuity of institutions and values. If the English constitution is "the superb edifice in which England prides itself, which attracts the jealousy of our neighbors,"this is because its "foundation is the work of several centuries."[20]

Both Hume and Burke have a theory not of abstract Liberty, but of concrete liberties: "The Tories appear to me to have had for liberty the feelings of all real British persons, resolved neither to sacrifice it for abstract principles, nor to the pretended rights of princes."[21] "In the famous law of the 3d of Charles I, called the *petition of rights,* the Parliament says to the king, 'your subjects have *inherited* this freedom,' claiming their franchises not on abstract principles 'as the rights of men,' but as the rights of Englishmen, and as a patrimony derived from their forefathers."[22] For Burke, to be free was to conserve the inheritance passed on to English subjects by their ancestors; it was to preserve an inherited patrimony and to transmit it to one's posterity. Communal belonging, the product of tradition, was more convenient for the individual than the abstract claim of liberty. Hence his interpretation of the Glorious Revolution and of the Restoration of 1688 conformed to that of the Whigs. These events, according to him, permitted the restoration of the tradition of liberties that the king tended to limit. According to Burke the origin of this tradition came from article 12 of the Magna Carta of 1215, which subordinated all tax levying to the agreement of the Council, and from article 61, which in permanence submitted the king to the control of a delegation of barons who were authorized to launch a revolt in order to obtain the respect of agreements taken. "All the reformations we have hitherto made, have proceeded upon the principle of reference to antiquity."[23] The Glorious Revolution at the same time affirmed the end of the royal absolutism, consecrated the preponderance of Parliament, but also the necessity of the presence of the king at the top of the political and social edifice. God could inspire the king, but he was from now on "king in his parliament." Far from marking a violent rupture, it was embedded in continuity.

The belief in the singularity of England, the nation which was itself invented by inventing the idea and institutions of liberty and the modern nation—makes of the English the new Chosen People. This property has not gone unnoticed by contemporary scholars who observe that: "Alone (the British system) represented a slow conventional growth, not like the others, the product of deliberate invention...Because it was first, the English—later the British experience remained distinct."[24]

The United States; or, the Invention of Democracy

Americans have prided themselves on having "invented" the first new nation in history. Harriet Martineau was not the only European traveler of the nineteenth century to be struck by the fact that all Americans shared this conviction. This theme was renewed in the age of decolonization, when in 1963 Seymour Martin Lipset saw in the United States *The First New Nation*,[25] that is to say, the first nation born of a revolt against a European imperial power. The United States therefore supplied, in his view, a model to all nationalist militants of those formerly colonized countries of the twentieth century.

Moreover, the United States entertained the idea that they gave to the world the first example of true democracy, the only nation wholly free from any ethnic dimension, open to all those who shared the ideal of liberty.[26] According to their collective myth, they created what in the language of that time they called a new "race," that is to say, a new nation, distinct from all European "races." In his book, *Lettres d'un cultivateur américain,* which was published in London during the Revolutionary War and which enjoyed large success throughout Europe, the American immigrant of French origin, Hector Saint-John de Crèvecœur, already evoked this new man who "without having any antique credulity, any dangerous prejudice, any old opinions, studies with care new discoveries of other nations, unites them to his, and adopts them with joy." And George Washington wrote with equal lyricism: "The bosom of America opens itself to greet the persecuted and the oppressed of all countries and all religions."[27] Until the publication in 1963 of *Beyond the Melting Pot,*[28] only a few marginal authors called into question the fact and the ideal—linked as in most of the nationalist literature—of the American *melting pot*. The national motto, *E pluribus Unum,* evoked this society founded on a principle which aspired to be entirely new.

Americans not only felt unique in their creation of a new "race," or nation. They also invented representative democracy. As Philippe

Raynaud summed it up: "Americans *democratized* the English theory of representation, they *republicanised* the English Constitution."[29] This is a conviction that contemporary American historians continue to validate. The idea of the sovereign people as the source of legitimacy was formulated by Rousseau. But the "delegation," that is to say the idea of representation, was conceived and implemented—according to the actors themselves and to contemporary historians—during the Revolutionary War. Madison affirmed that the American Republic was without precedent: it invented the idea of representation, that is "the delegation of the government to a small number of citizens elected by other citizens." These words reflected a judgment expressed by innumerable publicists of that time.[30] The historical birth of American democracy between 1776 and 1787 was indeed accompanied by a vast debate over ideas, in which various intellectual traditions clashed and converged: the political philosophy of antiquity, Christian theology, liberal English empiricism, the rationalism of the Enlightenment. The American project was simultaneously embedded within the biblical worldview, the English political tradition inaugurated with the *habeas corpus*, and the myth of a New World rid of the burdens and tyrannies of old Europe. For a decade an entire people collectively participated in the founding of a new form of society. The debate of ideas was immediately expressed in social forms, the confrontation between conceptions and institutions was immediate. During the course of this great confrontation, both intellectual and political, was formed an "entirely new conception of the political, a conception which carried them from an essentially classical and medieval universe of thought to a distinctly modern universe of thought."[31]

Throughout the nineteenth century European visitors reinforced this conviction: it was the very essence of democratic society that Tocqueville came to study and to appreciate by crossing the Atlantic. Moreover, his work itself contributed to maintaining the way that Americans formulated their own national myth.

Shared by an entire people, this myth was easily translated into a national project, as the newly independent American citizens already belonged to a homogeneous society, filled with biblical religiosity, formed by the same political culture, in an uncontested territory, with an already ancient history in common. The Declaration of Independence provoked no brutal rupture either in institutional structure or in social organization.[32] The independent United States not only had the will to manage their own affairs without the intervention of the motherland, they already formed a community of citizens, who entertained the goal of establishing the first true democracy founded on liberty. Both this sentiment of national unity and the constitutions of the thirteen colonies preexisted the organization of the federal state. Objective realities favored the birth of a novel idea of society.

This original myth and the political institutions stemming from the colonial period and the Revolutionary War assured the integration of American society for two centuries, despite the increasing heterogeneity of waves of immigration. Institutions were supported by the belief, shared by a whole people, of having invented "a political system so new, so complex, so well articulated, that one would not stop writing about it" (Harriet Martineau). Despite the "nativist" reaction and the xenophobia which erupted, first against Germans, Irish, and Scandinavians, then, at the end of the century, against Southern and Eastern Europeans (Italians, Hungarians, Czechs, Russians, Jews), the majority of Americans of European origin could recognize themselves in Franklin D. Roosevelt's formula: "Americanism has never been a question of ancestral race or origin. A good American is a man who is loyal toward this country and toward these ideals of liberty and democracy." This definition was rooted in the original political project.

But it is clear that neither blacks nor Native Americans were absorbed into this original political project. The extermination or exclusion of the Native Americans and the enslavement of blacks, was always present in the national consciousness and was fundamentally opposed to the essence of the democratic project as formulated by Americans themselves. This placed limits on the national project, limits whose weight historians tardily (but today abundantly) discovered in the historical consciousness and public life of America. Nevertheless Tocqueville had earlier perceived that the physical presence of blacks, excluded by fact from the national bond and absent from political life, would represent "the most fearsome of all harms which threaten the future of United States."[33] The presence/absence of blacks and Native Americans in democratic life until the 1960s, the cruel persecution of Asians before and also during World War II, and even the violent nativist reactions against non-British European immigrants at the end of the last century all found their inspiration in the political project, which was founded on universal principles, but which was concretely implemented by those known today as White Anglo Saxon Protestants (WASPs). Today, modern scholars denounce precisely these breaches of professed democratic principles—insofar as blacks, Native Americans, who obtained the right to vote only in 1924, and women were for a long time excluded from political participation—but the power of the national myth can nonetheless be admired.

France; or, the Invention of the Nation

"The French example relied on a history two millennia old, on a political framework which has existed for fifteen hundred years, on a millennium of centralized power, on a half millennium of national consciousness and on the prestige of the great *French* Revolution," as Istvan Bibo has observed.[34]

If one can discuss this almost epic evaluation of historical time, it is true that patriotic feelings and the primary statist institutions have existed in France since the end of the Middle Ages. National construction has for centuries been undertaken around and by the action of the state. Kings of France unified the nation long before the revolution proclaimed its sovereignty. Registers of grievances which preceded the meeting of the *Etats généraux* of 1789 testified to the attachment of populations to a homeland that they saw as inseparable from the monarchy. Yet it is also true that France pretended for some time to have invented the modern nation. According to the national myth, *its* revolution is the universal model. It affirmed before the entire world this new principle of legitimacy and proclaimed for the first time in the name of the entire universe the Declaration of Rights *of all men*. After having insisted on the privileged bond that the royalty and France maintained with the Catholic Church, when the principle of legitimacy was religious, the French after the Revolution now feel glorified in having given the world the first experience and the first ideology of the modern nation.

Even if the national idea was born in the Middle Ages, and if the monarchy for centuries led the national project and organized the first statist institutions, the Republicans of the Third Republic, upon assuming power in the 1880s, consciously created institutions charged with establishing the modern nation. National institutions—the School or the Army—organized collective life around regular practices and diffused a system of coherent national values. The unification of society by the centralization of education and administration—even if these were at least in some part inherited from the monarchy—were reinforced by the desire, transmitted from kings to Republicans, to build the modern nation around and by the state. In the only European country which has known massive immigration since the beginning of the nineteenth century, this policy, which is linked to the history of citizenship and democracy, permitted France to assimilate these foreigners, to recall the term used until the 1970s. The political project was carried by national institutions: the particularly open nationality law, which in a country of immigration transformed immigrants or, at least, their children into citizens and soldiers; the free, secular, and mandatory School of the Republic; the public administration; the army. Teachers of the Third Republic effectively nationalized the children of French provincial peasants and of immigrants by teaching them, even by force, French and calculus and by forbidding them to use the language of their parents. The army also contributed to this nationalization of populations, whose efficiency the war of 1914–1918 tragically demonstrated. After the establishment of conscription (1872) and of a nationality law (1889) which imposed French nationality on the children of foreigners born on French soil in order to recruit them, it mixed populations from all countries of emigration, all regions, and all social classes. It maintained the sentiment of national community with the help of teachers who carried on the schooling of recruits and the diffusion of the patriotism.[35]

The pretension of leading a politics of assimilation in the colonies, that is to say, of imposing a politics linked to characteristics of French society upon countries with different traditions—an ambition even more abstract than the colonial situation was founded on the inequality of political status between colonizers and colonized—reveals the force of that model.

The apparition of the citizen on the political stage—in contrast to the progressive acquisition of citizenship in England—constituted a rupture so brutal that it accounts for gaps between state and civil society, as well as conflicts over legitimacy. The state had for some time been the protector and the liberator of minority groups, eventually even against the prejudices and violence of civil society. The contest between the legitimacy of the Ancien Régime and that of the Revolution and the Republic—which was expressed by the succession of political regimes throughout the nineteenth century—finally ended with the reestablishment of the Republic at the end of World War II—the French state of Marshal Philippe Pétain had again established its legitimacy against the individualistic and democratic values of the Republic. Perhaps this collective and conflictual argument over the identity and meaning of the nation, which has monopolized French political history since the Revolution, also had paradoxical function of integration. For both the former and the latter groups invoked the "true" France, pretended to personify the real French nation, and conjured up equally passionate patriotisms. Since the Revolution, the opposition between the Right—conflated, perhaps unfairly, with the Ancien Régime—and the Left—assimilated to the revolutionary project—organized the world of political thought. Born from the battle of the Revolution against the Ancien Régime, this cleavage continued to influence the spirit and the political landscape of modern France.

This notion of having invented the nation and forging political modernity lies at the heart of the national myth and national pride. Born from values incarnated by the Revolution, which marks for the French "the beginning of the reign of truth on earth,"[36] the political project was founded on the fact and ideology of individual citizenship: it is thanks to this project—both as a system of professed values and institutions—that since the Revolution populations heterogeneous in term of their regional, social, and national origin were integrated. National integration was the product of a political desire, implemented by strong statist institutions and justified by a system of values regularly evoked in public life as the "republican model." More than in any other country, the model of integration "in the French way" is founded on the idea and the value of individual citizenship, on the formal, juridical and political equality of the citizen-individual. This model was ideologically founded on a conception by which all men, if they merely attained the necessary education, were capable of participating in a political project founded on universal citizenship. In this manner, patriotism might be founded on the myth of the Revolution, which allowed the national idea to be reconciled with the ambition of universality: the French conceived and experienced this as the purest form of the rights of man.

But the consciousness of having invented a unique nation is not reserved for great Western democracies; it is constitutive of any nation. The cause of liberating modern Greece mobilized intellectuals and even several European governments by means of a myth of prestigious origin—the invention of democracy by Athens in the fifth century. This myth remains alive in the historical consciousness of today's Greeks, who gladly flatter themselves with their direct affiliation with ancient democracy and repress the centuries during which they were subjects of the Turkish Empire. On the other hand, however, the Turkish "hereditary enemy" plays an essential role in the national consciousness. All nationalist thinkers similarly "rediscovered," that is to say, rebuilt or even invented the exceptional birth of their nation. Serb nationalists celebrated the memory of the battle of Kosovo in 1389, which became the symbol of their multisecular fight for independence. At the beginning of the nineteenth century, Païssi rediscovered the singular greatness of the Bulgarian empire, which had existed before the Bulgarians were for five centuries dominated by the Ottomans. Henri Pirenne attributed a glorious birth to independent Belgium, when plebeian cities in revolt against patricians halted the cavalry of Philippe the Fair in Courtrai in 1302: "Flemish artisans held out in front of the charges of horsemen just as the *sans-culottes* of the French Revolution held out in the eighteenth century in front of Austrian batteries, because both were conscious of fighting not only for the soil, but also for a political ideal."[37] A glorious birth, inextricably factual and mythical, supports the belief of nationals in their specific genius.

The Will to Independence of Small European Nations

Yet this process of political invention is not the only source of the political project. By way constrast, that of the small European nations was born from their refusal, demonstrated through centuries of wars and revolutions, to be annexed by major states, monarchies, or empires of Western Europe. The desire not to become a province of Spain, Germany, or France established the national project of Portugal, the Netherlands, or Switzerland. The feeling of being regarded as the object of contempt or condescension by a more powerful neighbor aroused the national will of the Danish against Germany and Sweden, and the Norwegians against Denmark. The aspiration to independence against more powerful neighbors constituted the heart of the political project—perhaps causing us to wonder about the future of this project when, today, these neighbors seem no longer to constitute a threat to national independence.

The "small nations" of Europe (Switzerland, Belgium, the Netherlands) were heirs to the municipal tradition of polycephalic Europe, which was maintained under the auspices of the Holy Roman Empire of the Germanic people, even while the great monarchies of Western Europe were being built. Switzerland was born only mythically from the pact signed on 1 August 1291 between the cantons of Uri, Schwyz, and Unterwald, but it is true that Switzerland was progressively constituted over centuries by gathering other political entities equally attached to their independence around the treaty of alliance between these three original cantons. The Netherlands was created by an agreement between provinces during the Union of Utrecht in 1759. But when Pirenne wished to found a common national myth which might unite Flemish and Walloons, he evoked in addition a very remote military victory against a common enemy in 1302 at Courtrai. This "civic camaraderie," according to him, permitted a Belgian nation to be constituted even before the construction of a state recognized by other European powers. "Contrary to what happened in many other countries, where the monarchy made society, where the unit of government produced national unity, one can say that, in our home, national unity preceded the unit of government...Moreover, the State was often the cause of a proper national life; here, this seems to have been the case."[38] In the case of Holland, Switzerland, and Belgium, Renan also evoked "the direct will of provinces" and the "deep municipal spirit which made the French royalty unbearable to these countries."[39] The "municipal" democracy—perhaps favored, in the case of the Netherlands and Switzerland, by difficult physical conditions which led men to collaborate in collective institutions in order to fight together against nature—resisted the will of more powerful neighbors.

But this will alone would not have been enough to ensure national integration, despite the antiquity of collective history, if three objective conditions had not been considered: ideas alone do not create nations. Great nations had to agree to recognize an independence which was rooted in the judgment they made of their own interests and their power struggles. Despite the objective diversity of populations and their political traditions, "small nations" were united if not by the feeling of belonging to the same historical collectivity, then at least by the same desire not to be annexed by one or other great neighboring powers. The practices of the "consociative democracies" (Belgium, the Netherlands, Austria, Switzerland)[40] allowed entities distinguished by their language or religion to participate in common political management in a way that respected the dignity of each of them and allowed them to preserve their own religious, philanthropic, and cultural organizations. The values of liberalism and pluralism, the sense of the "organized compromise" in the Dutch formulation, which were part of the national myth in the Netherlands and Switzerland, were inscribed in political institutions and in social practices.

Especially in Switzerland, the ability to manage a native democracy fosters national pride. Yet all the political and juridical dispositions of "consociative democracies" would be in vain, if they were not accompanied by what Uli Windisch termed "the intercommunitary historical know-how," forged by centuries of cohabitation and collaboration among different cultures and political collectivities.⁴¹ In their management of diversity, cultivated as a national art, the Swiss believe themselves to be unique. "There are none like us" is a very ancient formulation that ethnologists continue to hear in all environments. Everywhere one evokes "the traditional Helvetian values": strength of character and discipline, morality and ardor in work; public spirit; respect for religion, economic and familial common sense, and so on.⁴² This elevated opinion of their own singularity maintains the Swiss national project and contributes to their respect for practices which ensure the collaboration of various cultural entities.

Israel's Birth out of Tragedy

The uniqueness of the national project in Israel is a result of its double birth: the original Zionist project and its reformulation after the *shoah*.

The original Zionist project was forged in the Jewish communities of Eastern Europe from two essential ideas. When Eastern nations, in the image of those of Western Europe, become organized on a principle of secularity, on the market economy and on the universality of political rights, it becomes impossible for Jews to maintain their unique way of life and collective identity. This identity is national and religious, and has so far been preserved irremediably by social separation. On the other hand, modern democracies can never completely respect the universal and formal principles to which they refer. They will betray the very values they purport to hold, inevitably developing symbols and traditions more ethnic than civic; they will never completely accept Jews. "We always tried loyally to enter into the national collectivities which surrounded us, conserving only the faith of our fathers. But this is not permitted. In vain are we sincere patriots, and indeed, in different places, exuberant patriots; in vain do we make the same sacrifices in money and in blood as our fellow citizens, in vain do we strive to reinstate the glory of our respective homelands."⁴³ In Europe, Zionists fought against developments which, according to them, destroyed traditional Jewish community and assimilated its members to the ambient society, without, moreover, succeeding in dispelling antisemitism. They intended to build in Israel a largely secular modern society, territorially, economically, and politically independent, on the model of European nations. But one which would be "at the same time totally Jewish."⁴⁴ It would give Jews self-respect by making them respected by others, and would assure their liberty and their security. Until World War II, Zionist migrants did not look to better their lot by settling without personal or collective financial means in a poor country ravaged by malaria. They intended to create a new society and even a New Man, the Hebrew. But contrary to French and Soviet revolutionaries, they wanted to create the New Man as Normal Man, to consecrate the normality of Jews and of the Jewish nation. The "rising" (*aliyah*) of the Jews toward Palestine was essentially political. Herzl said "I consider the Jewish question to be neither religious, nor social, but truly national."

Because it is a matter of inventing a new society, the economic and social structures of Israeli society had to stand out clearly against those of diasporic communities. The Hebrew, contrary to the Jew of the Diaspora, would work the earth and would also become a worker of industry. As during the French Revolution, one dreamt of regenerating humanity. Undertaken by individuals who already kept their distance from the traditional religious community, this project was also related to dreams of social justice and solidarity which were inspired by socialism and a criticism of the individualistic and competitive character of the modern economy. Migrants from the third *alyah*, after World War I, created the kibbutz, direct democracy uniting free and equal individuals. The kibbutz was founded in the confluence of every dimensions of the Zionist project: the replacement of the Jew by the Hebrew or the Israeli, the first realization of the socialist utopia. It symbolically incarnated the political project, which explains why it is maintained today despite its contradictions and the criticism to which it is often subjected in Israel.

The great powers would never have accepted the creation of an independent Jewish state if, after the war, the governors—if not the populations—had not discovered the extent of the disaster. "The victors, as the Jewish tragedy was revealed, did not have a clear conscience. It was only at that time that one asked if one had done enough to help them and what one could do to help survivors.... The birth of the Jewish state was the realization of a Zionist dream. But it required the destruction of the Jewish community in Europe. Zionism had not been able to prevent the catastrophe. To the contrary, the state owed its existence to the disaster."[45] Beyond even the recognition of the state by the United Nations, the *shoah*, for Zionists themselves, renewed, albeit tragically, the original project and gave it new legitimacy. "As shocking as it might seem, Hitler was certainly the most powerful lever in the edification of the Jewish state."[46] From now on, it was no longer just a matter of returning their dignity to Jews, but of allowing the Jewish people to survive, and hence making a failure of Hitler's politics of annihilation. The commemoration of the *shoah,* a true civil religion, is maintained as a national cult. In April 1951, a decree fixed the date of the Day of Remembrance, whose commemoration was afterward made law on April 1959. Each year, on 19 April, all the media carry the commemoration exclusively; the entire country rests for two minutes to pay homage to the victims. The ritual visit of chiefs of state to Yad Vashem, the teaching of the *shoah* in schools, and university scholarship all further contribute to maintaining the Israeli political project. As Istvan Bibo wrote: "An autonomous local unit becomes a nation only if its autonomy is accompanied by notable and lasting political events..."

The Law of the Return, passed in 1950 just after the Independence of the State of Israel, gave to all Jews of the world the right of return to Palestine as Israeli citizens. But that project, although universal in ambition, was elaborated and concretely embedded in the new institutions of the *Yishuv,* and later of the state, by Jews of Central and Eastern Europe, mainly Russians, Polish, and Romanians: the Zionist project was thus political and European. However, in the 1950s and 1960s, it was a matter of integrating waves of immigrants native to the Middle East and the Maghreb. Some of them, in particular those who came from Arabic countries, fled persecution. Others primarily strove to better their lot; these oriented themselves to individualistic values and did not identify themselves with the collective ambition of Zionism. Others had, to the contrary, an essentially messianic conception of their coming to Palestine. All arrived in an already constituted society, balanced by its political organization, with a strong bureaucratic structure of European and socialist inspiration. Israel then experienced the classic problem of countries of immigration. Populations of the same national origin, in particular those who came from the three countries of the Maghreb, form the vast majority of the underprivileged social groups. Local administrations and national political parties have in fact organized "ethnic" sections. "Community" organizations were used as intermediaries between the political powers, the administration and individuals. Arriving in a society whose project was wedded to the European political tradition, "Orientals" had the feeling of being poorly received and misunderstood, of forming a minority looked down upon as inferior. Foreign to their traditions, the measures of "Israelization" to which they were subjected upon their arrival appeared brutal and humiliating to them. Tensions and conflicts in Israel between Ashkenazim and Sephardim—since the 1950s, the revolts of "Orientals" against the European and socialist political establishment—are closely linked to the very history of the Zionist project.

As in other countries, the political project is only revised by the occasion of common adversity. The danger of war that the country has known continuously since 1948 has maintained a patriotism, even if it appears weaker today, that other democracies ignore. Upon the arrival by plane of more than 30,000 Falashas thanks to the operations "Moses" and "Solomon," in 1985 and 1991, Israelis once again experienced the messianic élan which carried the first Zionist immigrant toward the land of Palestine. These black Ethiopian Jews had for two thousand years remained faithful to Judaism despite their isolation. On the other hand, the integration of Soviet Jews, arriving en masse since the liberalization of the former Soviet Union, appeared difficult insofar as they barely participate in the Israeli political project. Marked by their historical experiences, many among them have every desire to accede to Western life; Israel is for them nothing more than a substitute for the United States.

Citizenship and Nationalities

Since the Great Revolution, which aroused nationalist claims throughout Europe and later in the entire world, many have attempted to resolve the tension between the universalism of the civic nation and ethnic particularisms by the "overcoming" of the nation. Numerous thinkers have reflected on the possibility of a political organization dissociated from "national" belonging, that is to say, from ethnic belonging. In this manner one might hope to deflate ethnic and nationalistic passions by the pure rationality of citizenship. Since the beginning of the age of nationalisms—the age of ethnic claims to create an independent nation—one strove to conceive of an organization in which individuals would retain their identity in a historical and cultural collectivity while at the same time participating in a political entity with a universal aim which would transcend these cultures or these "nations." By this dissociation one might guarantee both cultural autonomy *and* political sovereignty, both "nationalities" *and* citizenship, or to adopt the modern terms, geographical, historical and cultural patriotism *and* juridical patriotism.

During the 1880s–1890s, Jewish nationalist thinkers gathered in the organization of the *Bund*, and others in the *Volkspartei* of Simon Doubnov, were militantly insistent that national and cultural autonomy be granted to Jews in a democratic Russia, or more broadly, in the Diaspora. This would be attached not to a territory or a political organization but to persons. Dragomanov, discussed by Max Weber, also proposed for early-twentieth-century Russia a political system in which the existence of particular "nations" would be recognized and their cultural rights respected. The conception of Otto Bauer, celebrated under the rubric of Austro-Marxism, is also founded on this idea of national/cultural autonomy. A Jew living in the supranational Austro-Hungarian empire riven apart by its "nationalities," Bauer dreamt of a new form of political organization, one in which entities would cooperate while maintaining their cultural personality and their right to self-administration. He imagined the "United States of Greater Austria," a confederal state "in which each nation would independently manage its national affairs, while uniting themselves in a single State for the protection of their common interests."[47] Each individual, in whatever territory he was situated, would be free to become a member of a community of culture (*Kulturgemeinschaft*) or "nation" by simple declaration. Common economic and political problems would be treated by a supra*national* government. Willingly chosen, nationality would be independent of a particular territory and state.

Today, the political order founded on the sovereignty of politically constituted nations stands in question. The collapse of the communist system allowed nations composed of several different ethnies—the U.S.S.R., Yugoslavia, Czechoslovakia—to decompose. The construction of the European Community (EC), on the other hand, tends to limit the sovereignty of the states of Western Europe and is founded more or less explicitly on the logic of a federation or confederation of nations. More generally, it is obviously impossible to organize a global order which recognizes as a politically constituted nation every ethnie which is capable of demanding recognition as an independent political entity—whose number risks increasing indefinitely insofar as it is nationalism which creates nations. Some 300 languages are spoken in Europe, whereas politically constituted nations number in the dozens. According to Ernest Gellner, there are 8,000 languages in the world, but only 200 nations recognized by the international juridical order, even though this number has increased since the end of the Soviet empire. Moral arguments about the hypocrisy of politically constituted nations coming into being at the expense of ethnies (as, for instance, in the case of Kurds, divided between Iraq, Iran, Turkey, and the former U.S.S.R.) are justified. Indeed, so too would be all claims on behalf of the 8,000 languages/cultures, if nationalist thinkers were merely to claim that they should be recognized as nations. Philosophers and jurists are therefore once again tempted to conceive of a form of political organization in which cultural belonging and political organization would cease to coincide, at least as an ideal and regulating idea; in other words, to question again the principle and the political ideal of the nation-state.

In this fashion Jürgen Habermas elaborated the concept of "constitutional patriotism" which, against the "conventional form of national identity," would refer "no longer to the concrete totality of a nation but to the contrary to processes and abstract principles."[48] By dissociating the order of citizenship and patriotism, the state, "place of the law," of the "nation," "place of affectivity," the civic or political participation of national identity, this "constitutional patriotism" would be capable of refounding German identity on an examination and an essentially critical reappropriation of its entire past. Patriotic feeling would no longer be linked to Germany, as a cultural and particular historical nation, but to the very principle of the *Etat de droit*.

Pursuing this inspiration and universalizing it, Jean-Marc Ferry developed the idea of "postnational" identity, which also would refer exclusively to "principles of universality, autonomy and of *Etat de droit*.[49] Citizenship would from now on be founded "on a moral reflexive identity whose principle is further inscribed in the French Declaration of Rights of man and citizen, with the right (for the human) and the task (for the citizen) to revolt against tyranny."[50] Individuals would adhere to principles of the *Etat de droit* and the republican order, to the exclusion of any reference to a territory and a concrete historical and cultural community. Any democratic state would be capable of inspiring this patriotism. Similarly, Jacqueline Costa-Lascoux proposes a European citizenship, one which would be defined by harmonized national legislation, in conformity with human rights and accompanied by a "contract of citizenship" between populations who would remain free, in all other respects, to remain attached to a particular culture. This assumes, of course, that social practices stemming from this culture are not incompatible with supranational principles of human rights.[51] Pierre Kende also suggested distinguishing the people (that is to say, the ethnie) from the political organization in Eastern countries, given "the impasse of traditional nationalism" in this region.[52]

Without underestimating what is linked, in the thought of Habermas, to the uniqueness of German history, to the "controversy about the singularity of the extermination of Jews by the Nazi regime"[53] and to his effort, against the revisionism of certain German historians, to found a historical consciousness which integrates democratic values into the national tradition, it is necessary to notice that it extends an older reflection which was born of the abusive and disturbing forms that nationalisms often assumed in history.

One can wonder, however, if it is possible in European countries to separate national belonging and purely political allegiance, as Habermas has attempted. If democratic society implies that there is a communicative and intersubjective space—to recall the Habermasian terms—where citizens, politicians, and experts may talk together, to understand one another and to attempt to persuade one another in order to confront common problems, this can not exist if all members do not share a language, a certain culture and at least some common values. Otherwise, how can one establish this communicative space? These ideas are vulnerable to the same criticism that Burke addressed to the French Revolution and, in particular, to the doctrine of human rights that Philippe Raynaud sums up this way: "It is radically impracticable because it takes no account of the real conditions of human life which occurs in *already* constituted communities"[54]

It is indeed within a particular national community that individuals developed their identity, inextricably individual as well as collective. For centuries in Europe each finds in himself his nation. Any sense of belonging or collective idea can only be the product of a long common history, even if it is, more often, either wholly or partially invented. It is not born from a decision, as desirable or as reasonable as it might be, because one cannot build a collective identity from a *tabula rasa*. An intellectual adhesion to abstract principles—human rights, respect for the *Etat de droit*—could not in the foreseeable future replace the political and emotional mobilization aroused by the internalization of the national tradition. Leaders of communist states knew this: even while pretending to adhere to a universal ideology and a universal political project, they nevertheless exploited national or ethnic rivalries and hatreds. The Soviet citizen had on his passport the category termed "national"—of "Jew" or of "Armenian." Hoxha organized the cult of Illyrians and Ceausescu that of the Daces. The abstract/concrete national—without speaking of the concrete character of ethnic belonging—is a more effective mobilizer than the pure abstractions of class consciousness, *Etat de droit,* or human rights. As Benedict Anderson humorously quips: "Who will willingly die for Comecon or the EEC?"

It seems utopian to conceive in the near future of a political desire dictated only by material interests or convictions founded on abstract reason—however respectable these are. Can we even imagine a politics which does not find its source in the unity of values, traditions, and specific institutions which define a nation? The political organization must answer to what Elias has called "the affective desire of human society." But as he himself observes, "the emotional tonality of the identity of 'us' is notably weakened from the moment that it becomes a question of postnational forms of integration."[55]

Some of the French revolutionaries had previously attempted the project of building an entirely new society, founded on the equality of free and reasonable men, according to the Kantian formula. During Federation Day, in 1790, they affirmed their spirit of tolerance and their desire to get along with representatives of all cultural minorities, without forcing them to abandon their cultural specificities. In a different way, their professed ambition was in conformity with the Habermasian concept: they wished for a political agreement to be concluded among culturally different groups, according to which each would maintain its identity. But rapidly, they joined those who favored a communal type of nation in order to mobilize energies around their political project, then to defend the "homeland in danger." Confronted by external danger, they participated in the organization of passions in favor of the Revolution and the nation in order to lead a national war. They thereby demonstrated that a citizenship which was neither embedded in history nor the subject of its own destiny, and which did not possess concrete instruments for the integration of populations and for intervention on the international stage, remains an abstract idea. The nation is a concrete social and political form.

This is also the reason why "postnational" projects—defined as perfect incarnations of the democratic nation—even if they were attainable, might not be politically desirable. On the one hand, the "disunity of political reference and of cultural belonging," to adopt Jean-Marc Ferry's formula, risks leaving essentialist nationalisms without any political control and arousing fragmenting markers of identity and violent conflicts. By losing any political dimension and any political authority, nations would no longer control ethnic passions. On the other hand, the total rationality and abstraction of the political project would render that "pure" nation excessively fragile. In a world marked by the fervor and sometimes even the ferocity of ethnic nations, could nations founded only on "constitutional patriotism" survive? It seems inevitable that, to ensure its existence and its vitality, the nation must build and maintain elements of ethnic order. Paradoxically, to create a civic nation whose ambition is rational, as Ernest Gellner has observed, nationalists invoke ethnic, racial, linguistic, religious or cultural arguments, thereby contributing to their creation and perpetuation. Nations have always reinvented an array of myths and ethnic values; they require a sacred territory, heroes of a golden age. In brief, they arouse a form of ethnicity which nourishes for nationals their feelings of belonging in the collectivity.[56] The invention of tradition is a condition of the existence of any nation.[57]

The example of Zionism is once again instructive. Three major nationalist projects were confronted during the 1880s–1890s: the first was the diasporic and cultural nationalism mentioned above; the second, of the Socialist-Zionist Labor party of Nahman Syrkin or the Jewish Territorial Organization of Israel Zangwill, favored the concentration of Jews on a territory—not necessarily in Palestine—in order to guarantee their cultural and national autonomy; the last one was Theodor Herzl's, who published in 1896 *The State of the Jews (Der Judenstaat)*, and did not distinguish the invention of the nation from the construction of the state. For him, the state would alone permit the Jewish nation to fully come into being. In the 1930s, in Palestine, partisans of the state, those around Jabotinski, were still a minority. It is nevertheless this last project which was given strength by the reality of World War II. Even before the UN recognized the new state in 1948, the general confederation of Jewish workers—the *Histadrut*—constituted a quasi-state in order to organize the economic, social, educational, cultural, and even sporting life of the new nation. Since 1920, it created an office of immigration, a labor bank, and economic enterprises. The majority of children were educated in its schools; it occupied the protective role of the welfare state. More than a union, it was a true bureaucracy, independent of the political parties. It managed the common life and possessed a labor militia, the *Haganah*, which gave it a monopoly of violence judged legitimate by the majority of members of the *Yishuv*, despite the opposition of the right. Ben-Gurion remained all his life obsessed by the necessity of the state. During the years 1933–1945, Jews learned to measure the collective destiny in the modern world of humans without recognized nation and without state.

The effort of philosophers to conceive a postnational identity permits us—at least by way of contrast—to specify what the nation is: the nation is not merely transcendence by an abstract political society, but it also entails a social reality, concretely situated in time and space. It is at once the product of the overcoming of ethnic belongings and identities by means of the political, of the articulation of an abstract civic society, and the concrete creation of the collective institutions of the state. It is only as an "ideal-type," and not in its particular forms, that the rational national "society" can be contrasted to ethnic "communities." Any national construction is elaborated from ethnic elements, which its strictly national institutions later operate to reinforce. As Max Weber observed to the German Sociological Society of 1910 (by identifying nation and nationalism), the Nation is a "community of the order of feelings whose adequate expression is an autonomous state and which normally strives to create it (the state)."[58]

One can neglect neither this ambition toward political transcendence nor its intrinsic limits, in other words, the concrete conditions for the existence of the nation that sociology brings to light.

Notes

1. Even if, concretely, the very conception of the universal "citizen" has evolved since its "reign" was proclaimed. Cf. Rosanvallon, 1992.
2. Renan, 1947 (1882), pp. 896, 899, 902, 903.
3. Gellner, 1983, p. 54.
4. Gellner quoted in Delannoi-Taguieff (ed.), 1991, p. 236.
5. Mauss, 1969 (1920?), pp. 595 and 596.
6. Mauss, 1969 (1920?), pp. 598 and 601.
7. Weber, 1947, (1913), p. 627. "'nationale' Zugehörigkeit nicht auf realer Blutsgemeinschaft ruhen muss," "vollends ist Gemeinsamkeit eines spezifischen anthropologischen Typus zwar nicht einfach gleichgültig," des anderren grossen 'Massenkulturguts'," "'Nation' ist ein Begriff, der, wenn überhaupt eindeutig, dann jedenfalls nicht nach empirischen gemeinsamen Qualitäten der ihr Zugerechneten definiert werden kann." One finds the same theme, on p. 242. (*Economy and Society*, vol. 2, pp. 922–923)
8. Mauss, 1969 (1920?), p. 54.
9. Weber, 1971 (before 1913), p. 427; Weber 1947, p. 22. "Offenbar ist also 'national'—wenn überhaupt etwas Einheitliches—dann eine spezifische Art von Pathos, welches sich in einer durch etwas Sprach-, Konfessions-, Sitten-oder Schicksalsgemeinschaft verbundenen Menschengruppe mit dem Gedanken einer ihr eigenen, schon bestehenden oder von ihr ersehnten politischen Machtgebildeorganisation verbindet, und zwar je mehr der Nachdruck auf 'Macht' gelegt wird, desto spezifischer."
10. Lipset, 1963, p. 7.
11. Greenfeld, 1992, p. 14.
12. Weber, 1971 (before 1913), p. 427; Weber, 1947, p. 226. "Immer wieder finden wir uns bei dem Begriff 'nation' auf die Beziehung zur politischen 'Macht' hingewiesen." (*Economy and Society*, vol. 1, pp. 397–8)
13. Weber, 1971 (before 1913), p. 427; Weber, 1947, p. 226; "Und doch ist z. B. bei den Schweizern das stolze Selbsbewusztsein auf ihre Eigenart und die

Bereitschaft, sich rückhaltlos für sie einzusetzen, weder qualitativ anders geartet noch quantitativ unter ihnen weniger verbreitet, als bei irgendeiner quantitativ 'groszen' und auf 'Macht' abgestellten 'Nation.'" (*Economy and Society*, vol. 1, p. 397)
14. Harzt, 1968 (1964).
15. Lipset, 1963, in particular pp. 73–78. Lipset, 1990.
16. The weakening of political projects in modern democracies and the decadence of the nation explain that they are often presented in the past.
17. Bibo, 1986 (1946), p. 134.
18. I follow directly Greenfeld, 1992, pp. 41 and following.
19. Hume, pp. 136 and 300.
20. Hume, pp. 333, 345 and 64.
21. Hume, p. 150.
22. Burke, 1989, p. 41.
23. Burke, p. 40.
24. Nairn, p. 18.
25. Title of Lipset, 1963.
26. T. Parsons in Glazer-Moynihan (ed.), 1975, p. 56; Greenfeld, 1992, p. 13.
27. These two quotes were borrowed from Schlesinger, 1991.
28. Glazer-Moynihan, 1963.
29. Ph. Raynaud in Furet-Ozouf (ed.) 1993, p. 59.
30. Wood, 1991 (1969), p. 684.
31. In that way Claude Lefort summarizes the scholarship of American historians in his preface to the translation of Wood, 1991 (1969), p. 33.
32. Hartz, 1968 (1964), p. 90.
33. Tocqueville, 1992 (1835), p. 394.
34. Bibo, 1986 (1946), p. 55 (italics added).
35. The nature of the French political project is the subject of Schnapper, 1991.
36. Dumont, 1991, p. 251.
37. Pirenne, 1917, p. 20.
38. Pirenne, 1917, p. 5.
39. Renan, 1947 (1870), p. 416.
40. See chapter 3, 2nd part.
41. Windisch, 1991, p. 84.
42. Hugger (ed.), 1992.
43. T. Herzl quoted in Laqueur, 1973 (1972), p. 106.
44. Eisenstadt, 1954, p. 39.
45. Laqueur, 1973 (1972), p. 606.
46. Barnavi, 1988 (1982), p. 27.
47. Quoted by Anderson, 1982, p. 101. According to Georges Haupt, Otto Bauer later modified this theory of cultural autonomy. Cf. Haupt *et al.*, 1974, p. 52.
48. Habermas, 1990, p. 238.
49. Ferry, 1991, p. 194.
50. Ferry, 1991, p. 195.
51. Costa-Lascoux, 1992.
52. Kende, 1991, p. 27.
53. To take the subtitle of the collections of texts, *devant l'histoire*, 1988.
54. Ph. Raynaud in Burke, 1989 (1790), p. XV.
55. Elias, 1991 (1986–87), pp. 261 and 263.
56. Smith, 1986, pp. 212–213.
57. See Szücs, 1986, in relation to Hungary in the thirteenth century.
58. Quoted in Beetham, 1985, p. 122.

3

Transcendence by Citizenship

The democratic nations of Western Europe are the product of a multisecular history whose uniqueness never ceases to arouse the wonder of sociologists. The modern democratic nation inherited not only its institutions, but also the very idea of political society and the values of democracy which were elaborated by the Athenians and reinterpreted in the Roman Empire. It also benefited from the historical experience of the medieval town and from the great monarchs which centralized, organized, and imposed the authority of the state between the thirteenth and the eighteenth century. In this way, the modern democratic nation benefited both from the ideas which founded the principle of political society and citizenship *and* from the political institutions by which these ideas are incarnated and transmited. That is, the modern democratic nations benefited from a specific political project.

It is important therefore to analyze in this chapter the principles of citizenship, which constitute at the same time the idea—the ideal and the reference accepted from political practices—before approaching, in the following chapter, the workings of national institutions which make each particular nation unique.

The Idea of the Community of Citizens

The Greek Polis *and the Roman Citizen*

For almost two centuries one has spoken of "the liberty of the ancients compared to the liberty of the moderns," to invoke the title of Benjamin Constant's famous lecture delivered to the Athénée Royal of Paris in 1819. Most generally one concedes that "the liberty of the moderns opposes itself to that of the ancients just as trade opposes itself to war, as representation opposes itself to participation, and as the pleasure of reflection is at odds with the pleasure of action,"[1] as assessed by Pierre Vidal-Naquet. Recent historians, however, allow us to add nuance to these affirmations.[2]

The Greeks "invented" the concept of the political in the sense of an autonomous domain of social life. Basing his reflection on the historical experience of the city, Aristotle believed that political activity, which alone dignified the human, allowed man to realize in himself that which was properly human. In Aristotle's definition, the *polis* represented the community of citizens organized by means of a constitution (*politeia*). *Poleis* were clearly distinguished at the time from peoples not organized in a political society—the *ethnè*—and from the society, a totality, what one would call in modern terms "civil society." Indeed, the *polis* excluded slaves, women, foreigners and Mettics, who nonetheless participated in various capacities in social life of the city. Mettics and visiting foreigners, in particular, played an important role in the economic activity of the city as artisans, tradesmen or farmers. Mettics were protected by the law and they were associated, in a certain fashion, sacrifices and with public banquets, or, one might say, with the civil cults. But the *polis* remained, by right, exclusively limited to citizens. Important positions of responsibility were in fact held by wealthy citizens who had been trained in rhetoric in the schools. The community of citizens was the sole source of legitimacy and held the sole authority over political and judicial decisions.

This conception led to the separation between the political or public sphere, in which each citizen participated, and the sphere of the private, in which everyone was free to live as it pleased him, so long as he obeyed the laws and did not harm his fellow citizens. This dichotomy appeared in all the aspects of life: the private person was distinguished from the citizen, the domestic house from public buildings, the interest of the individual from the good of the *polis,* and private financial affairs from public finances. Doubtless this had more the character of the opposition between the private and the public than that between the individual and the state which characterizes modern society. But the Greeks had elaborated the essential idea that the *polis* had to be limited, insofar as political society was conceived by them as distinct from society in its totality. Morgens Hansen has reconsidered the idea developed by Fustel de Coulanges of an ancient "totalitarian" city, one which controlled all aspects of the public and private life of its members, and concluded that this description would fit only the case of Sparta.[3]

The Greeks also invented the principle of the rule of law. Their contemporaries were of one mind as to the need to recognize the true *polis* in that it was governed by laws and not by men. The laws of the City were the only master that confronted the citizen. Condemned to death in a legal way, Socrates refused to escape: he respected the laws too much to violate them. The famous "prosopopoeia of laws" of *Crito* illustrates his thinking: the laws of the city gave everything to the citizen Socrates. He was free to leave the city; however, by remaining in it willingly, he accepted the responsibility of obeying its laws. "As you well know Athenians, in a democracy, it is the laws which protect the individual and the *politeia,* whereas the tyrant and the oligarch find their safety in mistrust and armed guards. Oligarchs and the ones who lead states founded on inequality must protect themselves by the strength of arms from those who want to destroy their state. But we, for whom the constitution is founded on equality under the law, we must isolate those who talk or act in a way contrary to the law."[4]

Greeks also formulated the values of liberty and equality, which formed the basis for modern democratic thought. The democratic ideal of Athens was composed of the idea of the liberty, or *eleutheria*. It not only contrasted the free citizen participating in democratic institutions to slavery, but it also implied, according to Hansen, the idea that the individual, in the private sphere, was free to live as he pleased: "A principle at base of the democratic constitution is liberty. One often says this, and moreover those who say it often imply that it is only in this constitution that humans partake of this liberty. One of the marks of the liberty is to be successively governor and governed...Another is to live as one wishes."[5] The Greeks elaborated the idea of the equality of all citizens before the law, their right not to be condemned without judgment, as well as the idea of the equality of opportunity. In other words, they spoke of the ideas of formal, juridical and political equality, which were for a long time those of modern liberal democracy. For them there was no conflict between liberty and equality, insofar as it was a matter of equality of rights, not of results. The contradiction appears only when one has the goal of assuring *also* the equality of outcomes in the distribution of political responsibilities and goods.

However, the Greek *polis* remained limited by a conception that we would characterize in modern language as ethnic. Citizens were defined by their birth and their belonging, determined by their filiation to a phratry and to a deme. From the age of three or four, a male child, son of a citizen of Athens, was part of his father's phratry; at his majority, he entered in his deme, introduced by his father. One was an Athenian citizen because one was a son, grandson, and great grandson of Athenian citizens. The political society of ancient Greece did not abandon this ethnic definition of citizenship because the *polis* remained at the time concrete and direct. Real groups, families, relatives or groups of friendship constituted the genuine elements of the political system, which defined itself in terms of community in the sociological sense. If one adopts the vocabulary of Philippe Gauthier, it was "structures of participation", which founded "homes of sociability," whose very existence was necessary for the concrete functioning of the *polis*. By far the most populous, even Athens was composed of only a limited number of members, between ten and twelve thousand. Other cities had thousands, and indeed some hundreds: Greek cities were face-to-face societies. A member of political society was defined by the fact that he personally and directly participated in the management of common affairs. For Aristotle, "the city is the community of the good life for families and for relatives, in view of an accomplished and self-sufficient existence".[6] What counted in his eyes was "'the function' exercised by 'political animals,' which is to say that participation, unequal according to the city, and within a city according to regimes, in the management of common affairs."[7] Yet if the fact of directly managing common affairs defined the ideal of citizenship, it is clear that one could not help but restrict the number of citizens. The accomplished character of the *polis* made it difficult to incorporate foreign elements: founded on an ethnic conception, the city remained closed. The acquisition of Athenian citizenship by foreigners was exceptional. Given this, Greeks defined themselves and were defined by others in ethnic terms: the origin, the language, gods and sacred places, sacrificial feasts and the way of life. On the other hand, because of their concrete and direct conception of public life, the idea of uniting themselves in only one political organization—particularly one in which citizens would not directly participate in political life—remained foreign to them.[8]

Modern democracy inherited from Rome the conception of citizenship heretofore defined in terms of juridical status. The increasing scale of territories and of populations controlled by Rome imposed a new type of relations between individuals: it was no longer a situation of face-to-face societies. The civic frameworks, classes, centuries, tribes were not real groups, but administrative categories. They functioned as "structures of integration" (Gauthier). Those intermediary groups upon which Aristotle founded the city no longer existed. The "men," that it is to say citizens, appeared. The *civis romanus* disposed of civil or personal rights: the *jus connubii* or the *jus commercii*. "For those who have between them community of law, there is community of right. For the ones who share these things (law and right), they must be considered as belonging in the same city."⁹ The essential criterion became that of the law, not of functions. While the Aristotelian *polis* was the direct expression of a social reality, the politicians and thinkers of Rome defined political society by the rule of law. It was no longer a matter of organizing the life and conflicts between groups of real individuals, but of regulating the relations between subjects of the law. The issue of the number of citizens no longer stood in the same terms as in the Greek city, and the principle of openness to foreigners was inscribed in the definition of political society. By definition, the juridical nature of status permitted Rome progressively to incorporate foreign elements—which was the case throughout the history of Rome, until the edict of Caracalla in A.D. 212, which sanctioned this form of secular politics by granting citizenship to the vast majority of free men of the empire.

If the horizon of citizenship was universal, the practice, however, remained aristocratic, and indeed oligarchic. Social integration by means of civil citizenship first of provincial elites, then of all men, did not allow for the right to participate effectively in political life. Citizens of Rome conceived of themselves as citizen-soldiers, but the immense majority of them did not have any part in public life. The practice of politics ceased being a lived experience. While open in principle, the Roman aristocracy was in fact restricted. Only a minority of citizens had the requisite property qualification for eligibility to the magistracies: the mass of citizens was excluded from all public duties, as well as the Senate. In the centurian meetings, where the most important magistrates were elected, the vote of the first, wealthiest class—and sometimes of part of the second class—was sufficient to ensure the majority of suffrage, which halted the very process of voting. In political assemblies, the vote was not individual, but collective: one counted by century or by tribe.¹⁰ Finally, in a society where all public actions were scanned by rituals, the Roman aristocracy reserved for itself the right of interpreting signs and supernatural omens, whose usage permitted them to direct, manipulate, or even suppress public debates.¹¹ Throughout the history of Rome, the direction of public affairs remained the monopoly of wealthy citizens. Clientelism played an increasing role: "Nowhere else in the world was political patronage of that kind held within the hands of so few families."¹² The rupture between the minority, which concentrated public responsibilities in its hands, and the mass of the population was one of right as much as of fact. Nevertheless, it is necessary to observe that it was not a matter of an aristocracy of birth: becoming wealthy, the citizen changed his class and century, allowing him to participate in public life and to enter then into the *cursus honorum*. This economic and social success might ultimately lead to political participation; the aristocracy was not totally closed. Because the size of the Roman society prohibited all citizens from directly managing the public thing and because the idea of representation was unknown, it became impossible to avoid limiting the number of those who, in right and in fact, directly participated in political activity.

Despite these oligarchic practices, it remains the case that the Romans, by defining the citizen in juridical terms, founded at least potentially the notion of an open citizenship and its universal practice. In that sense, it is possible to affirm that "we all are Roman citizens."[13]

Towns and State Institutions of Monarchies

The modern nation is the direct heir of the double history of the constitution of an independent political body in the medieval city-states and in the great monarchies of Western Europe. In both cases, horizontal ties were established between men. This contrasts with the feudal tradition, which united vassals and lords vertically by direct and unequal exchanges of services.

Max Weber illustrated the birth of the conception of a political domain, independent of any religious and dynastic dimension, in the medieval commune. The self-administration of the city-states of Western Europe permitted them to escape from the standoff between the feudality and the peasant stratums characteristic of Eastern Europe. A bourgeoisie of peaceful work and of free administration was formed there. The town was constituted as a political unit, and the bourgeois as a juridically and politically autonomous citizen, defined by his belonging to the city. "Here, at least in a new foundation, the burgher joined the citizenry as an individual, and as an individual he swore the oath of citizenship. His personal membership in the local association of the city guaranteed his legal status as a burgher, not his tribe or sib."[14] Differences of juridical status disappeared in the town, even if, in several northern cities, wealthy patricians in fact dominated the organization of common life. On the other hand, clannish and religious logics, or castes in India and the bureaucracy in China did not permit it to be constituted as a collective organization representing the community of citizens in and of itself. Concerning Islam, the works of specialists from the Muslim world confirmed Max Weber's intimations of Western uniqueness. Arabic towns did not give birth to communes. The Arabic city has never been either a political place of reference or one of political allegiance. The Koranic law ignores moral persons. In the history of Islamic countries, one finds no room for the idea of cities as subjects of the law, disposing "of privileges, of a status and of specific rights",[15] nor as organizations of free bourgeois. In Islam, religious power and civil power are not distinguished. Legitimate authority comes from God alone, the state is the state of God governing the people of God, the law is the law of God, the army is the army of God, the enemy is the enemy of God. Here the citizen did not replace the religious man. The absence of recognition of the legal person prohibited the emergence of a council or a form of assembly, according to which the members of a political body might participate in the conduct of government. In this regard, history explains why the idea of the community of citizens, "oriented toward a rational model of economic activity," according to the Weberian formula, was born in Western countries.

However, the Italian or German city revealed itself to be too weak to oppose itself politically to the church and the emperor. Weber observes that the greater the centralization of political organization, the lesser the development of towns' autonomy. The king could not fail to regard with distrust the independent power of communes. In fact, it is the king of great western monarchies, creator of the territorial state, who increased "the independence of the political body toward the church,"[16] against privileges of feudal lords and cities, against imperial ambitions, and against the power of the church. It is he who founded the political body as the human society *par excellence*. At the end of the eighteenth century, the citizenship of the town represented nothing more than one of the particular privileges that modern states, stemming from absolutist monarchies, dedicated themselves to destroying.

Transcendence by the political assumed different historical forms. One traditionally contrasts the pluralism of the liberal British tradition—which is embodied in orders, bodies, classes, and particular groups—to the unitary and total conception of citizenship which was violently imposed in France. English democracy was born from the idea of assuring liberties by the creation of countervailing powers, arising from the political representation of the principal social forces. This pluralism is perceived in England as the "natural" expression of public liberties. One is a citizen by virtue of belonging in a particular community. Assuring the representation of collectivities in Westminster, forms of multiple voting were maintained until 1948: until that date the Universities of Oxford and Cambridge possessed representatives in Parliament.[17] The British tradition rests on the idea that in order to assure the true liberty of men against the perennial risk of arbitrary power, one must respect the diversity of particular belongings and attachments. As formulated by Burke: "We begin our public affection in our families. No cold relation is a zealous citizen. We pass on to our neighbourhoods, and our habitual provincial connections." The nation can be nothing but the result of a long history, and one must respect the rights of particular groups which compose it and the local powers: "Such divisions of our country as have been formed by habit, and not by a sudden jerk of authority, were so many little images of the great country in which the heart found something which it could fill. The love to the whole is not extinguished by this subordinate partiality."[18] More generally, the general interest is composed of particular interests: "Each class knows things which are not known by other peoples and each class has more or less specific interests."[19] In the utilitarian logic of British democracy, various social groups are represented in the political domain for the very reason of their specificity, and, by defending their own interests, they contribute to the general interest and to the proper functioning of the entire society.

In their proclamation of the new reign of the "citizen," French revolutionaries were primarily inspired by the thought of Rousseau. For him, the dependency between men is the source of inequality; intermediary bodies between the citizen-individual and the state prevented man from being free, and as a result they must be destroyed. Contrary to English notions, the citizen as a direct expression of the "general will" must be independent of any intermediary links and must remain in intimate and direct relations with the state. Even if the revolutionaries had posed the problem of representation since 1789, they essentially retained the Rousseauean conception of a unitary democracy, hostile to pluralism. The interest and the will of each citizen are to be identified with the collective interest and the collective will. The general interest is not deduced from the sum or from the composition of particular interests. Like the nation, citizenship is an indivisible whole; it must be organized and guaranteed by a centralized state, expression of the general will, generator of society.

The concrete forms assumed by the principle of citizenship continue to engender different practices—for instance in the politics of immigration initiated in Great Britain and in France. In the first case, the British concede the existence of forms of socially recognized communities, in which interests are specific and whose representatives negotiate with the authorities in order to obtain particular rights; in the second, the French strive to integrate populations of foreign origin by individual citizenship, that is, by refusing to recognize the existence of communities in the public sphere. But, despite this diversity in traditions and social practices, it is a matter in all cases of creating a political domain ruled by common norms, whose function is to resolve rivalries and conflicts.

The very idea of nationhood, as an abstract place of political unity given legitimacy by the community of citizens, is intimately linked to modern individualism. The related emergence of individualism and of the nation, as idea and as reality, has often been noted.[20] The political national society strives to "construct a *whole* political body beginning from individuals supposed to be radically independent."[21] Moreover, it rests on the idea that this citizen-individual has the capacity to break away, at least partially, from his particular roots and to enter, by law, into communication with all the others. He can cease to be determined by his membership in a real group. The citizen is defined precisely by his ability to break with determinations that would stifle him in a culture and a destiny imposed by birth. It releases him from prescribed roles and imperative functions. It is this tension between the universalism of the citizen and the particularities of the private man as a member of civil society which shapes the principle—as well as the values—of the democratic nation.

Representation and Democratic Citizenship

Rediscovering the Roman law in the thirteenth century, modern political theory developed and transformed the conception of the citizen. In the societies of Greek and Roman antiquity, the individual was before all a *homo politicus;* the citizen was also a soldier. On the contrary, in the medieval town the individual was first and foremost a *homo œconomicus*. The individual sought the personal freedom linked to economic activity. Modern democracy prolonged this uniquely liberal tradition of defending the individual's autonomy. Even if one should not summarily contrast ancient democracy to modern democracy—the warlike and religious vocation of the first to the essentially economic vocation of the second. Modern democracy was born first from the claim of the liberty of the individual, acting as economic actor *against* political society, from the effort to guarantee the liberty of the private man by reducing the sphere of intervention by the state. This preceded a second intellectual tradition which suggested that one limit the power of the state by the active participation of citizens in public affairs.[22]

But, even beyond their rediscovery of the conception of political society inherited from Athens along with that of Roman citizenship, modern theorists of democracy also introduced two important ideas according to which the civic nation of today represents a fundamental break with antiquity. These were representation and a novel conception of the citizen.

Antiquity conceived only of direct democracy. With the exception of some experiences in the Hellenistic Confederations, antiquity ignored the idea of delegation. For Aristotle, to delegate one's power was to renounce one's liberty. Thinkers of the eighteenth century, in criticizing the experience of antiquity—the disunion of Greek cities defeated by Philip, the collapse of the Roman empire in the face of the Barbarians—excluded the idea of the republic. It was then commonplace to affirm the impossiblity of establishing a republic in vast modern states. The political dreams of philosophers were not republican. It was the invention of the idea of the delegation or, in modern terms, of representation, which allowed one to conceive of the republic as the regime of a great country. Contrary to those of antiquity, modern democrats perceived the necessity and the value of representation. They specifically invented the political institutions by which this representation might be assured. They did so in a way that strove both to guarantee the efficiency of government as well as to respect the sentiments of citizens who did not wish to be alienated from the politics now attended by their leaders. In so doing, they set forth the principle that political society might function in larger political units, accompanied by an increased abstraction of the public domain and of citizenship.

At the same time, they formulated the strictly democratic principles of modern citizenship: its universal character and the right of each person to exercise his rights concretely.

Since Hume, there has been a tendency to criticize the ancient city, founded on the distinction between free men and slaves, and which excluded the majority of the population from democratic practice. Modern thinkers progressively imagined and inscribed in institutions the potentially universal character of citizenship, extended by degrees to all individuals, whatever their characteristics of social class, regional or national origin, or gender. Insofar as the right to vote represents both the best instrument and the symbol of citizenship, the history of the development of universal suffrage, progressively accorded to new groups among the population, illustrates the essence of citizenship within modern democracy. Since 1792 the only limitations on the right to vote were justified by nature (women or children) or the naturally adduced boundaries of social ties (domestics, paupers, or vagabonds).[23] Actual debates, where some suggest giving the right to vote to children, mentally ill persons—also, theorists of *deep ecology* do not exclude animals and plants—serve to illustrate the logic of the idea of modern citizenship. Even if, in reality, the sole civic activity of the majority of citizens consists only in voting (some refrain or do not register), and even if professional politicians tend to the details of public administration, all individuals have, by law, the ability to be citizens and to participate in political life.

This is not to say that modern democratic nations have always permitted this calling to be effectively realized. But they were always required to justify their practices of exclusion by proposing a restrictive definition of the human. In this way one had to affirm that neither Indians, nor blacks in the United States, nor indigenes in colonized countries, nor women were truly "men," that is to say, human beings endowed with reason. During the era of positivistic and evolutionist thought, French jurists had no qualms about justifying the political and judicial inequality between indigenous and French in Algeria referring to the political and moral superiority of Western civilization. The existence of the Muslim statute concerning marriage, the repudiation, divorce, and the civil state of children seemed to justify in the eyes of contemporaries the refusal of full French citizenship to these indigenous populations, considered "subhumans." It is moreover the reason why one can not underestimate the power of symbolic measures—such as, for instance, the presentation of television news by an African-American woman in the United States—in inscribing the principle of the universalization of citizenship in everyday life.

Moreover—and this is the second characteristic of the modern ideology—citizens must possess the means necessary to *concretely* exercise their rights. It is this doctrine of positive rights which underlies the ideology and the function of the democratic school: the school provides the requisite intellectual training such that everyone can participate meaningfully in public life. This doctrine also legitimates the development of the welfare state: all citizens must possess sufficient material means such that their rights do not remain merely formal. Today the poor enjoy the right of material subsistence. The democratic society must respond to this privation because of the principles in which it locates its legitimacy (see chapter 4).

Modern democracy is an "empty space" according to Claude Lefort's formulation: an abstract place of power which is not identified with any particular person, a sphere of pure representation. It is in that sense that the nation can be interpreted in terms of the *Gesellschaft*, whereas ethnies belong to the order of the *Gemeinschaft*, in the classic dichotomy of Tönnies. There is a qualitative difference between ethnic belonging, experienced as an immediate given, and participation in the nation, which is a product of a departure from the given. In Hegelian terms, it is the product of a culture, or *Bildung*, which gives itself over to the object of making us alien to ourselves, and by means of this "dispossession," carrying us above the limitations inherent in our belonging to a particular people, by realizing the universal essence of man. That which Bergson said of democracy applies equally well: "an effort in the reverse sense of the nature." It is also a utopia in Mannheim's sense, that is to say, a theory of breaking with the existing order in order to transform it.

The Logic of the Civic Nation

The existence of the community of citizens—both as an ordering principle and as a common ideal—legitimates the rules according to which the governors attain power. This principle further legitimates these governors as they redistribute commodities (incomes, patrimonies, services) or public services (security, health, education, use of public services) between individuals and groups; regulate the conflicts necessarily aroused by that redistribution; and affirm the independence and the will of the nation among other political units. This presumes that citizens respect the laws and the constitution. That is to say, they respect the rules which govern the functioning of the public domain in the expansive sense of the term. This includes not only the political—the fight to assume power and to exercise that power—but also the collection of rules which govern the relations between individual subjects of the law in familial, economic, and social relations. The example of colonial Indonesia, where ethnic communities coexisted without forming a single political unit and which accepted common rules only to organize their market exchanges, demonstrates that the organization of the nation implies that the common space is not only political, in the strict sense of the term, but also administrative and juridical.[24] Integration by citizenship—what one can call political loyalty—presupposes a common apprenticeship of the political as a sphere of unity, a consensus as to the means to regulate by compromise, or even by force, conflicts of all natures. All this presumes, of course, that the citizen must also—at least ideally—contribute to the defense of the nation.

Instruments of Political Life

The democratic vote functions as more than just a means of choosing leaders, giving voters an occasion to manifest their trust or distrust towards politics, and regulating relations between society-at-large and political power. It is also the symbol of the new sacred, the sacralization of the political society itself, which affirms social ties and traces the destiny of the collectivity. By studying how particular voting procedures have evolved, French historians have shown that the sacred character of the act of voting has been emphasized for two centuries.[25] The increased solemnity of the voting location, the development of what one can call, by way of religious analogy, the ceremony, the obligation held by the elector to go in the polling booth (which has been seen as a form of confessional), and the placement of the ballot box in the polling place (that one could liken to an altar)—all this contributed to the sanctification of the electoral act. In this light, to vote is to demonstrate, by respecting a ritual, that one belongs to a national political community. When one asks the population, What distinguishes the national from the foreigner?, the right to vote is immediately invoked. This response comes before the possibility of being elected, of acceding to public office, or of doing military service—and hence the reason for the emotion and debate aroused by the possibility of giving the right to vote to foreigners. Beyond the consecration of social bonds, the democratic vote is a concrete manifestation of the abstract political domain in which each citizen is the equal of the other, contrary to any real and observable social experience. By manifesting in act the truth of the formula: "One man, one vote," elections reinvigorate the idea of the formal equality of citizenship, thereby legitimating the political order.

By institutionalizing and regulating the conflicts which confront real groups, political parties give shape to democratic life. Their organization and form of balloting, upon which the principle of representation depends, have more than a single technical function: one of forming a stable majority capable of governing, while at the same time giving the citizens a sense that they retain the right to choose their governors and to authorize their actions. Political parties are also the means by which political society discovers itself, putting itself on stage and incarnating itself in institutions. The integration of the nation is measured in the fact that by arousing the participation and mobilization of citizens, parties embody distinct political propositions. They are no longer solely the expression of particularisms and of regional, social, religious or ethnic interests. The rapid decomposition of Polish democratic life between the two world wars demonstrates this. When Poland was reconstituted as a national independent entity in 1919, it had been divided and subjected to an external power for more than a century and was unable to form a single tradition of civic community. The parties directly stemmed from certain social groups: the Communist Party, the Labor Party (PPS), two peasant parties, one radical, the other centrist, the Nationalist Party, and the national democracy, motivated by the bourgeoisie, or parties of national and religious minorities (Jews were considered as a religious minority).[26] But no one offered strictly political alternatives; no one organized debates on national problems. The sociologist John Rex recently suggested that in Great Britain, British citizens, former immigrants or descendants of immigrants from the *New Commonwealth*, that is to say from the nonwhite *Commonwealth*, who become for him the "new proletarians," look to their own independent political organizations to make their voice heard.[27] If understood as parties, founded on their national or ethnic origin, and represented *for their own sake* in the partisan life, this calls into question the traditional function of the democratic nation. The idea not of the representation of economic or political interests, but of particular, national, or ethnic identities, constitutes a changing of legitimacy.

In countries founded on immigration, the process of national integration presumes that different groups of immigrants do not constitute parties based on their origin. In the United States and in Australia, traditional political practice has insured that various national groups were absorbed by the two major parties. It is inside the Democratic party that the electoral machines of Irish and Italians were organized. Nowadays the "ethnicization" of public life—that is to say, the recognized social existence of groups defined by their national or "racial" origin— risks weakening the national unit. When Jews arrived in the Jewish establishment of Palestine, the *Yishuv*, they had already filtered into political parties. With their arrival in Palestine, they participated in the partisan life. This activity was organized around debates on the nature of the *Yichuv*, on the political strategies to pursue toward Arabs and European powers, and on the political and religious meaning of Zionist values. Power conflicts were rooted in the new society; they were not founded on particularistic claims. This tradition has been maintained, as the "ethnic" Russian party obtained less than 1.5 percent of votes and won no seats in the Knesset in the June 1992 elections. The extreme politicization of the new society—which persists today—was an essential factor in the creation of the nation.

The multiculturalism of social and religious life, much discussed today in Western democracies, did not arise from the large migrations of immigrant workers to Europe after World War II, nor from the discovery of the existence and value of ethnicity in the United States, nor from the acknowledgment of the rights of long persecuted minorities to obtain compensations. The "multiethnic" or "multicultural" society is neither an invention of American democracy, contrary to Parsons,[28] nor a recent characteristic of the nations of Western Europe, as eagerly affirmed by theoreticians of the new citizenship. Rather, it is inscribed in the very definition of the nation. This last one did not suppress ethnies, but it effectively interpreted other belongings, experienced as natural—even if they are, like nations, the product of a historical construction—as "ethnic." The multiculturalism of social life is a fact: any nation, by definition, is formed of populations differentiated by their respective culture, their social environment, their religion of practice or of reference, and their regional or national origin. Among populations recently immigrated, individuals might participate regularly in professional or collective life, all the while conserving the "core" of their culture of origin. They are able to retain a distinct conception of morality preserved since early childhood by the bond between parents—especially the mother—and the child, a system of norms and values according to which the honor of each is defined.[29] Directly stemming from ethnic inheritance and transmitted by the family, this cultural core does not preclude subsequent participation in political society, provided that these norms are not in conflict with the values of the community of citizens.

Multiculturalism is also a right, for the separation of the public domain from the private domain is at the foundation of the democratic order. Multiculturalism became the object of collective reflection, claims, and militancy since the 1970s–1980s only as a result of the recent weakening of the national ideals and realities in Western democracies.

If one retains only the *logic* of the operation of the civic nation, then debates about the nature and scope of multiculturalism are easily answered. So long as cultural distinctions of particular groups are compatible with the demands of common life, then citizens and foreigners regularly settled on national soil have the right to cultivate particularities in their personal and social life, under the condition of respecting the rules of the public order. This right is inscribed in the very principles of the *Etat de droit* and of modern democracy. Public liberties guarantee the liberty of association, the right to practice freely one's religion or to use one's own language. At the same time, however, these particularities must not form the basis of a particular *political* identity, respected for its own sake within the public realm. This last function must remain the task of the political unit and of the common political project—otherwise one falls back to the Lebanese situation, where the constitution merely organized a common life of "associated minorities" and where "Communities," persons created by public law, each possessed their own guaranteed representation at all levels of political and administrative organization. These constitutional provisions led to the collapse of the state and helped to dissolve national identity in the interest of particular communitarian belongings.

We should not forget that this is a response in principle only—that is to say, this response conforms to the logic of the nation. It must be understood as a regulating idea and as a principle of political organization. In practice, however, it is evident that one has always been forced to manage relations between political authorities and diverse social forces, among them ethnic groups in countries of immigration. It has also been necessary to compromise between the particular needs of certain populations or groups and the affirmation of the national unit in universal political terms. In its very principles, as Louis Dumont observes, "contrary to many thoughtless affirmations, a 'pluricultural democracy,' or even one that is bicultural, is in the strictest sense a contradiction in terms." But it is also true that the art of politics consists eventually in "violating our law, or rather to instill secondary dispositions which in themselves, if one did not limit their application, would contradict the law's general inspiration."[30]

Because the effort to constitute a political society, independent of the state, defines the nation, language is not merely one ethnic characteristic among others. Language is also the precondition and the means of political exchange. This dual nature makes it both the instrument and the expression of any historical and political collectivity. It permits men not only to partake of the same knowledge and the same emotions, but also to manage the rational exchanges of public life. In Switzerland, the principle of using each of the four languages recognized in the public space is universally accepted and is a necessary condition for the functioning of democracy in spite of the diversity of cultures.[31]

The Sense of the Consensus and Its Limits

The construction of a nation supposes that in order to be accepted by its members, a system of laws and common norms must provide what Edward Shils terms "moral consensus," political coherence, or integration. As Mauss more lyrically affirmed: "The Nation, there are citizens aroused by *consensus*."[32] This formulation may look somewhat grandiloquent in the age of social science, but if one translates it in modern terms, it simply consists of recalling that it is necessary to have a minimum of agreement between individuals about collective life. The notion of *consensus* can be retained to analyze the idea of nation, so long as one recalls that this term never implied that there were no rivalries, clashes, and conflicts. *Consensus* simply means that citizens accept explicit and implicit rules which permit at least the provisional resolution of their conflicts in a non-violent way. This occurs by discussion, compromise, and a commonly accepted reference to a general interest, proclaimed and accepted as such, which is not to be confused with the interest of individuals or particular groups. In this light, it was a commonplace throughout the whole second half of the nineteenth century to contrast the paper ballot to the gun. Victor Hugo himself formulated it: "Universal suffrage, by giving a ballot to those who suffer, takes away from them the gun. By giving them power, it calms them."[33]

The experience of those democracies commonly characterized as "consociative" is instructive in this respect. In four societies where languages, religions, cultures, or ethnic origins vary (Austria, Belgium, the Netherlands, and Switzerland) it was nonetheless possible to organize a democratic government. Four conditions contributed to the proper functioning of political society. First, in each case, all groups are represented in the political elite. Second, there is a reciprocal rule of veto which permits each group to make the others respect what it considers to be its vital interests. Third, each of the groups is represented in the administration and obtains a part of the public funds proportional to its number. And finally, each group retains the right to manage its own affairs.[34] In Belgium, the Christian, socialist and liberal "pillars" and in the Netherlands, the Catholic, Protestant and socialist "pillars" each manage their own schools, hospitals, housing, associations of social work, radio and cultural organs. For these they obtain public funds in direct proportion to their numbers. But merely respecting these dispositions would not be sufficient ground upon which to base a true democracy if there were not at the same time a single political elite stemming from all groups, which applies these unwritten rules and shares the same conception of the world and value system. In particular, this elite must manifest the will to maintain national unity and have a sense of moderation and compromise in public life. Moreover, in the two most stable countries, Switzerland and the Netherlands, the cooperation between the political elite of each particular group and such habits of compromise existed long before the modern political nation came into being. In fact, the political project was constituted around this very idea of negotiations and of compromise between groups. Consociative democracy can be maintained only if there is a common public domain based on a common origin and a shared conception of the world.[35]

Conversely, by destroying a number of the institutions of civil society, totalitarian, Nazi or Communist regimes, forbade that a community of citizens could be expressed in public life independent of the party-state. By striving to eliminate all other collective actors from political life—associations, unions, churches, local powers, competitive political parties—and by forbidding the development of authorities liable to consolidate a civil society distinct from the state, these totalitarian regimes prevented the political domain from functioning as a place where groups and particular interests confront each other and where the conflicts which divide them are remedied before new ones appear. Therefore, for example, only the social groups directly linked to power—the *nomenklatura*—participated in Tito's project to create a Yugoslav nation, before withdrawing, after 1970, in each of the republics. Since the collapse of communist societies, at least for the moment, one witnesses not the constitution of democratic nations but nationalist claims of the ethnies where were gathered into states after World War I.

In many countries which were colonized, the goal of breaking with the colonizing power and the battle for independence are alone insufficient to create a political project. Identities, defined by religious or linguistic markers, resist being overtaken by a citizenship linked to a colonizer's artificial territorial and political unification. These prove too abstract. The overtaking of ethnic solidarities or of communities by citizenship is not self-authorizing. So long as the idea of distinguishing between private and public domain and of instituting essentially political relations between men—from the order of "society" rather than of "community," to recall the Weberian vocabulary—remains incomprehensible to the majority of the population, the state is incapable of overcoming familial, village, or ethnic solidarities, and of organizing social life.

The democratic nation is in its principle formed by citizen-individuals who are united only by their recognition of a political contract. Hobbes long ago demonstrated that the fragility of the social bond was implicit in the contractual principle of modern society. The ongoing dialectic between various religious, regional, or ethnic roots and the national project, between particular interests and the arbitration of the state, is the source of the unique stability and instability of democracy. The fundamental instability of the nation, often revealed, and implicitly condemned, merely reflects the instability of modern society, founded on the sovereignty of the individual and devoted to change, where any notion is historicized, where roles and statuses are not definitively prescribed, and where technical innovation leads to a continual revision of employment as well as social behavior. Citizenship can be nothing more than a regulating idea.

The nation is defined and, implicitly or explicitly, condemned as abstract, in contrast to the concrete realities of tribes, towns, or ethnies. In the epic terms of Mario Vargas Llosa's above-cited lecture, "no nation emerged from the natural and spontaneous development of an ethnic group, religion, or a cultural tradition. All were born from political arbitration, invasions, imperialistic intrigues, violent economic interests, and brute force allied with chance." According to Aristotle, the *polis* was also composed of abstract individuals, detached from their sociological conditions of existence: the citizens. The nation is indeed following Benedict Anderson—an "imagined community." Marx long ago denounced its abstraction. But why must one necessarily interpret this product of "the imagination" as a fiction or a masquerade, and not as a creative invention? Any political society is by nature abstract, precisely insofar as it is constructed by the will of men and insofar as it is neither able to be measured or directly perceived. Neither is it an issue of quantity: even members of a small ethnie do not necessarily maintain direct relations. Rather, the nation and the ethnie are qualitatively different. The ethnie, or communalism (according to Geertz's terms), are experienced as naturally given or prescribed. Whereas the nation supposes a self-constituting political space within which one strives to overcome past differences between populations by means of public discussion and respect for a law founded on an idea of the common good. It is not size which differentiates the ethnie from the nation, but the nature of the tie that unites men.

The nation is considered artificial, particularly in non European countries. It is true that the idea of the nation was initially elaborated in Western Europe, more precisely, in England. The English example, so deeply admired and praised by Montesquieu and Voltaire, contributed to the emergence of both the American nation and the French nation as historical subjects. The battles of the Revolution and of the Empire, in turn, diffused the model of the revolutionary nation throughout Europe, then to countries born from the overseas installation of European colonies: the genesis of the nation in European countries was the result of a relatively endogenous process. In the rest of the world, however, the national model was imposed by the direct or indirect domination of the European powers. In these countries the nation is not the direct product of an endogenous history and political invention, but a borrowing, in the anthropologist's sense. This alone is not sufficient to condemn it: for anthropology taught us that culture is a dynamic founded on exchanges, borrowings, and approximated reinterpretations between cultural entities. Borrowed does not necessarily mean "artificial" in the pejorative sense of the term. Everywhere, the nation is a historical construction. Even in the old nations of Western Europe, all those who are accorded the rights of citizens do not participate fully in democratic life. The nations of North America and Western Europe are not distinguished from the various newly constituted countries of the rest of the world by a natural/artificial opposition. Rather, it is the number of formal citizens who have effectively internalized the idea that there is a public domain whose rules and existence must be respected. Beyond just "importing the state,"[36] it is even more difficult to import the rules that accompany the functioning of a political society, whose development is the product of tradition. In the case of the state, it is a matter of institutions that a minority of the population can organize and make function, at least apparently, by imitating the European model. In the case of the nation, it is also necessary that an important part of the population knows, internalizes, and respects the norms of a rational political society, in the Western sense of the term. It is impossible to construct a political society without taking into account initial social conditions. If the number of those who conduct themselves as formal citizens is too small, as is the case in certain non-Western countries where the state has been unable to transcend ethnic solidarities, it is clear that there can be no democratic nation. If the indifference of citizens and the corruption of politicians and civil servants becomes so pervasive that it undermines the principles upon which public life is founded, then this proposition applies equally well to the established democracies of Western Europe.

The democratic nation became concrete insofar as it serves as the source of identity, morals, emotions, and collective behaviors: the national integration created, according to the Norbert Elias's terms, a socially specific *habitus*.[37] The internalization of the norms of national society means that the dignity of individuals is no longer linked solely to their particular place in a familial or statutory group, but to their character as universal man and citizen. By mobilizing and shaping collective memory and its transmission from one generation to the next, statist institutions indissolubly maintain the individual and collective identity of the nationals. Patriotism in old nations might arouse the same emotions as belonging in ethnies, as demonstrated by the war of 1914–1918. This holds true even if the objective and sentimental relation between the individual and family or his particular community, religious community, or historical communities and the State is not the same according to the history of the nation.

It is currently fashionable to condemn the closing of the nation, defined as a system of exclusion of non-nationals.[38] This is to emphasize one dimension and to neglect the relation of inclusion/exclusion which characterizes any political organization. It is clear that by including and by integrating some, the nation, at the same time, excludes others. The inclusion of the first implies the exclusion of the second, as the collective identity of nationals is defined against the otherness of foreigners. This property distinguishes any group and even, more generally, any identity which is affirmed by opposing itself to others. Any characterization has as its function the separation and the classification of individuals. This discrimination is not however necessarily "discriminatory," that is to say, founded on a pejorative motivation judged illegitimate.[39] In order to appreciate the uniqueness of the nation, it is necessary to compare it to other modes of political organization.

The nation is by its very essence more open to others than any other form of ethnies, and it is even more so than it is, in its concrete forms, closer to the idea of nation. Because it is defined primarily in political terms, and hence juridical and administrative, the national community is in principle able to legally incorporate foreigners, depending on the more or less rigorous stipulations established by the state. Even if the state imposes disproportionately severe demands for one's "assimilation"[40] to the common culture—symbolized by the very term "naturalization"—conditions for acquiring nationality nevertheless remain primarily legal and political. One can not enter into the Corsican or Welsh "people"—that is to say, into an ethnie—if one does not partake of it by birth, whereas one can possess all rights of the French or British citizen once one has been naturalized. The term naturalization refers to the idea of nature, but one must not forget that it is in fact a case of the opposite. If Corsica or Wales constituted themselves as politically united nations, they would elaborate legal rules to transform some foreigners into nationals. Rabbinical tribunals complicate the entrance of non-Jews into the Jewish people defined by the religious tradition. The State of Israel nevertheless admitted as Israeli citizens not only Christians and Muslims, but in the name of Judaism, some individuals who would not be recognized as Jewish by the rabbinical tribunals: for instance children of "mixed" marriages in which only the father is Jewish (according to rabbinical tradition, only the children of a Jewish mother are Jews). All nationality laws allow for conditions by which foreigners can acquire that nationality. However, as a function of the history of the nation's construction, of collective values, and economic and demographic needs, the criteria imposed on the candidates for naturalization vary widely. Among European countries, these differences remain a sensitive matter.[41] In particular, in Germany and Switzerland, nations still premised on the idea that there are ethnic ties between nationals, according to a definition perceived as natural, the juridical and administrative obstacles confronted by foreigners who wish to acquire nationality remain difficult to surmount. Nonetheless, even those countries which refer most directly to the ethnic conception of the nation must anticipate and make provisions for naturalizations.[42] Since the new law of 1990, German authorities have extended the possibility of acquiring nationality, essentially to young foreigners who were born and educated in Germany. They are heretofore allowed the *right* to a virtually free naturalization, on the condition of their renouncing their original nationality. Similar provisions were adopted in Switzerland. Despite the resistance of some groups, Germany and Switzerland have evolved slowly but inevitably in the direction of the so-called political or civic nation. One cannot totally ignore the effects of the principle of universal citizenship, according to which nationality is open to those who demonstrate that they want and are able to participate in the public domain.

It is also common to complain of the constraints related to political organization and centralization—to the existence of the state—while neglecting to take into account the uniqueness of the nation among other political units. In fact, any centralized political organization leads to limits on the liberty of individuals. What one must analyze are the *particular* forms that these constraints assume in the democratic nation, with its community of citizens relatively independent of the state. Accused throughout the last decades of being tyrannical the democratic nation is, on the contrary, essentially fragile insofar as it is founded on a principle of abstract rationality; it is this fragility which requires the reinterpretation of references and of identities associated with the ethnies which predated the nation, as well as the action of the state to reinforce those ethnic dimensions directly linked to the construction of the nation itself (see chapter 4).

Citizen-Soldiers

In the democratic nation, universal citizenship leads to conscription, as was already the case in ancient democracy. Armies composed of citizens succeeded the aristocratic and professional armies of the great monarchies of the Ancien Régime, which engaged only aristocrats and the poor enrolled by force, who participated in battles whose meaning was foreign to them. Even today, the model democracy of Switzerland maintains the pretense of being defended by an armed people, as each citizen keeps his gun in his home. In France, universal suffrage (1848), conscription (1872), the right of foreigners (1849), and the nationality law (1889)—these latter two directly linked to military imperatives—were parallel and related stages in the nationalization of society.

Because their armies are composed of citizens, it has been a perennial source of contention whether there is anything unique about the foreign policy of democratic nations. "There are two things that a democratic people will always have difficulty doing: beginning a war and ending it."[43] Tocqueville's celebrated formula was brilliantly confirmed by events of the twentieth century. The civic nation, whose own values are more industrial than military, often delayed "beginning a war." The French and British resisted Hitler's will neither in 1936 nor in 1938. The United States entered World War I only in 1917, and World War II only in 1941 after the shock of the Japanese attack on Pearl Harbor.

Neither Europeans nor Americans have intervened in Yugoslavia from 1991 to 1995. Yet the Allies of 1917 and of 1945 pursued the war to the point of completely annihilating their enemy, just as Tocqueville predicted. The democratic nation is unique in the fact that it must give to citizens the feeling or the illusion that they decide their own destiny. In order for them to enter into war, they must believe they are participating in a truly national community and that they may identify themselves with their governors. Only this support is sufficient to justify the state's demand that they eventually sacrifice their lives. To mobilize citizens, in practice and in principle, it is necessary that they be committed to the professed goals of war: "During World War I, the aggressors discovered that civilians 'dressed as soldiers' did not accept as easily as professionals the call to die without knowing for whom and for what."[44] Governments must obtain the agreement of the masses. From this follows the importance assumed by the war of propaganda: radios, tracts, and newspapers were used to affirm the effort of citizens and to attempt to discourage the enemy. These tactics are necessary both to convince combatants of the validity of their engagement as well as to arouse opposition to the war in the enemy camp, to employ the pressure of particular groups and public opinion against the enemy. More recently, the powerful effects of information proved more efficient than any enemy propaganda: the live presentation by U.S. television of American soldiers dying in rice fields contributed to protest demonstrations against the Vietnam War and made way for the abandonment of South Vietnam. However, this same patriotic mobilization makes it difficult afterwards to halt wars before their completion, which is seen as a compromise with the enemy. But the ideological character of the wars of the twentieth century was only secondarily linked to the characteristics and requirements of democracies. It was primarily the ideological ambitions of the Nazi regime and of the Soviet Union which insured that wars were ideological.

On the other hand, the workings of democratic life founded on negotiation and compromise does nothing to render decision making any easier. The case of consociative democracies—Switzerland or the Netherlands—is instructive in this respect. Their internal integration is based on a meticulously organized balance of power between groups by the same political organization. More than in any other democracy, any decision there is the product of compromise. Accordingly, their foreign policy is extremely limited. Weber, who confounded the nation with the affirmation of the will to power, accused Switzerland of being an "incomplete nation." The longstanding legal neutrality of Belgium, Switzerland, and also the Netherlands, guaranteed or recognized by large neighboring powers, was one condition for the survival of small European nations. These were founded on a political project that foreclosed the aspiration of direct and active intervention in world politics. Moreover in the United States today, some go so far as to question whether the exaltation of quasi-ethnic values does not rend the political body "to the point that it is almost impossible in United States to have an external politics, insofar as internal politics has practically become a diplomacy among various echelons of power and among ethnic communities."[45] This communitarianism, even when it is not formally recognized by political institutions (as it was in the case of Lebanon), is only doubtfully compatible with a genuine foreign policy, because it presumes various compromises and negotiations between groups, linked to assorted loyalties, each susceptible of becoming antagonists.

But "these same democratic nations that it is so difficult to lead onto the battlefields, sometimes do prodigious things there, once one has finally succeeded in putting arms in hand."[46] When the respective wills of belligerents confront each other in war, an army founded on the ardor of men who are determined to defend their collective identity and their independence is potentially more efficient than an army organized by interest, discipline, or fear. Citizen-soldiers of Israel during the Independence War in 1948 and during the Six Days War in 1967, citizen-soldiers of the French revolution, who fought armies of mercenaries, seemed invincible. But the latter were defeated when their victories aroused in other peoples—Spanish, Prussian or Russian—the same patriotism. In the twentieth century, democracies finally won wars against armies which were the instruments of an imperialist will. Yet they politically lost wars against their former colonies. The victory of the French army in Algeria was followed in 1962 by the government's surrender of sovereignty to the *Front de libération nationale* (FLN). One part of the population, convinced that the colonial project was adverse to the professed values of democracy, sympathized with those who fought for their independence. In order to succeed, the states of democratic nations must make certain that the citizen is convinced of the fairness of their cause.

Once launched, it seems possible that war conducted by a democratic nation, by transforming all citizens into soldiers, might culminate in the total mobilization of the country's human, industrial, and political resources. This is a fear expressed earlier by Renan, who summoned up with nostalgia "these temperaments, these civilities that admitted small political and dynastic wars of the past."[47] In reality, armies before "the principle of nationalities," to recall Renan's expression, produced wars no less destructive than those conducted by armies of citizens. The total character of the wars of the twentieth century was linked, first and foremost, to the demands of military and industrial mobilization, which required progress in the technology of building the means of destruction, as well as to the ideological dimensions of World War II.

Ideal-Type and Concrete Forms

If he is to conduct himself according to the principle of the democratic nation, each must first and foremost respect rules which govern the workings of political society, in particular, those which ensure the formal and juridical equality of those individuals at the foundation of political order. But it goes without saying that particular examples of citizenship will never and have never conformed to the rational ambition of citizenship. An idea cannot be totally realized. Rousseau and Locke, those early theoreticians of the social contract, understood that in practice the contract would always prove imperfect. The universalist idea put forward by proponents of integration in the French style—by pure individual citizenship—has always been an idea or a goal—a political project or a regulating idea—and never an empirical description of social reality. It is easy to denounce it in terms of its obvious limits and failures in Western nations, not to speak of colonized countries which were subjected to the imperialism of European powers. Looking no farther than southern Italy, familial solidarities continue to prevail over civic demands: southern peasants in the 1950s still refused to participate in a common activity not exclusively consecrated to the immediate good of their direct family, the only object that they judged worthy of their interest and their activity.[48] The Mafia has never submitted to the rules of the *Etat de droit*. It is a regrettable fact that in countries that remain pre-national—even if they are recognized as politically constituted nations—individuals express their solidarity toward the family and the particular groups to which they belong at the expense of their loyalty toward the state and the abstract political community. We characterize these attitudes and behaviors as clientelism. But within every civic nation, these forms of ethnic, clannish, or familial solidarities have in practice always existed, even if, in principle, they ought to have surrendered in the face of respect for individual equality and the preeminence of national allegiance. The national state has never been able to mobilize populations exclusively around a purely political goal or to impose behaviors linked to the priority of citizen allegiance over communautarian ties.

Particular examples range from the simplest passive sense of laws ensuring public order up to the total political participation whose extreme form is war. Max Weber earlier suggested these various degrees of adhesion to the national community. Concretely, it is necessary that citizens understand and respect—at least passively—the rules by which politics functions. Modern citizenship must submit to three conditions, according to Jean Leca: the belief in the intelligibility of the political world, the empathy which authorizes negotiation and deliberation, and the civility which allows one to manage "the tension between social differentiation and common belonging."[49] In particular, it is true that more and more often, "to an increasing degree national unity is maintained not by calls to blood and land but by a vague, intermittent, and routine allegiance to a civil state, supplemented to a greater or lesser extent by governmental use of police powers and ideological exhortation."[50] One must add the real and symbolic role of electoral participation which is periodically manifested.

Transcendence by citizenship—or the principle of the tearing away from particular belongings accomplished by political society—can never be fully realized. It is a matter, as has been said of inequality, of a "challenge of the spirit to nature." There exists an essential contradiction between the universal principle to which the civic nation refers and the efforts of each to establish its uniqueness, many times even against the others. Each nation tends to conceive of itself as exceptional or "Chosen" and pretends to be the best possible synthesis of particularism and universality. Americans have devoted an entire body of literature to their *exceptionalism,* transfiguring the crossing of the Atlantic into a new Exodus and interpreting their national experience in light of the Old Testament, which made of them the new chosen people, in whom God had invested the task of creating the New Man. Other nations have also discovered arguments to justify their exceptional existence and mission. Even when the claim of exceptionalism is justified in the name of the universal, the nation is defined by this tension between its regulating idea whose aims are universal and the constant effort to institute and reinforce national distinctions.

Notes

1. Vidal-Naquet, preface to Finley, 1985, p. 6.
2. I base my account on Hansen, 1991, and on my exchanges with Philippe Gauthier.
3. Hansen, 1991, p. 62.
4. Eschine, 1. 4–5 quoted by Hansen, p. 74.
5. Aristotle, Pol., 1317 a–b 17.
6. Aristotle, Pol., 1280 b 32–35.
7. Gauthier, 1981, p. 167.
8. Finley, 1954, p. 256.
9. Cicero, *De Legibus*, 1, 23, quoted and translated by Gauthier 1981, p. 172.
10. Gauthier, 1979, pp. 318–319.
11. Finley, 1985 (1983), pp. 139–140.
12. Weber, 1982 (1921), p. 209; Weber, 1947, p. 600. "Nirgens in der Welt ist eine derartige politische Patronage in den Händer einzelner, formell rein privater Familien einigt gewesen." (*Economy and Society*, 1978, ch. 3, n. 12)
13. Nicolet, 1976.
14. Weber, 1982 (1921), p. 62; Weber, 1947, p. 534. "Der Bürger trat wenigstens bei Neuschöpfungen als Einzelner in die Bürgerschaft ein. Als Einzelner schwur er den Bürgereid. Die persönliche Zugehörigkeit zum örtlichen Verband der Stadt, und nicht die Sippe oder der Stamm, garantierte ihm seine persönliche Rechtssellung als Bürger." (*Economy and Society*, 1978, p. 1246)
15. Lewis, 1988 (1968), p. 344.
16. Manent, 1987, p. 26.
17. Rosanvallon, 1992, p. 333.
18. Burke, 1989, p. 252.
19. John Stuart Mill quoted in Rosanvallon, 1992, p. 453.
20. For instance, Mauss, 1969 (1920?), Dumont, 1983.
21. Manent, 1987, p. 170.
22. Philippe Raynaud analyzes these two traditions with much clarity in Furet and Ozouf (ed.), 1993.
23. Rosanvallon, 1992.
24. Furnivall, 1939.
25. Garrigou, 1992; Gueniffey, 1993; Ihl, 1993.
26. Mendelsohn, 1983.
27. J. Rex in Wieviorka (ed.), 1993, p. 343.
28. T. Parsons in Glazer-Moynihan (ed.), 1975, p. 55.
29. Schnapper, 1991, pp. 155 and following.
30. Dumont, 1991, pp. 269 and 270.
31. Windisch 1991, 1992. See also, pp. 108–109.
32. Mauss, 1969 (1920?), p. 593.
33. Quoted by Rosanvallon, 1992, p. 337.
34. Lijphart, 1968; Lijphart, 1977, passim.
35. Lijphart, 1977, p. 168.
36. Badie, 1992.
37. Elias, 1991 (1986/1987), pp. 235 and following.
38. For example, Balibar, 1992, p. 113.
39. Costa-Lascoux, 1992.
40. According to the formula, for example, of article 69 and the Code of French Nationality.
41. After many others, I have insisted upon the differences, in particular, between West Germany and France. Schnapper, 1991, pp. 51–71.

42. 15,000 foreigners acquire German citizenship each year.
43. Tocqueville, 1992 (1840), p. 787.
44. Aron, 1962, p. 170.
45. Villars, 1991, p. 425.
46. Tocqueville, 1992 (1840), p. 797.
47. Renan, 1947 (1870), p. 434.
48. Banfield, 1958.
49. J. Leca in Birnbaum-Leca (eds.), 1986, pp. 172–174.
50. C. Geertz in Geertz (ed.), 1963, p. 110.

4

The Institution of National Uniqueness

No matter how objective or mythical are the circumstances surrounding the birth of a nation, these alone would not be sufficient for its integration if the original political project were not renewed from generation to generation by common institutions. It is the state and political institutions which give form to the nation: they maintain the distinctness of the public domain as the site for the transcendence of particularisms. Not only do these institutions impose norms on domestic public life, they also act in an international context where decisions are made regarding war and peace. Inevitably, the state develops the national political project and directs a politics based upon the principles of assimilation—one refers to it today in French public life as the politics of integration—a constant renewal of the process by which new populations have been integrated through participation in common life and the practices of citizenship.

These policies are commonly seen as tyrannical. But one must not confuse the authoritarian forms of nationalization that lead to cultural or real genocide—by definition, destroying the community of citizens—with the acculturation of populations, who rearticulate their culture within a new political organization, one founded on the principle of citizenship. Hegel earlier made this distinction by reserving the term "assimilation" to refer to biological phenomena, and by employing the term *Ausgleichung* to designate non-violent assimilation, fruit of the movement proper to individuals. He showed that it really was "the goal that a state cannot fail to set for itself, which is concerned with preserving the unity and the cohesion with respect to the differences which are the center of identification."[1] The state must attend to the preconditions for political society and the formation of national singularity upon which the allegiance of its citizens depends. By their permanence and their stability, independent of individuals, these institutions both perpetuate and give a particular shape to the original political project.

The very idea of political nationhood implies tensions between the abstract citizen and particular individuals—insofar as they belong to a particular ethnie and to a particular social group. The tension between the unity/universality of the public domain and the ethnic and social diversity of national society finds expression in the process of national integration. In Western Europe, after having integrated provinces by transcending preexisting collective belongings, the modern state furthered democratic integration by successively including various social groups in collective life when these groups successfully fought to have their rights recognized. In the East, on the other hand, it was necessary to overcome historical individualities, diversities, and social fractures born of a later industrialization. In the West, the two stages succeeded one another, whereas in the East and in other countries of the world, the two processes often were concomitant. They are, however, different by nature.

In the first case, it is merely a matter of replacing the loyalty of individuals to extant ethnies by encouraging their real and symbolic participation in another collectivity: the writing and diffusion of a common history and memory and, more generally, common education play a preeminent role. The transcendence of the particularisms of the economic and social order by political society is qualitatively different. I will discuss the conditions which allow the overcoming of tensions, inevitable in any democracy, between the principles of equality and the universality of the citizen, on the one hand, and the visible inequality of the socioeconomic order, on the other. In a society that professes to value equality, is it really possible to forge a nation when these ideals of legal and political equality are belied at every turn by palpable socioeconomic inequality? So long as it is true that "the rational state cannot be edified by artificial dispositions and from any available material."[2]

The Overcoming of Ethnies

The Concrete Nation: Space and Time

The state inscribes the nation in space: the nation is tied to a particular territory. Contrary to the Greek *polis*, founded and formed by a group of men who could carry it with them overseas, the modern nation ties a political organization to a territory. Herzl, creator of the Zionist idea, was obsessed with physical space: the organization of the city and architectural styles. Israelis plant trees to manifest their faithfulness to the dead and to celebrate the Just who protected persecuted Jews. Even if they retain their cultural, religious, or economic ties, diasporic populations do not form a nation. Conversely, territory is at odds with the logic of social organizations founded on familial or clannish solidarities. A particular space defines the limits within which laws are applied and within which common practices are exercised which give shape to the inherently abstract political domain. The *jus soli* is always partially recognized by the nationality law. From the sixteenth century onward, when large Western nations were constituted in and by a territory, Germany continued to refer to the idea of the universal sovereignty of the Holy Empire. Here lies the origin of the much observed delay in the formation of the German nation. The kings of Western Europe conducted a politics of borders and invoked the legitimacy of the natural borders of their countries for centuries. By way of contrast, fluctuations of borders contributed to the political instability of the nations of Eastern Europe. All borders are arbitrary but, handed down by history, this arbitrary element becomes more or less naturalized, that is to say, considered as normal or inscribed in the nature of things, and so accepted: the good border is the one which is embraced by the nations it separates.

Similarly, the symbolic role of territory cannot be underestimated. One had envisioned, in the course of years and conflicts, the settlement of a Jewish colony or state in Uganda, Argentina, Tripolitania, Texas, Mexico, Australia, Surinam, Canada, and other parts of the world, not to mention the Jewish republic created by Stalin in Birobidzhan.[3] But it appeared that one could not mobilize Jews toward the Zionist project without echoing the formula repeated for centuries: "Next year, Jerusalem."

The state constitutes the nation, in the full sense, by giving it body and by ordering the social system around it. The nation cannot remain the pure abstraction that is the community of citizens, even if relations between civil society and the state were specified in each instance. According to cases, it is the state, collective values, and common institutions which were the motivating forces, or it is one or other ethnies which, as in Eastern Europe, claimed to constitute themselves as a nation, and so to possess a sovereign state. The institutions of the state anchor the nation in historical continuity.

The Sense of Dignity

During an age when one accepts the right of peoples to self-ownership and to be independent of any form of subjection, the political's overcoming of ethnies, which, gathered in a nation, retained consciousness of their singularity, presupposes that individuals believe their collective dignity to be recognized and respected. Dignity, it has been said, is the value of modern democratic man. The national claim is associated with this aspiration to emancipation. Between the fifteenth and the nineteenth century, when empires annexed historical communities or preexistent ethnies, by "Francofying" them, "Anglicizing" them, or "Hispanicizing" them, kings did confront resistance and revolts. Nevertheless, the right of peoples to self-possession was not yet proclaimed. Nations of the East, on the other hand, were constituted only after the principle of modern political legitimacy was affirmed in the West. Nations created in the twentieth century, then, could be stabilized only if a political project was able to unite the ethnies which composed them by recognizing their equal dignity.

It is difficult to elaborate a common political project when ethnies insist on making reference to different histories and national ideas. When in 1848, Kossuth strove to build a Hungarian nation-state on the Western model, he actually called on the notion of citizenship. But the history and the historical consciousness of peoples settled on the Hungarian territory made it impossible for them to immediately accept the Hungarian citizenship that transcended their historical or national belongings. More generally, the intellectual lesson that can be drawn from "the misery of the small states of Central Europe," is that not all diversities are susceptible of being overcome by a political project, in particular when peoples have the feeling of belonging to a historical collectivity which is not recognized in its own way and whose concrete national forms (statist institutions, political culture, national elite) do not exist. In 1919, Serbs and Croatians shared neither the same historical inheritance nor the same national symbols. These were linked for the former to a national Church, and for the latter to a secular and intellectual project. Serbs wished to found a nation-state inspired by the French model, Jacobean and assimilationist. Croatians, on the other hand, meant to create a federation that would reunite various groups of Southern Slavs while respecting their diversities. Similarly, beyond their religious and economic differences, Slovaks and Czechs, gathered in the Czechoslovak state of 1919, even if they spoke related languages, nonetheless had not known the same history for a thousand years. The first group, which formed a rural province of Hungary, aspired to be part of a federal state which would respect their specificity. The latter, annexed in the seventeenth century to the Habsburg Empire, sought primarily to form a democratic nation on the

Western model. In both cases, political conflicts reached directly to values of individual and collective dignity constitutive of the democratic order. Czechoslovakia would have been able to maintain itself after the collapse of the Soviet empire only if each of the two peoples, Czech and Slovak, had entertained the feeling of being equally and justly recognized in its personality within the common nation. The integration into the German federal republic of the *Länder* which made up East Germany was a similar experience: East Germans felt collectively humiliated when faced by the Westerners, who saw themselves as wealthier, more efficient, more "democratic," and who imposed their political and economic norms on all German *Länder*.

Since the treaty of 1759 whose terms were renewed by the agreement of 1867, the Canadian federation rested on the effectual economic, cultural and political domination of British Canadians over French Canadians. The former and the latter formed two distinct societies. For the French Canadians the British conquest remained an open wound. Their heroes were linked to that dramatic history. Yet it was impossible to discern there a pantheon common to all Canadians. Until 1960, they entertained the sole ambition of what they themselves termed the *survivance*. Immersed in the vast world of Protestant tradition, Anglophone culture, and capitalistic spirit, French Canadians wished to preserve, under the authority of the Catholic Church, their religious and linguistic identity, their traditional values, and their rural way of life. When the economic and cultural foundations of their project collapsed and the values of modern and industrial life were imposed upon them, they violently reinterpreted their collective experience as that of minorities, victims of a situation of colonization, which made them subjects and not citizens. They felt that their dignity was not recognized. Their revolt, since the Silent Revolution and the claim of Quebec's independence, has thrown into question the Canadian national project.

The case of Belgium is similar. The political pact of 1830, which founded the Belgian nation, was born of an uprising of prominent Catholic and liberal Walloons against the king of Holland. It consecrated the political, economic, and cultural domination of the Walloons, prosperous people of industry, participating in the grand French culture, over the Flemish whom the Walloons regarded as poor, rural, and intellectually and politically behind the time. The instruments by which one builds a unitary nation were introduced slowly: conscription in 1909, followed only in 1919 by public and national schools and universal suffrage. The original unifying plan met successive failures: Dutch was recognized as the official language and equal with French in 1898; admitted in the Crown Court of Brussels in 1906 and in the industrial courts in 1907. A whole series of laws between 1932 and 1935 consecrated unilingualism in Flanders, and in Walloon, the bilingualism of Brussels and the *flamandization* of the University of Ghent. The relative situation of the two groups was indeed progressively overturned and the phenomenon was accentuated after World War II: Flemish economic activity and culture—the "cultural *flamingantisme*" was born at the turning point of the century—peaked, whereas the heavy industry of the Walloons collapsed. The Flemish resented the contempt, embedded in the Belgian political project, always manifested toward them by the Walloons. In 1970, the prime minister declared that the unitary state was overcome. The unitary Belgium founded in 1830 belonged to the past. The constitution now recognized three cultural Communities (French, Dutch, and German) and three Regions (Flemish, Walloon, and the one of Brussels). There are those who dream of a European construction which would permit one to surmount the obsolete national framework. The federal Kingdom of Belgium was instituted 14 July 1993. In the words of Renan: "Nations are not eternal things...."

If all nations formed by several ethnies perpetually tend towards dissolution, the danger seems particularly great when they gather no more than two. The existence of several groups permits one to make the boundaries between those groups more vague, to multiply varied modes of exchange and the number of populations who belong to different entities. It permits varied coalitions on different subjects and avoids the excessive crystallization of particular belongings. When there are only two historical collectivities, the boundaries which separate them are more stable. The reciprocal position of the two groups is a constant threat to national unity: one of the entities is objectively inferior on all levels to the other and it nourishes a feeling of collective humiliation and a need for revenge. Constitutionalists have remarked for some time that federations constituted by two entities are the most fragile. Transcendence by citizenship appears to the humiliated as purely formal, serving only to consecrate, under pretensions of universality, its domination by the other.

From the Religious to the Political

The principle of secularity is constitutive of the democratic nation, for it is the political and no longer the religious bond which hold society together. This secularism permits all individuals, whether or not they belong to a church, or whether they are part of the majority church or of a minority church, to participate equally as citizens in public life. But it is clear that this principle can never be completely applied; it represents a regulating principle, not a concrete reality. According to the case, the state must inevitably coordinate its relations with ecclesiastical institutions. Concretely, there are inevitable compromises and accommodations between the modern state, whose secularity is affirmed or simply applied, and the social forces of religious groups and churches.

By its extreme severity, the French example illustrates the transfer of legitimacy from the religious to the political. Revolutionaries proclaimed the sovereignty of the nation, but the separation of church and state could only be enacted after more than a century of conflicts, all the more violent in that they pertained to the very principle of political legitimacy whose sacred was transferred in the eyes of many from religion to the nation. The latter became the object of a genuine cult: the nation and the republic were developed by means of a civil religion, with its own rituals, altars, temples, and saints. Stages of secularization were played out in an atmosphere of religious war. Yet even in a country which vehemently proclaims that "secularity" is an integral part of its political tradition and which embodies this principle of secularism in its foundational texts—one could hardly imagine that the churches receive, as in Switzerland and in Germany, subsidies taken on the product of the general taxes or that religion is mentioned on an administrative document—the persons in charge of religious organizations nonetheless maintain regular relations with representatives of the state and negotiate with national and local authorities the conditions of religious schooling, the observance of holidays, and the process of ceremonies.

In a different way, the case of the United States and Great Britain shows that the logic of secularity must be imposed, at least in principle. The United States has always known a multiplicity of churches and sects; its society was impregnated with religious spirit, and for some time religious institutions organized social life. Tocqueville attributed to their internalization of Protestant values the ability of Americans to join "the spirit of religion and the spirit of liberty." The social activism of churches and religious groups, the oath on the Bible pronounced by the newly elected president, the invocation of divine will in some historical presidential speeches even today testify to that ambient religiosity. Nevertheless, the separation of church and State was declared at the time of political independence. In 1790, George Washington wrote to the Jewish community of Newport (Rhode Island): "The government of the United States, which gives to bigotry no sanction, to persecution no assistance, requires only that they who live under its protection, should demean themselves as good citizens, in giving on all occasions their effectual support."[4] The American tradition has always defended in the name of liberty and the principles of the democratic nation, the political and social rights of non-Christians and of those not affiliated with any church. A high official of the State of New York, himself a believer, affirmed in 1853 that "prayers could not be required as part of the school exercises" and that *"religious education must be banished from the common school and consigned to the family and church....* Not only have the Episcopalian, the Presbyterian, the Baptist, and the Methodist met on *common* and *neutral* ground in the school room, but with them the Unitarian, the Universalist, the Quaker and even the *denier of the creed."*[5] Whatever the social realities, secularity appeared necessarily linked to the constitution of the democratic nation.

From this point of view, the English example is even more demonstrative, since the national feeling is born not only within the parliamentary institution, but in and by an indissolubly monarchical and national church. Separating himself from Rome, Henry VIII resolved not only his conjugal problems. He also responded to the feeling of a nation, concerned to limit foreign intervention on its territory. His politics of independence had the further support of the Parliament. English Protestantism, significantly known as "Anglicanism," and its rationalist individualism—having a structural affinity with the individualism of citizenship—reinforced national feeling and contributed to maintaining among the population the idea that the English were the new chosen people. Nationalism sanctioned by religion and the religious faith in its national dimension supported one another. Moreover, the politics of Mary Tudor ended up confusing for her subjects (in majority, Anglicans) national identity and anti-Catholicism. The church, of which the king of England was—and remains today—the leader, consecrated the union between the organized religion and the nation. And nevertheless, despite this long history and the respect of the tradition which underlies the political project, the equality of Catholics in public jobs was recognized in 1829; universities as well as the civil service were opened to men of all beliefs in the 1860s. Even today, this secularity is not legal, but is imposed de facto.

Secularity is from that point of view so linked to the democratic project that outside of Europe, Mustapha Kemal, when trying to make of Turkey a nation-state in the European style, imposed in an authoritarian manner a separation between state and Islam. Whereas Turco-

Ottoman identity seemed indissolubly linked to the Muslim tradition—non-Muslims, constituting the *millet*, that is to say, recognized minority cultural entities—Kemal affirmed the Turkish citizenship of non-Muslims, removed the Koranic law, prohibited religious education, adopted the European civil and penal codes, nationalized pious foundations, sought to eliminate the power of ulemas, demanded the transformation of clothes, hair style, and the calendar linked to the Muslim tradition, and finally, eliminated from the constitution, in April 1928, any reference to Islam.[6]

As another example, tensions within the State of Israel demonstrate the logical contradictions of a plan with national aspirations, but where those politicians in charge were unable to secularize the country. Put forward regularly by members of the Labor party since 1966, these proposals to separate religion from the state never succeeded. Neither Ben Gurion nor Golda Meir supported them, so much did they fear making explicit the contradictions embedded in the original project and dividing a country in which the tie between the nation and the religious tradition appeared as constitutive of a singular political project. Zionists wished to emancipate the political from religious tradition. In the age of nationalism, they meant to reinterpret the meaning of the "Jewish nation" in political terms and to banish the literal truth of the formula of the Babylonian master of the tenth century, Saadia Gaon: "Our nation is a nation only by its *Torah*." This also accounts for the hostility, sometimes passionate, manifest toward the State of Israel by some Orthodox believers, for whom only the respect of the *Torah* and of Jewish Law continues to define the "Jewish nation." But the Zionist officials could not eliminate the religious dimension of the definition of the chosen people without reconsidering their very project: for it is only in the name of a tradition both religious, in the modern sense of the term, and national could they mobilize the Jewish masses. From that fact, religion plays an active part in the political life of Israel. It is the rabbis who answer the question: "Who is Jewish?" But from their response arises the law of Israeli citizenship. The services of the rabbinate are public services, rabbis are remunerated by the state. National holidays and days of rest are those of the Jewish tradition. Marriages and divorces of Jewish citizens are the concern of rabbinical tribunals. The religious are opposed to the fact that there is a written constitution. Their interests are represented at all levels of the administration and of political authorities and their role in the Knesset is well known: given the system of proportional representation and the fact that opinion is divided approximately equally among the two major parties, it is often the small religious parties which determine the formation and collapse of governments.

The case of Spain can be used as a counterexample. The inception of the democratic nation was delayed by, among other factors, the fact that Catholic kings founded the national unit of the peninsula by expelling Jews and Muslims in 1492 in the name of religious unity, then, in the following century, eliminated the New Christians who were forcibly converted, in the name of the "purity of blood." In 1992, the king of the new Spanish democracy symbolically paid homage to the principle of the nation. He solemnly denied this religious and ethnic conception and denounced the mistakes of past monarchs.

Political Institutions

Beyond its secularity, the nation-state also coordinates the means of recruiting governors and of assuring proper political functioning. The administration, the parliament, parties, local powers, or unions all contribute to national integration by organizing public life according to commonly accepted rules.

Whatever the ideology of the Founders of American democracy, new immigrants were integrated due to the stability of political institutions, essentially by the respect accorded to the Constitution and by the balance between powers which a presidential regime and federalism allowed. Owing to the pluralism of civil society, to local liberties, to voluntary associations, to morals suffused by religious values and tinged with public spirit, and to political participation, Tocqueville admired a nation that was integrated, "formed by all nations of the world...all persons with a language, a belief, different opinions, in a word a society without roots, without remembrances, without prejudices, without tradition, without common ideas, without national character."[7] If all these ethnies—to return to my own vocabulary—really formed a democratic nation, it was because at all levels of political organization they participated actively in public life: "From where does it arise that each is as interested in the affairs of his commune, of his canton and of the entire state as much as his very own? It is that each one, in his sphere, assumes an active part in the government of society."[8] It is by political participation that large waves of immigrants, successively more distant geographically and culturally from the original WASP culture, were, until recently, and despite the force of nativist reactions, integrated into collective life. Moreover, it was by refusing to allow them to exercise the right to vote—the primary condition of citizenship—first by law, then by fact, that blacks and native Americans were excluded from public life until the 1960s.

The republican model, invoked in French public life, was also a model of integration by means of political institutions. The nationality law, particularly open, favored the acquisition of nationality, extending citizenship if not to immigrants then at least to their children born in France. Republicans of the nascent Third Republic conferred the task of educating French children in patriotism to the secular, free, and mandatory school system. They charged the army with a specifically civic function by instituting mandatory military service. Those national institutions which organized collective life around regularized practices and which diffused a system of coherent values were renderred more efficient by the myth of the Revolution, which permitted the reconciliation of the national idea with the goal of universalism. Beyond national institutions, the organization and activity of labor parties and unions provided their members a system by which to interpret the world. They helped integrate working-class population and foreigners. Integration in the French style was based on a political project, born of values objectively and symbolically incarnated in the Revolution, that is to say, according to the principles, the values, and, within limits, the practice of individual citizenship.

The politics of Switzerland may be contrasted to French statocracy. Even today, communes and cantons remain essential political entities, collecting the majority of direct taxes. All citizens are able to organize "a gathering of signatures" in order to launch a referendum of "popular initiative." Direct or semi-direct democracy at the communal level assures at least the symbolic participation of all in public life. Members of the minority can perpetually goad the majority; the political forum is permanent. Aggressive minorities force majorities to respond to them and thereby contribute to setting the political agenda. More often, the majority element makes larger efforts to encourage contacts with members of the minority. Alemannics, a strong majority at the federal level, study French more often than the other way round. "It is rather rare, indeed exceptional that, in situations of cultural contact, it is the member of the majority who more willingly learns the language of the minority member than the opposite."[9]

The Swiss pride themselves on the fact that their political project promotes the cooperation—within a single institution—of a population using four languages, belonging to two major religions and several churches, whose political traditions were various, some democratic, others formed of a federation of autonomous communes, others still oligarchic or aristocratic, not to mention the special cases of the principality of Neufchatel, of the bishopric of Bâle, or of the abbeys of Saint Gall or Engelberg. But this cooperation was built on objective conditions and out of respect for principle. Objective conditions: Given the immense variety of minority-majority combinations at the various communal, cantonal and federal levels, those who are in the majority in one situation are in the minority in another. Members of the majority are less likely to abuse their position when they are perpetually in fear of being victims of retaliatory measures in another commune or canton. This presumes that the differentiations are not superimposed, that linguistic borders do not coincide with religious borders, and that neither coincides with political borders. When this proved the case, for example, in that part of the Jura—francophone, Catholic, and rural—which was united to the canton of Bern, there was no other remedy but to introduce a partition. In principle, it is the "territoriality which assures the durability of a language on its traditional and historical territory of utilization." This means that one cannot alter linguistic borders, whatever the evolution of the population. A commune where francophones represent no more than 20 percent of the population remains nonetheless officially francophone; French remains the language of public life. This principle is truly fundamental, since it takes away any justification for one of the groups to abandon itself to linguistic or religious propaganda: "Without a strict application of the principle of territoriality, Switzerland could be destined to disappear."[10]

These practices assume their meaning within a national project, itself premised on the idea and the value of the intercultural, on the pride of being the only nation which has understood the practive and respect of multiculturalism for decades or even centuries. There seems to be great satisfaction in resolving by negotiation the conflicts raised by common life; in demonstrating the requisite ability to foster collaboration, despite tensions, among different groups; and in peacefully regulating those rivalries born of the diversity of linguistic and religious belongings. Foreigners are just as happy to celebrate the success of Swiss democracy. Like so many others, André Siegfried paid homage to "this exceptional political spirit, born of experience, kindness, aptitude for compromise, which deserves and won the admiration of the world."[11] This national project is maintained as much by the practices of political life as by the consciousness that the Swiss have of their originality.

The state must define the population which is legally and politically included in public life, hence the role and the meaning of the nationality law, in both its practical and symbolic dimension. Each democratic nation defines the legal criteria for nationality and anticipates that foreigners may acquire this. But the conditions imposed on candidates vary according to economic and demographic needs of the country, as judged by officials. Countries of immigration—for instance, Australia, Canada, or Argentina—allow legal immigrants to easily acquire nationality. When the French government decided that meagre fertility and the needs of the infantry demanded an increase in the number of citizens obliged to military service, they adopted, in 1889, a new law, such that children of foreigners born in France could not escape conscription. The values which are part of the political project also play an important role. The French nation or the American nation, founded on a strictly political and not an ethnic idea, imagine themselves open, at least ideally, to all who are prepared to accept their political values. That is, those who adhere to the principles of the rights of man. The United States and France conceived of themselves as political and moral examples. They presume themselves to be charged with a universal mission, destined to spread the benefits of civilization. On the other hand, Germans or Swiss primarily define their national idea in cultural and ethnic terms. In all cases, the nationality law expresses and consecrates the conception of the nation and reinforces the homogeneity of national populations.

In countries formed by immigration, it is crucial that various groups of immigrants be politically integrated before they become organized into particular, politically mobilized communities based on their respective origins. In Israel, the messianic force of Zionism rapidly eliminated all forms of particularisms. Since the beginning of the 1930s, Hebrew was the daily language of 90 percent of Palestinian Jews, the number of translations in Hebrew has steadily increased. By way of contrast, the languages and traditions linked to the cultures of the Diaspora were relegated to private life. Associative, cultural, literary, and civic activities were from the very beginning oriented on the Zionist project, not on the experiences of a past with which all immigrants wanted to break. Organizations of immigrants from a particular country, the *Landsmannschaften*, were reduced to a charitable role and did not preserve the national identity of their origin. New immigrants were scattered in different sectors of economic life without forming "ethnic niches."[12] The extreme politicization of the Jewish masses, one which was at the origin of the migration, was maintained in the collective life of the *Yishuv* (one still says that politics remains the favorite national sport in Israel). Conflicts between groups did not oppose the "newly arrived" to the "settled," as is so often the case in countries of immigration, but rather different parties, each of which pretended to be the "true" defenders of "true" Zionist values. Zionists of the Left and the Right were opposed, often violently, on issues such as the form of society, the destination of funds collected in the Diaspora, the goals of the movement (Home, binational, or mono-national state), their stance on Arabs and the imposed power, and relations with the Jewish communities of the Diaspora.[13] A secular form of religious mysticism, Zionism aroused the same fervor and conflicts as religions. One must also recognize that the very struggle for existence, pursued since the first waves of immigration, against the imposed powers and the Arabs, also contributed to the integration of the society of the *Yishuv*. The army, *Tsahal*, was previously and still remains the site and the primary instrument for the integration of different populations. Today's new immigrants continue to participate more vigorously in *Tsahal* than in the rest of public life.

Integrated by a messianic and political project, the Jewish society of Palestine suffered until 1948 from the lack of a real state, in particular from not being governed by a single legislation: Ottoman or English law regulated public life, Jewish law regulated personal relations, in particular, marriage. But the Histadruth, the syndicate, as has been observed, functioned as a proto-state; it allowed the development of those institutions which would become the State of Israel. The nation preceded the state, but, without the Histadrut—without this pseudo-state—as bearer of the political project, the Zionist movement, even when recognized in 1948 by the United Nations as an independent State, would probably not have been able to conduct a successful war against Arabic armies and to effectively ensure the existence of the new politically constituted nation.

Teachers of the Nation

Whether it is directly organized by the state or merely administered by it, the School is the institution *par excellence* of the nation. In Greek democracy, the absence of the public school limited real political participation to the wealthy citizens: the idea that each citizen must be able to exercise his rights effectively is unique to the modern nation. It is since the French Revolution that school teachers ceased to be called "regents" and became known as *"instituteurs,"* because they were now in charge of "instituting" the nation.

The public school must prepare individuals to participate in economic life, requiring a high degree of technical competency, as Ernest Gellner rightly observes. The school is also charged with training competent civil servants, by means of whom the state can manage conflicts between individuals and groups over the distribution of common goods and can intervene internationally. Because the state is the instrument by which the nation maintains itself, permitting it to act externally, the control of public administration and the methods of recruitment of civil servants are a major issue in public life.

But, most importantly, it is in the school that one forms citizens and arouses and nourishes their loyalty to the collectivity. It is in school that one gives citizens the concrete means necessary to fully participate in public life; it is there that one guarantees the democratic character of politics. The school transforms members of a small, provincial community into citizens.

All those concerned with nation-building have devoted a veritable cult to the school. In order to found the Republic, French republicans of the 1880s systematically detailed a system of education. Jules Ferry's school system was a political instrument in the service of nation building. This is why the school in France completely belongs to the public domain—which explains the symbolic value of conflicts over the secularity of the school. Durkheim, himself a republican, insisted as a sociologist on "the primordial importance of the School in the moral formation of the country."[14] Contemporary supporters of the republican tradition continue to maintain the cult of the school, as was the case with the authors of the report of the Commission of Nationality, created in 1987. They implicitly celebrated the school's function in nationalizing students, suggesting that one should encourage the acquisition of nationality by all who were educated under the auspices of French schooling, whether on national soil or abroad.[15] In the course of the nineteenth century, the first Turkish reformers also began to give a central place to education, creating an academy of sciences and a literary academy. Conversely, the fact that a common Belgian school, free and mandatory, was introduced only recently is probably one of the factors which impeded the development of the Belgian nation after the French model.

Since its creation, Israel has known violent conflicts whenever the new state has attempted to nationalize educational systems, which were organized by the institutions of the *Yishuv*. On such occasions, all the ambiguities of a Jewish state, created on the model of an European nation, but which could not eliminate the religious dimension of its political project, were expressed. A compromise was negotiated in 1951, then again in 1953, which established three schooling networks: the "state schools," the "state religious schools," and ultra-orthodox schools, autonomous but subsidized by public funds. This conflict, which occasioned the new state's first ministerial crisis, directly mirrored the confusion over national identity and the specific tie between religion and nation. It revealed the importance of the school in the construction of the nation.

But, beyond these examples, the school does more than merely provide a common national ideology and historical memory by its educational content. More fundamentally, like political society itself, it also forms a fictive domain in which students, as citizens, are treated equally, regardless of their familial or social characteristics. It is a space, in the physical and abstract sense of the term, which exists in spite of the real inequalities of social life, resisting the vagaries of civil society. As is the case with citizenship, the order of the School is both impersonal and formal. The abstraction of the school's society should ideally shape the child to understand and control political society.[16]

Inventors of Nations

"In a sense, it is the historians who create nations."[17] As such, the teaching of history has been directly entrusted with the task of creating that feeling of historical community which is directly given in the ethnie. On the basis of real facts, it is the historians who elaborated on the glorious birth of the great Western democracies, Israel's birth out of tragedy, and the myth of the municipal liberty of the small European nations. In the era of nations and nationalisms at the end of the nineteenth century, the retelling of corroborated historical events, was given the task of affirming collective identity and exhorting contemporaries—consecrated heirs of this glorious history—to extend the inheritance of the past and to pursue common action. In every European nation, national history traced the development and the triumph of the nation, imposing the idea that the nation must become the exclusive object of individual loyalty at the expense of any other form of identity or belonging. In Germany, higher learning served the idea of German superiority. In France at the time of the triumphant nation of the Third Republic, history was the queen discipline. After the defeat of 1870, scholarship was rehabilitated in service of the intellectual and moral reform of France. At the turn of the century Ernest Lavisse wrote a *History of France* in twenty-seven volumes, meant to demonstrate how a secular destiny found its necessary and glorious culmination in the republican nation: the history of France was that of national fulfillment.

Likewise, in his urge to build a new Turkish nation on the European model, Kemal dissolved the Ottoman historical society and created a historical society charged with writing new texts and manuals for schools and universities. This historical society was required to spread the idea that the Ottoman Empire was a burden and that Anatolia was, throughout history, the only true homeland of Turks, the only one deserving of their efforts and sacrifices.[18] In Israel, since 1955, the teaching of history was charged with awakening national consciousness. Biblical history, taught as national history, justifies the Zionist project by reference to the antiquity and legitimacy of the *Torah*. Curricula emphasize the periods of the First and Second Temple, during which Hebrews were established in Palestine, and subsequently focus on the history of the Zionist movement, neglecting the period of the Exile. The *Torah* is no longer merely a text revealed to believers, but it is the book of history of Israeli citizens, witness and evidence of the historical permanence of the Jewish nation, and the source of legitimacy for the occupation of the territory of Israel by the descendants of the Hebrews. As another example, writing at the beginning of the century based on Lavisse's model, Henri Pirenne authored a history of Belgium in six volumes in which he also strove to detail the Belgian national myth. In so doing he combined three grand themes: the antiquity of the Belgian nation, its culture of syncretism, and the fact that it was founded on the political will of its members. "Our history begins therefore squarely in the midst of the ninth century, and if one is determined to have it opened by a treaty, it is not the conference of London in which one must locate its origins, but rather the partitioning of Verdun." He repeatedly emphasized this foundational aspect of the Belgian nation, which he attributed to the victory of the communes in Courtrai against armies supported by Philip the Fair. He strove to demonstrate the position assumed by the country "among nations of Europe" with the construction of the state by the dukes of Burgundy: "Modern Belgium is really the continuation of ancient Netherlands." He underscored then the qualities of a people of "borders," whose "race" was "half-Roman, half-Germanic" and a syncretic culture, a "fusion of Romanism and of Germanism," "where one finds again, mixed together and modified one by the other, the genius of the two grand races"; "in these chosen places for the fusion of the races and the exchange of ideas," populations "number among the most intelligent and the most brilliant." Subsequently, Belgium could pride itself on being a "nation without ethnographic basis," where one was able to assist in the "fusion of races," a nation which ignored racism and was "the product of the will of its inhabitants."[19]

Contrary examples: in the State of California it was impossible to agree on the same history text for use in all schools; one teaches therefore an African-American; Native American; "Hispanic"; and "white" history. In Canada as well, "national history fell from favor since the 1960s." It has been replaced by the history of Quebec and, more generally, by social histories of ethnies (the Italo-Canadian, Ukraino-Canadian, Germano-Canadian, etc.), the history of social classes, and of gender.[20] This appears to be an indication—as well as a potential instrument—of the "ethnic" fragmentation of the two great North American societies. In the Netherlands, where the existence of "pillars" is part of the original political project, the history of the revolt against Spain and of the independence of the country are liable to be presented differently in Protestant and Catholic schools.[21] But are the United States and Canada sufficiently unified that they are able to follow that example?

The democratic nation belongs to the rational political order, but—in a notable paradox—it must borrow numerous symbolic and ritual characters from the religious order. Insofar as it is the will of citizens which legitimates the democratic nation, it depends more than other political units on the fact that these citizens have internalized common values. It is founded, to recall Durkheimian vocabulary, upon morality rather than constraint. If it is constituted by transcending particular roots, it nonetheless maintains itself by cultivating and developing emotions, immediately given in the ethnie by familial socialization, but which must be formed in the case of the nation, in order to create those sentiments of belonging and of participation according to which the nation can perpetuate itself as a collectivity. Public and private national institutions have always worked toward this goal. The work of homogenizing the culture of populations carried out by the state was without a doubt justified by the need to make all individual citizens participate in public life and the demand of forming competent civil servants. However, in order to personify the abstract community—that is, the nation—and to ensure collective mobilization, the state also had to support the national élan by appeals to an ethnicity—national language, history, and mythology—that it had helped to build.

The Elaboration of Identifying Markers

The school was not the only source of this ethnicization by reference to a historical past, a pantheon, and a common culture. The nation-state took pains to arouse or impose markers that would be exclusively linked to the national entity.

As part of this process, a national language is invented or employed which differs from that of each ethnie. In their effort to distinguish their country from West Germany, leaders of East Germany strove to create a different language. As proclaimed in 1970 by the first secretary of the unified Socialist party of East Germany: "We must above all notice this: the language of Hitler's generals, of neo-nazis and of vengeful politicians does not belong in our German language, in the language of the peaceful citizens of East Germany that we admire, respect and cultivate."[22] For the leaders of East Germany, the socialist language became an instrument to create a new national identity. Currently, West or East Germans recognize each other by their accent, their use of certain terms and certain turns of phrase. This policy is not reserved to totalitarian states, though they implement it more thoroughly and eagerly. When Greece became independent in 1827, the creators of the new nation strove to impose a "pure" language, borrowed from classical Greek and purged of all Turkish influences. This symbolically associated modern independent Greece with the direct heritage of a glorious antiquity. Two languages had coexisted for some time: one of national construction, the other of the Greeks or "language of the people." In Israel, Hebrew was reinvented as the everyday tongue, despite the fact that 90 percent of the first waves of immigrants spoke Yiddish. The migration of populations from non-Germanophone countries in subsequent decades might retrospectively justify this choice as rational. But the essential point lay not merely in the efficiency of adopting one common language to cement the nation (Yiddish could have served just as well). Rather, adopting Hebrew as a national language was a political act. So too was the decision to require new immigrants to give up the first and last name of the exile and to select a Hebrew first and last name, or to adopt Jewish religious holidays as national days: it was important to break symbolically with the unfortunate destiny of Jews in the Diaspora and to give birth to Hebrew. In former colonial countries of Africa, English or French is retained in public life—ethnically neutral—sometimes because there is no other common language (as is the case, for example, in the Indian States), but above all to increase the homogeneity of the people, to symbolize the overtaking of ethnies by the political nation and the solidarity of the political elite, whatever its ethnic origin.[23] One of the first decisions of Ghana's new government was to reduce the number of years in primary school devoted to the local language and to impose English after the second year of primary school.[24] For his part, Mustapha Kemal ordained that the Turkish language, inherited from the Ottoman Empire, was to be modified: excluding foreign words coming from Islamic or Eastern languages and retaining words of European origin, or even importing them to replace words which were suppressed. The universal language of citizenship is opposed in that way to the particularistic and coded language of the *Gemeinschaft*.

In other cases where the language was fixed, a new writing was invented. There were practical reasons for the reform of language and writing in Turkey after World War I. But the adoption of the Latin alphabet, officially imposed in November 1928, also had symbolic value: Kemal meant to break with the Ottoman past. By learning a new writing and by forgetting the Arabic writing, by employing a simplified and Europeanized language, the new generation would be opened to the values and norms of a modern nation based upon the European model.[25]

The decision to establish a new capital rather than to promote to the rank of capital one of the largest preexisting cities derives from the same logic. To build Washington, DC, or Brasilia rather than to locate the headquarters of the new power in New York or Rio de Janeiro; to choose Ankara, a modest village in the center of Anatolia, rather than Istanbul, which was for centuries the political center of the Ottoman Empire—was again to affirm that a new political entity was created, distinct from ethnies, previous states, or a previous regime.

Similarly, concrete markers are established by means of objects destined to symbolize the nation itself. Names given to places, streets, airports, or monuments crystallize the national pantheon. The hymn, the national day, or the flag arouse feelings which draw upon the sacred: one shows his respect by standing up, by respecting the silence when the national colors are flown, or by singing the national hymn. National ceremonies, whether the military parade on Bastille Day or the eternal flame under the Arc de Triomphe in France; the changing of the guard and the birthday of the Queen in England; or the collective oath of newly naturalized Americans—all concretely inscribe the idea of the nation within the collective rhythm. All these rituals have as their goal the maintenance of the sense of community, the feeling of belonging to the collective, and the belief in the unique superiority of their own national values. Like religion, the nation would not perpetuate itself if it did not organize positive or negative practices, symbols, and rituals, through which it incarnates itself in daily reality.

The work of cultural unification has inevitably faced limits, as the examples previously studied should suffice to illustrate. In Jacobin France, unanimously cited as the nation-state *par excellence*—one which had experienced many attempts at linguistic unification since the sixteenth century, (efforts finally institutionalized by the laws of the Third Republic)—there were nevertheless still fourteen different languages spoken on the national territory in 1914. Even today, Corsican politics retains its particularities. The Jacobinism of the French administration was in fact limited, tamed, and reinterpreted by local elites.[26] In Greece, the pure language, reinvented by nationalists in 1830, vanished in the face of the popular language that Greeks continue to speak today. The secularization led by Kemal in the 1920s–1930s did not prevent Turkish identity from remaining closely linked to Islam in social life today. Non-Muslim Turkish citizens are socially regarded as if they were still members of the Jewish, Greek, or Armenian *millet* which have been legally suppressed since Kemal transformed the ancient Ottoman Empire into the modern secular nation. The work of Henri Pirenne on the antiquity and values of the Belgian nation was insufficient to overcome Flemish and Walloon identities. Despite efforts since 1920 by the new Yugoslav state to constitute Southern Slavs into a single political entity, Croats and Serbs continue to cherish their particular identities. By writing their common language, Serbo-Croat, the former group with Latin characters, the latter with Cyrillic characters, they reaffirm their Catholic and Roman identity, on the one hand, and signify their faithfulness to orthodoxy and the Byzantine tradition, on the other. As with any other cultural community, the community of language may prove impotent to unify traditionally distinct collectivities which share neither the same historical consciousness nor the same political project.

Cultural Homogeneity and Political Transcendence

From Aristotle to John Stuart Mill, the homogeneity of populations has seemed a necessary condition for assuring the stability of political units. Depending on the era, homogeneity has been either celebrated or reviled. During the era of the triumphant nation and nationalisms, the nation-state, which united the cultural unit and political unit—in other words, by which the ethnie became nation—appeared to be the "best" form of that old idea of homogeneity, according the Mauss's formula. Currently, however, the very same process is condemned—in the name of the modern values of diversity and of the authenticity of each individual and culture. In the passage already quoted, Mario Vargas Llosa does not fail to denounce the fact that "the nation maintains itself only by a system destined to produce uniformity," which "imposes the homogeneity."

Cultural diversity *in and of itself* does not prohibit the creation of a nation. The overcoming of particular roots by a political, abstract, and impersonal society does not imply the suppression of these entrenchments—such a suppression is probably neither possible nor desirable. In contrast to ethnic identity, citizenship is not founded on cultural identity. One can, once again, invoke consociative democracies and regional diversity—Corsicans, Bretons, Basques, or Welsh—which are maintained in the oldest unitary nations. Objective diversity, that of languages, religions, and cultures, is not, in principle, incompatible with the creation of a common political space. The homogeneity of populations is only one of the conditions favoring political collaboration. Institutions of the state, if they carry a political project and form (or are carried by) a political society and no longer merely by a particular ethnie—are capable of surmounting cultural differences and eventually—albeit with more difficulty—ethnic identities. The existence of nations depends on the capacity of the political project to resolve rivalries and conflicts between social, religious, regional, or ethnic groups according to rules recognized as legitimate.

Nevertheless, historical experience has demonstrated that the minimization of cultural and historical differences has been the most economical, and probably, the most effective means of transcending ethnic identities. Objective homogeneity of population is not enough to create a nation, but it is true that it favors the interaction of social life and of political society. This is why the formation of the nation was always accompanied by policies aimed at reducing particularisms, not only political, but cultural. Even though one must not confound any process of political organization with the cultural genocide of preexisting entities, it remains no less true that the civic nation, insofar as it is a political unit, necessarily imposes constraints and a form of violence. It is true that the action of the state tends to depreciate differences and that the logic of equality always risks turning into the logic of similarity.

However, one should not merely reduce national construction to this single dimension. When it functions to reinforce the homogeneity of the population, the state of the democratic nation tends to prohibit or, in any case, regulate preexistent cultural and political forms, but it also gives individuals the means to participate in political life. The common culture, maintained by the action of the State, is not only the product of the technical demands of industrial society, it is also the way to maintain political society. Language may be an ethnic marker, but it is also the essential instrument by which democratic life is instituted and maintained.

The few stable nations founded from heterogeneous populations were always the product of a multisecular history, in the course of which the members of each group not only internalized the obligation to respect others, but also slowly developed political institutions which objectively perpetuated this reciprocal respect. The example of consociative democracies can without doubt be generalized: federalism, in the juridical or political sense of the term, was able to ensure national stability only when it was integrally part of the original political project, as was the case in the United States (where it survived the rifts and hatred of the Civil War), in Switzerland, and in West Germany. It has never succeeded in organizing the common life among peoples who were confronted by violent conflicts. Neither legal provisions nor the internalization of political practices, which are the preconditions of the existence of consociative democracies, can be improvised, as is shown by the divergent examples of Switzerland and the Netherlands, on the one hand, and of Yugoslavia and of Czechoslovakia, on the other.

Because the nation is not purely abstract, and hence is situated within a particular society and culture, it is imcompatible with forms of particularisms which call into question the principles of political society itself. Two demands must be respected in order to preserve a nation of citizens. First, it is necessary that individuals acknowledge that there is a unified public domain, independent, at least in principle, from religious, clannish and familial ties and solidarities and that they respect the rules of its functioning. Second, it is also necessary that the principle of equal dignity which is at the heart of the democratic nation should not be contradicted by *status* inequalities in other domains of social life, in particularly in personal law.

In function of the first demand, differences in the order of the private must not prevent the logic of political society from being respected. In other words, citizenship must be separated from religious practice and be imposed finally even at the expense of other solidarities. It is the religious character of the political which raises the question of the compatibility of the democratic nation with Islam. In the Muslim tradition, the state is, to recall Bernard Lewis's formulation, "the State of God governing the people of God, the law is the law of God. Only God has rights; man has only tasks." The construction of a democratic nation on the basis of Islam presupposes a reinterpretation of the tradition, a reconsideration of the tie between the religious and national dimensions of common life (the problem of Muslim populations settled in a Western nation is different).

The values of the private domain, on the other hand, might not in the long term be at odds with those that establish the practices of the public life without challenging the national project. Respect for the rule of law—or "constitutional patriotism," in Habermas's terms,—is not compatible with every cultural tradition. Political equality is inspired by a philosophy of the individual, as the "complete citizen." The principles according to which the public domain functions—the idea of the essential equality and dignity of each citizen—are built on values which can be judged incompatible with certain traditional cultures, for instance those rooted in the inequality of status between men and women. "English judges have emphasized that tolerance is bounded by notion of reasonableness and public policy and that foreign customs and laws will not be recognized or applied here if they are considered repugnant or otherwise offend the conscience of the court."[27] In this way, British tribunals did not recognize marriages where one of the partners was less than sixteen years old, forced marriages, divorces by repudiation of the woman, the interdiction made to Muslim women for marrying a non-Muslim, and all practices judged at odds with individual liberty. British Muslims were not allowed Islamic law because some of its laws are judged contrary to the European Convention of human rights.[28] British judges limited by law some forms of cultural pluralism. In France too, judges deny the application of foreign law whenever it is seen as incompatible with the public order, whenever it is a matter, for instance, of repudiation, polygamy, or refusal of marriage because of the religion or the nationality of the conjoint. More generally, the "contract of integration," which was settled on the occasion of the round table of 29 May 1990, under the authority of the prime minister, questioned the principle that "France did not mean to accept on its territory practices incompatible with fundamental principles, particularly toward women."[29] Any inequality of status—of which the inequality between men and women is a notable example—is held as a challenge to common values, when one takes the natural equality of any citizen as the fundamental principle of democratic practice.

These principles notwithstanding, one must still resolve practical problems. Even in nations already based on the principle of state neutrality and unity, the difficulty of the boundary between public and private domain and of the recognition of particularisms remains an open question. Despite the individual right to practice all languages in private, can this plurality of languages be recognized in public life, in countries where this multiplicity is not part of the national pact as it is in Switzerland, without challenging political unity? Can one respect the expression of regional and religious differences in the school, where one must first learn the common shared rules of national life? There is an inevitable tension between the necessities of common apprenticeship—any national construction tends objectively to eliminate particularisms and risks surrendering to the urge to stifle them with force—and the perpetuation of particular cultures, when these are no longer confined to the order of the private. Hence arise the dreams cherished by some regionalist militants or supporters of the right to difference, who claim that cultural or religious singularities are not only entitled to the liberty of civil society and its tolerance, but that these differences should be recognized in public space and subsidized by the state.

This analysis suggests that "the optimum of diversity" evoked by Claude Lévi-Strauss in *Race et histoire* of democratic nations can be defined as that which does not prohibit the participation of populations in the common political domain. It is clear that this optimum varies according to the national tradition and, in particular, according to the history of statist institutions and of patriotic sentiment. One may very well cherish the ambition of exporting the Swiss model to other countries, so long as one does not forget that it is the result of a tradition, where historical facts and reconstruction by the national memory intertwine.

Nationalist Temptations and Peaceful Vocation

Insofar as the state works to homogenize the population that it gathers and to reinforce their consciousness of a unique history, institutions and common values, it effectively seeks the reinforcement of national uniqueness and the political project. This last one always risks leading any constituted nation to affirm its superiority over others, to pass from national affirmation to nationalism. But the will to power, described by Max Weber as necessarily linked to the nation, not only characterizes democratic nations, but *all* politically constituted nations.

In the era of nationalisms, the democratic nation strove to impose its political will on other politically unified nations, or, at the very least, to prevent these others from submitting it to their own will within the "European concert," or the system of relations between the political units of Europe. Democratic nations were also those that conducted colonial wars and imposed their political domination throughout the world, contrary to the logic which underlay their own existence.

What is at stake in such armed conflicts is often the existence, the creation or the elimination of politically constituted nations or states. Because the relations between ethnies and nations are directly linked to the legitimacy of the government and to the very principle of common life, nationalisms were one of the essential sources of political conflicts since the nineteenth century. The principle of the right of peoples to dispose of themselves nourished conflicts. In these, various ethnies which had achieved consciousness of their collective identity sought, with guns in their hands, to insure that this newfound consciousness coincided with political independence. The largest wars of the twentieth century were not aroused by democratic nations, opposing them to one another. They first pitted democratic nations against politically constituted nations organized according to other principles, and secondarily, they placed some democratic nations against their former colonies which claimed their independence in the name of modern principles of legitimacy (decolonization was not always or necessarily violent). Hence it is nationalisms rather than democratic nations which originated the wars of the twentieth century.

Besides the very existence of states, the nature of their political regime is often what is at stake in armed conflicts. If the start of World War I was directly aroused by rivalries between politically constituted European nations, one part of which was organized in national communities-of-citizens, the object of war was also the very principle of their political organization: democratic nations fought the German and Austrian Empires—the latter made unstable by nationalist claims—with the initial help of Czarist Russia. In World War II, democratic nations, allied after 1941 to the Soviets, led the war against another ideological empire, one which was animated by the will to impose its law and its political regime. Since 1945, military conflicts were never purely national or nationalist; they always possessed an ideological dimension, linked to the existence and the military and ideological preeminence of the Soviet empire. Rivalries between democratic nations, since 1945, were peacefully solved by economic competition and, eventually, economic cooperation. The collaboration between the United States and Europe as well as the efforts to build the European Economic Community (EEC) symbolize this overcoming of conflicts between civic nations, which were at that time also confronted by the ambitions of communist leaders. The biggest conflicts of the twentieth century were ethnic, imperial, and ideological.

By its own characteristics, the democratic nation is less disposed to armed conflicts than other politically constituted nations. Contrary to the democratic man of antiquity, modern democratic man is primarily a *homo œconomicus.* Tocqueville likewise observed that "democratic peoples are naturally carried toward peace by their interests and their instincts..."[30] During the era of exacerbated nationalisms at the end of the past century, it seemed necessary to make of "manufactures" the pillars of the power of the nation; European colonial expansion seemed at the time directly tied to industry's requirements of primary goods and new markets—a theme which was developed by the Leninist theory of imperialism. Industrialization, by nature, ignores political borders and imposes transnational exchanges of persons, knowledge, primary goods and products. Founded on the application of the scientific spirit to production, industrial society is virtually universal. Its internal logic transcends the boundaries of races and of peoples. Schumpeter advanced the notion that a regime functioning according to the pure logic of capitalism would not be imperialistic. Similarly, by recalling the idea formulated by Saint-Simon and Auguste Comte of the antinomy between war and the new industrial society, Mauss attributed to the nation an essentially peaceful vocation: it was "the young societies badly placed which aspired to the national life" which were, for him, imperialist.[31]

These theorists were largely correct in their description of the essentially peaceful vocation of the democratic nation, but their general optimism was erroneous. They supposed that the democratic nation would become the universally accepted political form. Nothing today has arisen to reinforce that optimism. Democracy is currently the effective political regime of only a minority of countries; inequalities of development between developed countries and the rest of the world have not decreased and will not decrease in the foreseeable future; ideological antagonisms are not about to disappear; and battles of ethnies that wish themselves to be recognized as nations are multiplying. Nothing heralds a global pacification.

The Democratic Integration

Different social groups have always participated unequally in the national political arena. Some, as Max Weber put it, had interests "indirectly material...as well as ideological" in the democratic nation becoming the universal political form.[32]

Overcoming Inequalities of Status

Those who belong in politically and juridically dominated ethnies or minority groups have a direct interest in seeing to it that juridical equality and political rights are universally acknowledged—an equality which offsets, at least partially or symbolically, the inferiority of their status. Because juridically or politically subordinate populations understand better than others what protects them, they were particularly attached to the principles of democratic citizenship. For instance, one can see the strong participation of Protestants, a minority in France, in public life and their attachment to the principle of secularity, which offsets their numerical inferiority. Holding socioeconomic levels constant, African-Americans maintain a rate of electoral participation superior to that of other ethnic groups in the United States; this is also the case of the Untouchables of the Indian States.

Similarly, this can also explain that, in all European countries, Jews adhered to national projects wherever they were granted citizenship— that is to say, political and juridical equality with those who always persecuted them. While nations were being built in Italy or in Austria against preexistent nationalities, the majority of Jews, belonging to none of them, fully and passionately participated in the national project. Not only were Jews the only truly Austrians, but they were also the only true Italians, the others remaining before all Piedmontese, Lombards, or Sicilians. Neither Walloons nor Flemish, Jews may also be counted among the only Belgians, even though there is one Jewish-Flemish community and another Walloon. During the entire duration of the unified *Reich*, German Jews were convinced that their political failure, such an obvious contrast with their successes in intellectual and cultural life, was linked to the nascent state of the national consciousness, and hence that it would end when the German nation was completed.[33] In all European countries during the 1930s, one witnessed the emergence of professed anti-semitism as civic nations and the principle of citizenship were weakening. If the democratic nation was not always faithful to its own principles, these principles remain nonetheless the best ramparts against ethnic passions, of which anti-semitism is a prominent example.

Bourgeois, whose social status was inferior in traditionally aristocratic countries, had a similar interest in the nation, one which was at the same time political and economic. While it is correct to emphasize the ties between the capitalist bourgeoisie and national construction—this does not mean that the bourgeoisie is the simple reflection of capitalist relations, as argued so many times by Marxist thinkers. What is true, however, is that the industrial and commercial bourgeoisie was agent and beneficiary of both the democratic regime and the capitalist regime, which arose simultaneously. According to Norbert Elias, the delayed development of the German nation inheres, among other factors, in the fact that the Bismarckian empire consecrated the domination of the economic bourgeoisie by the military elite and its model of life and thought. But the intellectual bourgeoisie had just as much interest in nation-building. Jurists of the king were essential in establishing the statist institutions of the English and French monarchy. Since the sixteenth century, its historians and poets celebrated the glory of England. In all countries, once institutions were established, historians exalted and amplified patriotism by building a teleological vision of the national destiny. It is the intellectuals who, throughout the nineteenth century, contributed, by their scholarship and ideas, in transforming the "protonationalisms" or nationalities into nationalist assertions. In order to transcend concrete belongings—which necessarily implies that individuals give up or reinterpret preexistent particularisms—it was necessary that a common ideology, system of values, and perception of the social world be elaborated as a necessary element of the political project. In all nations of Western and Balkan Europe, the national renaissance was composed of three steps: the first where intellectuals invented or reinvented the culture, language, and history of the oppressed people; the second during which a small minority of patriots were inspired by the work of these writers and reinterpreted it in political terms; and, finally, where the work of diffusion, led by these acting minorities, reached the masses who launched in turn the popular movement for claims to independence.[34] The making of a common memory, from now on a national and no longer ethnic basis, was a necessary dimension of any national construction. Academic historians and patriots of the Third Republic, intellectuals of Central Europe from the last century, and Westernized intellectuals of colonial countries after the end of World War II—all elaborated the national ideology and served as priests of the new religion of the nation. But historians and intellectuals also possessed, along with the whole intellectual bourgeoisie, the means of participating in democratic life founded on juridical competence, then economic, as well as on the controlling of discourses. This last one requires the handling of words and concepts. Intellectuals, like the industrial and merchant bourgeois, really had the "half-real, half-ideological" interests, evoked by Max Weber, in the construction of nations. The call to universal values is never alien to historically constituted social interests, even if it is not reducible to these interests.

The Citizenship of Workers

How does one integrate populations made subordinate by their economic or social status in a nation founded on the principle of political and juridical equality? In every European nation, few among the first generations of industrial workers in the twentieth century adhered to the ideal of the nation. In the poor and disrupted world of the first industrial revolution, legal and political equality was not enough to compensate either materially or symbolically for the brutal inequalities of the economic order. The Marxist critique of formal democracy as well as the aspiration for real democracy were born then, at the same time as the theory of the political as superstructure. The material conditions workers experienced at that time explained how one could denounce the constitutional liberal state as a basic fiction, indeed as an impostor. Officials of international labor never ceased to condemn national bourgeois society and called for worker solidarity across borders.

Nevertheless, with the nation the masses effectively acquired the means to participate in political life when universal suffrage was given to them, between 1848 and 1919 according to the European countries. They next obtained, after the end of World War II, the protection of the welfare state. The British example is a perfect illustration. The English parliamentary regime, essential source of power since the Revolutions of the seventeenth century, progressively admitted representatives of entrepreneurs and capitalists into the House of Commons by means of the electoral reform of 1832, which suppressed the "rotten boroughs," then those of the new urban laboring classes by the reform of 1867, and finally the whole working class, agricultural workers or minors, by the reform of 1884, which gave the right to vote to all adult men. The initial provisions for welfare and social security, the creation of unions, and the birth of the Labor party—in which unions were represented in and of themselves—contributed also to the organization and integration of the working class into political and social life. In France, the historical role of Jaurès was to reconcile socialists to the national idea. It was nevertheless a "divine surprise" for all the governments to see the European masses going to war in 1914 without revolt, and often even with enthusiasm.

In fact, the modern nation is distinguished less by national feeling, which already existed in the nobility, than by the democratization of that feeling by the mobilization of masses around national values and affirmations. It was an English historian, George Trevelyan, who observed that the French Revolution filled with pride and haughtiness the most humble peasants and bourgeois, who became, thanks to the new regime, citizens and patriots, to whom all civil and military careers were now open. Nationalist militants always insisted on the necessity of mobilizing the entire people. The Zionist project truly took shape when the Jewish proletariat of Central Europe massively participated in the messianic hope, originally articulated by an intellectual, of building a Jewish nation on the model of European nations. But beyond this mobilization lies a matter of a claim for equality which is strictly political.

In contrast to those partisan differences which mirror ethnic, religious, cultural, or regional claims—therefore contrary to the proper logic of the nation—the labor parties relied on the universal idea of citizenship to justify their demands. They demanded that political structures be reformed in the name of the very principles upon which the legitimacy of democratic nations was based. Whereas representatives of the popular classes once denounced formal democracy, the right to vote, parliamentary representation, and participation in government, one currently notices that individuals of the most modest social origin have become the most attached to the nation, from which they obtained, at least symbolically, a form of equality denied to them in social life. In every European country, the commitment of voters to the EEC, manifested in the treaty of Maastricht referendum, was greater among those belonging to an advantaged group, whether defined in terms of employment, income, or educational level. National belonging is a source of prestige for all, but it may eventually come to be the only source for those groups economically and socially least favored. Weber observed that national prestige was the only one accorded to those who occupied an inferior place in the order of the market, status and power. The phenomenon of "poor whites" in the Southern United States, forming a modest population particularly hostile to blacks or recent immigrants with whom they are in direct contact, speaks to the fact that their color or their nationality risks becoming the only foundation of their social status. Until now the political nation has been alone in responding to the properly democratic aspiration of men to recognize the equal dignity of all.

Empires and Nations

It is the demand that citizens identify with their governors which placed democratic values at odds with empire. In fact, it is as a result of the internalization of these democratic values that, today, "men prefer to be condemned, even severely, by members of their religion, nation or class, than to be under the tutelage, as kindly as it is, of masters of another country, another class or another environment."[35] Some empires could in fact be more tolerant than nations toward cultural particularisms, but they did not permit "the participation of all the governed in the state"; they did not respond to "the eternal claim of equality."[36]

This was the case, in particular, of the colonial empires created by European nations. The colonial project was intrinsically in contradiction with the principles of democratic nations. Nevertheless, the majority of contemporaries in France did not see the essential contradictions of a policy called the "assimilation" of indigenous populations which, at the same time, reserved citizenship to colonists. In Algeria, partially integrated to France, one could see this juridical monstrosity forming an affront to the principles of modern democracy: nationality without citizenship. In 1862, the Court of Algiers affirmed indeed that "even while not being citizen, the indigenous is French." Throughout the history of French Algeria, the citizenship of Muslims remained partial, and unequal institutions lasted almost to the day of independence. Because the project of formal democracy contradicts the realities of the social order, it is more likely to betray its own values.

Colonial society was founded on the juridical and political status inequality of the members who composed it, whereas the legitimacy of the modern democracy consists in giving this equality to all. The failure of the project of building a "French Algeria" as an integrated part of the French nation, shows that the nation could not contain both citizens and subjects at the same time. Not only did the colonizers educate at least partially the "indigenous," who became capable of controlling modern technical means, therefore calling into question the material superiority of Westerners which had allowed them to dominate vast territories with few material and human means. But, above all, the colonizers could not help but acclimate a westernized minority to democratic values. This minority then claimed for the subjugated group the same civic rights possessed by the colonizers. It was inevitable that at least a few of the colonized should internalize the culture of the colonizer, and that they should invoke in their turn these values of liberty and equality, claiming that the universal principles of the rights of men be applied to them. In all countries which were colonized, nationalist thinkers exalted the ethnic specificity of their country—the authenticity of the original culture—and at the same time demanded that one recognize their dignity by claiming Western values against Westerners. The decolonization, after 1945, seemed to be the outcome of the conflicts of World War I and World War II and the collective weakening of European nations. But this is not the essential point: if the empires built by European democracies before World War I were short-lived, it was because the territorial and direct political domination imposed by colonial powers were at odds with the logic and values of the democratic nation.

1789 and the Welfare State

During the revolution, one proclaimed that "society is obliged to provide for the subsistence of all its members either by giving them jobs, or by assuring the means of subsistence to those who are incapable of working." The right of the citizen to work or to public assistance replaced once and for all the idea of individual and private charity whose original inspiration was religious. When each individual is a citizen, moreover, he has the right to possess the means to food, shelter, and to decently raise his children such that they are capable of exercising their political rights. For if the professed equality of citizens were contradicted too much by observable inequalities, would this ideal continue to have any meaning? The impulse universally known as social democracy was not solely inspired by political necessity, but also by the need of Western nations after World War II to respond to Marxist critics of formal liberties and real liberties. The revolutionaries of 1789 obviously did not anticipate the development of the Welfare state. However, this development is a consequence, retrospectively evident, of the proclamation of the new sovereignty and equality of citizens. In the end, one could not make political and legal equality the basis of the social bond without at the same time setting into motion a dynamic which seeks to make economic and social conditions less unequal. The politics of liberal democracies, acting in that way by fiscal redistribution and the politicy of social intervention, is implicit in the very conception of the modern democratic nation, which differs here fundamentally from ancient democracy.

The Welfare state is not opposed to the liberal state: rather it extends and develops the implications of its principle of legitimacy. Charged with correcting the most striking inequalities and with lending concreteness to the abstract notion of citizenship, it illustrates its own logic. The citizen must partake of the material conditions which will permit him to concretely exercise his rights. This strictly political dimension legitimizes social policies and the various efforts undertaken to integrate by compensatory measures those whose exclusion from professional life threatens to lead to their exclusion from collective life.[37] Citizenship is not reduced to "economic and social citizenship," but this element has become one of the conditions for the exercise of true democracy. The term "liberalism," linked since the founding of the United States to the idea of political, civil, and economic liberty, now designates those principles and public policies whose goal is to intervene in economic and social life and to redress the most striking inequalities. For twenty-five years, throughout Western Europe, the right to social assistance has progressively been extended to new categories until it has become a form of minimum income given to the poorest, regardless of any relation to a past, future, or indirect job, or any physical or social handicap. The politics of social intervention entails the worthy goals of ensuring every citizen, beyond merely juridical equality and political liberty, the material conditions of life requisite to this dignity. For several decades, the Welfare state seemed to be the means of resolving the tension between the political order, founded on the legal and political equality of citizens, source of political legitimacy, and the perhaps inevitable perpetuation of inequalities within the economic and social order; in other words, the welfare state sought to manage tensions, implicit in the definition of the nation, between abstract citizens and concrete actors in economic and social life.

The feeling of "ethnic" belonging and the passions that it arouses are the direct expression of the natural attachment that men have to the land and to the immediate familial or ethnic collectivity in which they were raised. What is familiar tends to become a value in itself. Patriotism transferred this primordial sentiment on to an inherently abstract historical community and a political organization. To require of the individual that he be prepared to "die for the homeland," the action of the state consisted in arousing an identity which transcended that of the natural and social environment and in maintaining the intimate patriotic relations, at once mystical and instrumental, which defined the relations between the individual and the nation. It is necessary indeed to transcend the opposition between the instrumental and the expressive relationship, between the institution and the representation: the relation of the individual to the national was indissolubly both. The nation could answer that need for group belonging which is, according to Herder, one of the elementary needs of man; it could respond, if one adopts Elias's vocabulary, to "the affective desire of human society," to "the need to share and exchange affective relations with others," which "is part of the most elementary conditions of the human existence."[38] In so doing, the nation, the political form of democracy, created a new human type, a unique relation between the individual and the collective. But those other preexistent identities, subnational or supranational, were never wholly eliminated by the rationalistic ambition of modern democracy. Man is an animal of passions as much as of reason. It was impossible to found the nation simply on the rational and universalist ambition of citizenship. Instead, it was imperative that the nation appeal to those emotions linked to the historical and cultural singularity of each national entity.

Notes

1. Saint-Germain, 1993, p. 64.
2. Fichte, cited by A. Renaut in Fichte, 1992 (1806), p. 33.
3. Laqueur, 1973 (1972), pp. 452–453.
4. Goldenberg (ed.), 1990, p. 59.
5. Lipset, 1963, p. 165.
6. Lewis, 1988 (1961), pp. 354 and following.
7. Tocqueville, 1991, p. 29.
8. Tocqueville, 1991, p. 190.
9. Windisch, 1992, Vol. 2, p. 441.
10. Windisch, 1991, p. 83.
11. Siegfried, 1947, p. 199.
12. Eisenstadt, 1954, pp. 52–58.

13. Laqueur, 1973 (1972).
14. Durkheim, 1925 (1899), p. 90.
15. Long, 1988.
16. Durkheim, 1925 (1899), p. 170.
17. Guenée, 1971, p. 123.
18. Lewis, 1988 (1961), pp. 314–315.
19. The expressions in quotations are borrowed from the preface to the 1917 and 1918 editions.
20. Perin, 1993.
21. D'Iribarne, 1989, p. 226.
22. Cited in Hagège, 1992, p. 86.
23. Lijphart, 1977, p. 169.
24. Wallerstein, 1960, p. 138.
25. Lewis, 1988 (1961), p. 378 and following.
26. Grémion, 1976.
27. Poulter, 1989, p. 7.
28. Poulter, 1989, p. 5.
29. Higher Counsel on Integration, 1993, p. 81.
30. Tocqueville, 1992, p. 786.
31. Mauss, 1969 (1920?), p. 588.
32. Weber, 1947, p. 627. "teils indirekt materiellen, teils ideellen Interessen." (*Economy and Society,* vol. 2, p. 922)
33. Laqueur, 1973 (1972), p. 36.
34. Hroch, 1968.
35. I. Berlin in Delannoi-Taguieff (ed.), 1991, p. 311.
36. Aron, 1962, p. 299.
37. Paugam, 1993.
38. Elias, 1991 (1986/7), p. 261.

5

Conceiving the Nation

Most recent scholarship in the social sciences—like the preceding analysis—appears to neglect the debate pursued in Europe from generation to generation, since the beginning of the nineteenth century, over the dual conception of the nation. In different terms, virtually every author has concluded by opposing the idea of the "political" or "civic" nation, born in Western Europe, to the "ethnic," conception which stems from the German tradition and, more generally, from Eastern Europe, and which is founded on the belief in a common ancestry, culture and language. Because these two interpretations say something important about the underlying nature of social reality, one must take these issues seriously by seeking to understand why the modern nation was conceived in these terms.

Two Histories and Two Ideologies

The contrast between these two ideas shapes in large part the intellectual history of the nation.

The History of Western and Eastern Europe

In the West, political unity came into being long before the emergence of nationalisms in the nineteenth century. Monarchs united a territory over which they exercised authority. The political unification of England, and, more recently, of Scotland and Ireland, was completed by the English monarchy. Over the course of the centuries, kings progressively united the small kingdom of France with the provinces which would later form the national territory. This was done by means of military conquests, coupled with an artful policy of marriages, exchanges, and negotiations. State institutions slowly emerged after the Middle

Ages in France, England, or in Spain, aroused by the necessity of maintaining an army which imposed a heavy burden on the populations. It was necessary that the agents of the king levy taxes, enroll men, and requisition goods. The result of taxes, first gathered to wage war, permitted them to reinforce the royal territory, to centralize the administrative organization, and to differentiate the state instruments of control and of coercion. "War made the State, and the State made war."[1] Against the power of feudals and against popular revolts, the king's civil servants, jurists, and military progressively constructed the State in an intimate symbiosis with the nation. Indeed, national sentiment was expressed in France as early as the thirteenth century.[2] The national idea was progressively born in England and France as a result of the Hundred Years War which pitted them against one another and in Spain with the Catholic *Reconquista* of the Iberian peninsula at the end of the fifteenth century, of which the expulsion of Jews and Muslims in 1492 was at the same time the instrument as well as the symbol. Arising from a multisecular process of development, the French nation-state existed under monarchic form long before the nationalist idea of the right of peoples to dispose of themselves was formulated. The monarchy was so intimately bound up with the nation that, as Renan observed, when France was transformed into a republic, the nation was maintained: "This great French royalty was so highly national, that, the day after its collapse, the nation could hold without it."[3] France and England knew a parallel history of the birth of the national idea and of the elaboration of political and state structures, which, within the relatively stable borders, embodied and symbolized the unity of the nation.

Similarly, the close relationship between dynastic and religious principles magnified their integrative capacity: religious unity reinforced the royal power. Mirroring the dual human and divine nature of Christ, the doctrine of the King's Two Bodies constituted a truly royal Christology. By elaborating the fiction of a mystic royal body distinct from the natural body of the king, but united to him in a mysterious fashion, English jurists forged the abstract idea of a Royalty whose existence transcended the person of the king. In this way, the secular power was affirmed against the church by founding the conception of the state, naturally superior to its agents and independent of them. The king, image and instrument of God on earth, was often at the head of the religious organization of his kingdom. The king of the United Kingdom became the chief of the church. The very Christian king of France, who chased Jews and Protestants from the Kingdom, held his position by divine right. The Catholic monarchs of Spain founded their political legitimacy on the religious unity of their kingdom. "The State had more and more the tendency to become a quasi-Church or a mystic corporation upon a rational basis."[4] But, at the same time, faced with the political ambitions of the church, the monarch of divine right established and jealously guarded the independence of the political body as "wholly *one,* essentially distinct from the Church."[5]

In 1414, at the council of Constance, the five leading nations of Western Europe—Italy, France, England, Germany, and Spain—presented themselves as fixed and acknowledged political entities. But, in the following centuries, the imperial ambition of the Roman Saint Empire of the Germanic people, which officially perished only in 1806, and the subsequent Ottomans invasion forestalled the creation of stable national units in central Europe. From the Baltic to Sicily, in what S. Rokkan and D. Urwin called the "polycephalic" zone of Europe, city-states, independent towns, kingdoms, and ecclesiastical or dynastic principalities were perpetuated under the shelter of the imperial dream until the nineteenth century. In the historical consciousness of Germans and Italians, for example, cultural belonging was always distinct from political organization. Germany and Italy were constituted as nation-states only after 1870, and even then imperfectly. It was a German, Meinecke, who elaborated in 1907 the opposition between the nation-state (*Staatsnation*) and the cultural nation (*Kulturnation*). Germans, at different times in their history, made, more or less eagerly, various formulations in which nation and State were separated, either as "two states, one nation" or as one of "several states, one nation."

Between this polycephalic Europe and Central and Western Europe, the Austro-Hungarian Empire remained in 1914, a "conglomerate of heterogeneous States and without any internal cohesion."[6] The Habsburg monarchy, heir of the old imperial dream, was in principle supranational. Charles I, emperor of Austria and apostolic king of Hungary, was also king of Bohemia, Dalmatia, Croatia, Slavonia, Galicia, Lodomeria and Illyria, king of Jerusalem, archduke of Austria, grandduke of Tuscany and of Kraków, duke of Lorraine, Salzburg, Steyr, Carinthia, Krain and Bukovina, grand-prince of Siebenbürgen, margrave of Moravia, duke of upper and lower Silesia, Modena, Parma, Plaisance and Guastalla, Auschwitz and of Zator, of Cieszyn, Frioul, Ragusa and Zara, count of Habsburg and of Tyrol, Kyburg, Gorizia and Gradisca, prince of Trent and of Bressanone, margrave of upper and lower Lusatia and in Istria, count of Hohenzollern, lord of Triest, Cattaro, and so on.

The emperor neither comprehended nor wished to become involved with a particular national project. The Empire, established in its last political incarnation by the Austro-Hungarian Compromise of 1867, reunited peoples who were distinguished by their historical consciousness, convinced of the singularity of their destiny and separated by their religious belongings. Catholics, Protestants, Orthodox, and Muslims formed a mosaic, one in which churches divided peoples rather than uniting them. From the perspective of languages, too, of the distribution between majority and minority languages, European history shaped a world where the West tended toward unity, and the East toward dispersion.[7] Moreover, the tormented history of the region prohibited the development of a free bourgeoisie, which made these diversities even more resistant to a single, national project. The feudal tradition remained firmly in place for a long time, putting the noblesse and the peasantry face to face, allowing no place for a political society founded on bourgeois citizenship.

Confronted by invaders from the East, peoples submitted to conquerors and were able neither to be organized into independent political entities, nor to be separated by rigid borders. While the modern State emerged in the grand monarchies of the West between the fifteenth and the eighteenth centuries, Germany and Italy remained politically divided. Similarly, victorious Turks destroyed the national institutional frameworks of Hungary and of Bohemia, as well as of the medieval kingdoms of Serbia and Croatia. When the nationalist idea was diffused throughout central European countries in the nineteenth century, these ethnic belongings were even more difficult to surmount, as the instability of borders prohibited the birth of truly political institutions. They possessed neither a capital, state machinery, an autonomous economic organization, a national elite, nor a political culture. On the other hand, during the age of nationalism, Romanians or Germans settled on Hungarian territory, for instance, had no reason, in the name of the people's rights to dispose of themselves, to accept the domination of the Magyars. As a result, traditional peoples were unwilling to renounce their political identity, as had other peoples before the birth of nationalism: for instance, Brittany in the sixteenth century; Alsace, Artois, and Roussillon in the seventeenth century; or Scotland at the beginning of the eighteenth century, by the conclusion of the Treaty of Union of 1707 and Home rule.

While invoking on the one hand the right of peoples to self-possession—a principle born in Western Europe—Central European nationalists also justified their claims by ethnic and linguistic arguments. Their traditional uniqueness was affirmed by a passionate hostility toward their immediate neighbors, of which the hatreds between Romanians and Hungarians or between Hungarians, Serbs and Croats are notable examples. Isaiah Berlin was not the first to notice that nationalist excesses are felt less in societies which have benefited from political independence for long periods of time.[8] The fear for the very existence of the national community, deeply internalized by the collective consciousness, nourished collective hysteria and exacerbated unfounded national vanities. It pitted one people against another and prohibited the formation of a democratic nation.

It is impossible to understand the formation of nations if one neglects the relationship between internal integration and external sovereignty. Spain, Portugal, England, the Netherlands, and France were conquering nations; they discovered the non-European world and built immense colonial empires throughout the world. The will to international power effectively reinforced the process of internal integration. Eastern countries, on the contrary, were conquered by non-European invaders from the East. Throughout Central and Baltic Europe, populations were moved, deported, or subjugated, and borders varied according to the advance and retreat of Turkish armies. Submitted to the domination of an external power, peoples were for centuries subjects in vast, partially non-European empires. They were unable in so few years to be forged into a community of citizens.

The Western Ideology and the Ideology of Eastern Europe

This dual experience of European history has stayed our conceptions of the nation. Arguments put forward by militants at the occasion of conflicts between nationalisms—that which opposed England to its American colonies in the eighteenth century, and, then, France and Germany since revolutionary wars until the annexation of Alsace to the German *Reich* in 1870 and the war of 1914–1918—were transfigured in Ideas.

Nineteenth century thought was marked by the political and ideological conflict between the *Grande Nation*, which invoked the new principle of legitimacy, and the older "nations," in the medieval sense, or empires stemming from a dynastic or religious history. But the new principle itself seemed to admit two interpretations. The claim of peoples to self-possession might be legitimated in the name of the "people composed of citizens" or in the name of a "people" stemming from an original history and culture. By linking itself to the same revolutionary principle, a dual ideology of the modern nation was elaborated. The first invoked the will of men, the other, their ethnic and linguistic belonging. The French conception, stemming from the thought of the Lumières and the revolutionary experience, was political, individualist, rational, and voluntarist. After their military defeats, in 1806 and 1807, however, Germans defined their nation in organicist terms. Founded on the community of an original people (*Urvolk*) stemming from a common ancestry, sharing the same culture and the same past, the ethnic nation was inherited by individuals.

After the war of 1870, the controversy between French and German historians elevated the tension between two distinct ideas of the nation to the level of ancient tragedy, thereafter seen as essentially "ambiguous." On the one hand, Theodor Mommsen justified the Bismarckian policy of annexation by the ethnic, linguistic, and cultural "Germanness" of Alsace, whatever the provisory will of its inhabitants. On the other hand, the French affirmed that "it is neither race, nor language that makes nationality" (Fustel de Coulanges), invoked revolutionary principles and, in the name of the legitimacy of the "vow of nations" (Renan) and of the "will" and of the "free agreement" of peoples, affirmed that Alsace was "French by the nationality and the sentiment of the homeland" (Fustel de Coulanges). The role played by the annexation of the Alsace in shaping German, French, and even Italian theorizing about the nation demonstrates the degree to which that theoretical controversy was both polemical as well as analytical.

Forged by nationalists in order to justify and to orient collective action, these ideologies were afterward accepted as "ideas," in the analytical sense of the term. The existence of two ideas, first formulated by German romantics to edify their own nation against the French, was imposed, then, in varied vocabularies, as concrete evidence; it was analyzed by theoreticians, then sanctioned by the historians of nationalist ideas.

In different national and scientific languages, one inevitably distinguished the nation according to the "French" ideology (or "Italian," or "American") and the nation according to the "German" ideology. Or, in other terms, "Western" nation is contrasted to "Eastern" nation; civic nation to *Volk*; "nation-state" (*Staatsnation*) to "cultural nation" (*Kulturnation*); the people of citizens to the people of ancestors; political will to organic nation; elective nation to ethnic nation; contract-nation to genius-nation; public spirit to populism; the individual to the nation as a collective individual; Enlightenment to Romanticism; or holism to individualism. Yet behind these various terms lurk the same elements that Eric Weil summed up so well. He distinguishes the Western nationalism of "politics, preoccupied with the liberation of the individual, cosmopolitan in its intentions, affirming the plurality of values under those supreme of the liberty of thought and expression, which has its roots in a progressive society, living under the law which is freely accepted (at least in principle)"; but on the other hand, the nationalism of Eastern Europe is "the expression of a feeling of inferiority of linguistic groups which do not own a political organization of their own, constituting themselves by the myth of a *natural* value, in an idealized prehistory, in a 'consciousness of oneself' composed only of rights (always unappreciated by the others), in an ideology which is not destined to justify a reality but to transform the one with which they are confronted."[9] The first great historian of nationalism, Hans Kohn, consecrated this opposition in historical science by advancing that "liberty for the Germans was founded on history and on particularism, and not, as in France, on reason and equality." When a Hungarian historian wished to introduce the idea of a "third Europe," designating Bohemia, Hungary and Poland, he characterized it by its struggle between the "Western" and the "Eastern European" model.[10]

This series of binary oppositions particularly shaped the intellectual climate because they were entrenched in the entire reflection of the nineteenth century about the new society stemming from industrial and political revolution and modern political legitimacy. They were further inscribed in the philosophical discussion of liberty and necessity.

Even contemporary thought has not fully escaped the tendency to leap from historical description to abstract theory which seems to characterize all thinking about the nation. Anthony Smith, after having described the two historical "trajectories" which effectively led to the formation of nations, draws from it the conclusion that there are thus two "concepts" of the nation, the one territorial-civic, the other genealogical-ethnic: "The concept of the nation is found to be inherently unstable and dualist."[11] John Plamenatz, by contrasting German and Italian nationalisms of the nineteenth century to the claims of Balkan peoples, also rediscovered the dual idea of the nation: the former, already united around a grand culture, requiring recognition as an independent political entity to form a civic nation; the latter, in the rediscovery of a common culture, with historical allegiances and unstable and concurrent ethnies, aspiring to form an "ethnic" nation.[12]

Yet is is impossible to overlook the fact that in reality, every national tradition is dual—in terms of intellectual history or historical reality. Germans did not entirely ignore the political conception of the nation: Louis Dumont recalls that "the affirmation by Hegel of culturally distinct communities represents an aspect of German acculturation to the developed form of individualism and combines a holistic aspect with an individualistic aspect."[13] In France, counterrevolutionary thinkers, such as Joseph-Marie de Maistre or Louis de Bonald, extended Burke's passionate criticism of the revolutionary idea of the nation in the French style. But these very criticisms implied that for better or worse, these two ideas of the nation really existed, even if they were eventually merged in the concrete forms of historical nations.

This intellectual tradition is perpetuated even more because it does shed light on certain concrete realities. The comparative analysis of the nationality laws and immigration policies in France and in Germany demonstrates that the contrast between the contract-nation and the genius-nation has not lost all meaning, and moreover, that it continues to motivate the national spirit and to influence legislation. In France, provisions for automatic or semiautomatic acquisition of nationality, the place occupied by the simple declaration (for instance, for foreign spouses of French citizens), the right to reintegration (for those who have lost nationality) give rights to the individual against the state. The low cost and liberal application of the nationality law continue to make French nationality very widely open, not only to individuals born or educated in France, but to almost all settled foreign individuals who apply for it.[14] French politics retains its goal of integrating foreign populations around a civic project in the name of citizenship. Germans, on the other hand, have preserved an ethnic conception of the national bond. Many contemporary writers continue to evoke the linguistic and historical community, rather than political will.[15] The idea of the "German blood" is still alive in the population. The almost exclusive respect of the *jus sanguinis,* as translated into the nationality law which is essentially founded on a law of 1913, effectively denies citizenship to foreigners, even if they have been regularly and consistently settled, sometimes for two or three generations, and even acculturated to the German society and culture. On the other hand, the law grants citizenship to descendants of Germans settled for centuries in Poland, Russia or in the Sudeten Mountains, who sometimes completely ignore German language and society.[16]

Yet this intellectual and political heritage is not enough to explain why this contrast continues to mark the national spirit. However, the argument developed in previous chapters does take us some distance in understanding why these terms continue to shape our thinking. Even beyond the intellectual comfort offered by binary oppositions, the "theory" of the two ideas of the nation is founded on the tension, constitutive of the idea of the nation, between its proclaimed universality and the specificity of pre-national ethnies that the action of governments tends to reinforce. Partisans and theoreticians of the civic nation stress citizenship; conversely, defenders of the ethnic nation invoke the strength, the value, and the authenticity of particularistic ties.

European history therefore crystallized in fundamental and irreducible ideological opposition—defined as a system of ideas and values orienting political action—what was essentially the result of the two different histories. Ideas of the nation, socially constituted, were used in Europe since the French revolution as instruments of nationalistic battles. If ideas are necessarily historical objects, insofar as they were one of the means used by social actors to conceive and build nations, one must not confuse their study with sociological analysis. "Binary oppositions are an analytic procedure, but their utility does not guarantee that reality is divided up in that way. We must be suspicious of anyone who declares that there are two kinds of persons, or two kinds of reality or processes."[17]

Moreover, to interpret the classic texts of Fichte or of Renan within this opposition simplifies or even betrays their thought. Although an acknowledged supporter of the "ethnic" nation, Fichte nevertheless integrates in his analysis elements of the civic nation. Renan, for his part, is not simply the ideologue of the contract-nation.

Rede an der Deutschen Nation, composed by Fichte after the rout of Prussia in Jena in 1806, has traditionally been taken as the first formulation of the conception of the ethnic nation, one which romantic thinkers will develop throughout the course of the century.[18] In fact, one finds there three large romantic themes: first, language founds the national idea: it is from "the natural generating strength of language" that the nation is formed. Second, the German nation finds its source in the civilization of the Middle Age. Finally, German defeat in the face of the French armies is the result of the destruction of religion by the rationalism of the Enlightenment. But nevertheless, in 1797, in *Grundlage des Naturrechts,* Fichte adopted an idea of the nation very close to the revolutionary idea, "totally foreign to the idea of genius-nation,"[19] even before he advanced the arguments in favor of the ethnic nation after the defeat of his country in 1806. But, even in 1806, these themes remained linked with others embedded in the logic of the civic nation, in particular its axiologically fundamental foundation: it is open to all who participate in common values. "Whoever believes in the spirituality and in the liberty of this spirituality, and wants to pursue by liberty the eternal development of this spirituality, this one, wherever he was born and whatever his language, is of our species; he belongs with us and will make common cause with us."[20] One can now see in Fichte's text a first outline of the conception that "nationality is indeed conceived in terms, not of pure and simple adhesion, nor of pure and simple belonging, but of *educability*," thereby overcoming the "simplistic alternative of nature and will."[21]

Renan's position before 1870 represented a criticism of the egalitarian philosophy of the Revolution, his first essays invoked "race." His position is not exhausted by the mere expression of a pure will, of a willing adhesion which would ignore everything of national traditions or culture, which would be an absolute opening, risking the loss of identity. Renan became the champion of the civic nation, founded on popular will of people, only after the war of 1870 and the annexation of the Alsace and part of Lorraine by the German *Reich*: he meant to defend the rights of France on the annexed provinces. But, even in the lecture of 1882, *Qu'est-ce qu'une nation?*, it is consent, i.e., "the desire clearly expressed to continue the life together" which prolongs the transmission of a "long past of efforts, sacrifices and devotion," insofar as "ancestors make us what we are." If historical circumstances led Renan to formulate the elective theory of the nation, the present adhesion and the collective will toward the future was founded, for him, not-only on the will, but also on the fact of knowing and of adopting the inheritance of the past, "the inheritance of shared glory and sorrow." He wrote of "the plebiscite of every day life," which seems to sum up the very principle of the contract-nation, but within a common inheritance of history and culture. The will of men was forged in and by particular social conditions.

Examining Renan's analysis as "problematic"[22] from the point of view of an essential contrast between "ethnic" nation and "political" nation, the apparent ambiguity is less a result of the insufficiency of the author than of the abusive simplification which the traditional binary opposition has introduced into the analysis of the national idea. It is significant that neither Weber nor Mauss participated in this ideological debate.

The Political and the Sciences of Man

Scholars in the social sciences also avoided this debate. They were first dedicated to the history of national or nationalist ideas. Then they attempted to explain why modern nations were born, in other words, to analyze nationalisms in the sense of demands to create politically constituted nations. They had the worthy goal of objectively studying the fact of nationality, but this quest for rational knowledge had the unintended consequences of underestimating the strictly political dimension of the nation.

The example of Durkheim is the best illustration of this. His early work presumed the nation as "naturally" as Aristotle took the Greek city as the model of political society. But, after his first essays and his trip to Germany, he no longer treated the political as the site of conflicts and their regulation; he was not much interested in the institutions which assure the choice of governors and control their actions. Durkheim did not postulate even the relative autonomy of the political. He did not distinguish political society, in its particular historical and national form, from society in general. In his main works, he prominently illustrates—and hence contributes to founding—the sociological point of view: the primary object of his research is no longer the political regime and the consequences of this regime for social life. Rather, it is the social bond and sociability, or in his terms, *social cohesion*. This latter is for him the product of the moral and of society, not of constraints and the state. If one finds no systematic theory of the state in his work, it is because the state reflects the condition of a society rather than being autonomous of it: the state is its representation.[23] More than Tocqueville, "he tends to reduce the political to the social."[24] By failing to distinguish between the social and the political, Durkheim was unable to pose the problem of the democratic nation.

Under the influence of the work of Hans Kohn,[25] scholars were dedicated traditionally to the history of nationalist ideas: to conceptions of the nation in different Western countries and their diffusion in Europe and throughout the world. This tradition is maintained in the English language with the work of Elie Kedourie[26] and Liah Greenfeld.[27] In France also, historians who studied the nation initially privileged ideological and doctrinal contents by dedicating themselves to the analysis of written texts by nationalist thinkers.[28] More recently, they prolonged this tradition by studying the specific ways that extended collective memory, coextensive with the construction of the nation, was elaborated and diffused in France, finding its incarnation in "places," some material or institutional, others symbolic or emblematic.[29]

At the same time, within English and American political science, an entire field of research devoted to nationalisms was developed, probably because, as Anthony Smith wrote, "in many ways it is easier to 'grasp' nationalism, the ideological movement, than nations, the organizational cultures."[30] For three decades, English and American political scientists have tended to monopolize the theoretical study of nationalist claims and movements. However, despite their efforts to minimize the effects of their national belonging, they are nevertheless imbedded within a particular intellectual culture and refer to their own historical experience. Traditional English-language political thought tends to neglect the specific role of the State and statist institutions in producing society, insofar as, in England and the United States, political society preexisted the State and where, more generally, the liberal Anglo-Saxon philosophy holds that individuals are prior to and produce the political organization. Moreover, often heirs by their own personal destiny to the history of Eastern Europe or of Middle Eastern countries and, for Americans, of the history of American independence, they dedicated the bulk of their research to the emergence and the formation of nations. That is to say, to nationalisms, but not to nations. Elie Kedourie distinguishes the British or American "nation" from the nationalisms that he implicitly denounces,[31] but he analyzes the diffusion of the latter in the world, by showing the similarity of themes developed in the nineteenth century by nationalists in central and Eastern Europe and in the nations born from the decomposition of French and English colonial empires after World War II.

Theoreticians of economic and political development in countries of the Third World, especially Americans, studied the history of the formation of nations and stages of their economic "take-off" (Rostow) in countries stemming from direct or indirect European colonization (schools of nation building or of national development). They transferred onto the analysis of political development the same models that they used to explain the stages of economic development. Their analysis focused on the birth of politically constituted nations, not on the reality of the nation. More militant anthropologists highlighted the transformations that nation construction imposed on regional[32] or non-Western populations, the infranational claims in Europe. Sociologists, for their part, studied interethnic relations in United States and the development of ethnicity.[33] When they evoked the countries of Western

Europe, American specialists of ethnicity addressed the conflicts between Flemish and Walloons, the claims to independence by Scots or Welsh and problems raised by the presence of immigrant workers, that is to say, all forms of the contestation of contemporary national States.[34] Yet no one has yet studied the idea of the nation-state, or the concrete forms that it assumes today in Western countries, where it was born and knew its most developed examples.

Even historians, who should be professionally more sensitive to the political dimension of nations and nationalisms, are reluctant to treat the nation.[35] Charles Tilly and his collaborators studied the stages of state making in large European monarchies. Clearly setting the analytical distinction between the process of the formation of the nation (nation building) and the state (state building), they observe that they abandoned the project of analyzing the first so as to concentrate their efforts on the second, because "the 'nation' remains one of the most puzzling and tendentious items of the political lexicon."[36] They were extending the Marxist tradition, in which all thinkers, with the exception of Friedrich Engels and Otto Bauer, were embarrassed to imagine a reality capable of transcending what were to their eyes the true realities, namely, social classes and their conflicts.[37]

The distinction between the democratic nation and political unit is obviously well-known in the English and American tradition. It is in England that the very idea of the nation as a community of free and equal citizens came into being. It is even more significant that the social sciences, for thirty years, have abandoned it. The opposition between the subject and the citizen, which was for a long time one of the essential themes of political literature, was again formulated during the war, as democracies were fighting against Hitler's regime. "A state becomes a nation when instead of its members being primarily divided between sovereign and subjects, government and citizenship become a common task, demanding not passive citizenship but active cooperation from all."[38] This definition was once again employed by Edward Shils and Clifford Geertz more than thirty years ago in their study of the birth of "new nations" in "old societies." Shils defined the modern nation as "a mode of integration of the whole society"[39] and analyzed the functioning of new States stemming from the end of colonial British and French empires, noting that they did not constitute "civil societies,"[40] that is to say, nations. Clifford Geertz referred to the same conception when he defined "the nation—in the sense of the whole society encompassed by the new civil state"[41] which implied the "transformation of the whole pattern of political life, a metamorphosis of subjects into citizens,"[42] and, more generally, when he evoked the process of the creation of new nations as an "integrative revolution." Shils and Geertz thereby clearly defined the dual economic and political dimension of nationalist claims. Here the desire of peoples to be recognized as autonomous, socially responsible actors and their desire to better their lot by creating a modern and efficient State are intimately related.

But this point of view was subsequently neglected. It is a description more than an analysis that Talcott Parsons proposed, defining "societal communities or nations" by four characteristics: "The societal community presumes a relatively definable population of membership, which at this level we ordinarily call citizens for the modern case, and presumes as well that the collective organization of reference is politically organized on a territorial basis, that is, it maintains normative order and certain political decision-making processes covering the human events which occur within a defined territorial area. Finally, as a third primary criterion, at some level it is characterized by a common cultural tradition."[43] This common cultural tradition is, for him, composed, from case to case, of elements linked to "blood" and others stemming from "contract." It leads to a "diffused enduring solidarity" which is transmitted from generation to generation by a common language, the feeling of a common history and a goal of a common future. Parsons assimilated "societal community" and "nation." The ethnic affirmation was for him a simple atavism, destined to disappear, one which was contrary to the spirit of the complex, universalistic "society," where roles are less often inherited and more often acquired.

Since the works of Clifford Geertz and his collaborators and with the triumphant age of statistical measurements in the social sciences, reflection on the nation has been neglected. This is largely an effect of the inherently value-laden subject, as well as the fact that nationality studies are not undertaken in quantitative terms.[44] Specialists in the social sciences study the birth of politically constituted nations, which they do not distinguish from the democratic nation. Without specifying this, like Charles Tilly did, they presume the state to be the equivalent of the nation. They take nationalisms as the primary object of their reflection, that is to say, the emergence, in the name of the democratic nation, of politically constituted nations. One can sum up the meaning of their research with Karl Deutsch's formula: "How and when do nations break away from larger political units, and how do they triumph over smaller units, such as tribes, castes, or local states, and more or less integrate them into the political body of the nation?"⁴⁵ Historians analyze the birth of politically constituted nations which emerge from larger political units, namely, empires; political scientists and anthropologists concentrate their research on the relations between the politically constituted nation and the ethnie or preexistent ethnies. In any case, it is not a matter of the democratic nation.

The most eminent political scientists—Karl Deutsch, Ernest Gellner, Benedict Anderson, and Anthony Smith—lend to downplay the political dimension and interpret nationalist claims essentially in light of the conditions and demands of technical and economic organization.

For Deutsch, nations are founded when economic development mobilizes populations by progressively inserting them in ever denser networks of exchanges of all sorts. "A decisive factor in national assimilation or differentiation was found to be the fundamental process of social mobilization which accompanies the growth of markets, industries, and towns, and eventually of literacy and mass communication."⁴⁶ The "people" is born from the fact that there are complementary modes of life and that mass communications intensify relations between individuals. Applying to the political domain the model of stages of economic development, to recall the title of Walt Whitman Rostow's book, Karl Deutsch discerns, in all cases, the same "stages" in the construction of nations from ethnies: "open or latent resistance to political amalgamation into a common national state; minimal integration to the point of passive compliance with the orders of such an amalgamated government; deeper political integration to the point of active support for such a common state but with continuing ethnic or cultural group cohesion and diversity; and, finally, the coincidence of political amalgamation and integration with the assimilation of all groups to a common language and culture—these could be the main stages on the way from tribes to nation."⁴⁷

For Ernest Gellner, it is nationalisms which create nations; yet for him too they are born from objective conditions of modern societies and the exigencies linked to them. The infrastructure is no longer, as for the thinkers who are directly inspired by Marxism, the economic system, but the educational system understood as the necessary condition for the unique economic development of modernity. This is prefaced upon the mobility of men and upon their technical competence; men must share the same general and universal "high culture," and be capable of occupying a variety of jobs in a continuously changing economy. "Nationalism is rooted in a *certain kind* of division of labour, one which is complex and persistently, cumulatively changing."[48] Only the state can assure their formation. "The educational infrastructure is too vast and costly for any organization other than the biggest one of all, the state. But at the same time, though only the state can sustain so large a burden, only the state is also strong enough to control so important and crucial a function."[49] This is why the state "monopolizes legitimate culture almost as much as it does legitimate violence, or perhaps more so."[50] This statist centralization is primarily the consequence of the necessary centralization of education.

Gellner distinguishes three kinds of nationalism. In the first, characterized as "classic Habsburg," it is a matter of the construction of nations from supranational empires: this is the case of the nationalist claims in the countries of central and Balkan Europe. The second kind, that of Germany and of Italy, designates the construction of a nation-state from ethnies, which already belong in the same "high culture": nationalists demand that a single central political organization correspond to the extant cultural entity. Diasporic nationalisms constitute the third kind: in preindustrial or "agrarian" societies, minority or "pariah" groups exercised financial, commercial, or administrative functions. In modern society, where each individual becomes capable of occupying any profession, they lose their role and their monopoly and, as a result, the protection from which they benefited. They face a choice between assimilation or the creation of their own state. In the "Habsburg" variety, the nationalist claim is born when intellectuals belonging to marginalized ethnies, without controlling the "high culture" which assure the development of the more advanced center, perceive their interest in claiming the independence of their ethnie and its recognition as nation. In the second kind, German or Italian, it is the necessity of organizing and maintaining the "high culture," the precondition of economic development, which leads intellectuals to claim that the cultural unit and the political organization should coincide. In the third kind, the Pariah groups, becoming useless to the society in which they are settled, claim hereafter a national expression. In any case, nationalist claims are produced by the demands of education imposed by the continuing development of the economy. The nation offers the best solution to problems raised by the organization of a society which sets for itself the goal of unlimited economic progress.[51]

Kedourie has made historical objections to these analyses: the origin and diffusion of nationalist movements did not correspond in time and space to the stages of industrialization.[52] Nationalist claims appeared where no economic discrimination existed. Historians have demonstrated that the emergence of the national idea and national institutions—in England, France, and colonized countries—preceded industrial development. These gaps in the time between industrialization and the birth of nationalisms serve only to reveal a more general fact: industrialism does not alone define modern societies; modern societies are also democratic. Material interest is not the *only* source of nationalist claims; the claim to dignity is also essential. English national sentiment was born out of the opposition to the major Catholic monarchies of the continent and from the rivalry with Scotland. Nationalist intellectuals of colonized countries claimed political independence in the name of democracy that Europeans proclaimed even as they refused to apply democratic values and practices in their own colonies. Politics is irreducible to pure power. By accounting for nationalisms only in terms of material interests, Gellner underestimates the role of the passions and the will. He neglects the idea and the ideal of popular sovereignty, the aspirations of men to equality, and their desire to affirm their dignity. Finally, he grants no place to the role of nations acting as historical subjects of the international order.

Benedict Anderson seems, to the contrary, to grant a place to the political dimension, for he begins from a definition of the nation that he characterizes as "anthropological": "it is an imagined *political* community—and imagined as both inherently limited and sovereign."[53] He then seductively traces the birth of this "imagined community" mentioned in the title of the book. This imagined community develops through the printing press and mass communication, which institute an abstract tie between men: by reading his newspaper, each one knows that all the others do the same, without needing to establish a concrete form of exchange between them. Civil servants, on the other hand, who throughout their career go from one city to another, from one part of the country to the other, also brought the existence of this abstraction into being. There is a structural affinity between this imagined community and the modern conception of time: linear, empty, and homogenous. Yet after having defined this imagined community as *political* at the beginning of the book Benedict Anderson subsequently neglects this political dimension. The role of the state is never mentioned. Surely, one must consider the relationship between the spirit of the community which cements a nation and the political power which expresses it and reinforces it? When Anderson shows how patriotism is incarnated in the practice of a language, the source of shared knowledge and emotions, his analysis could just as well apply to the ethnie as to the nation.

In that sense Anderson joins Anthony Smith, who tends to reduce the nation to a mere extension of the ethnie. Smith insists, for good reason, on two facts: first, the existence of ethnies preexistent to nations, or in his words, "the ethnic origin of nations." On the other hand, he also calls attention to the preservation or even the renewal of ethnic consciousness in the modern nation, concluding that this does not possess a true social reality. In fact, it did nothing more than use extant ethnic ties to build, out of them, political units on a given territory. "Apart, then from the question of attitudes to the masses and their inclusion in the community, it is clear that modern nations and nationalism have only extended and deepened the meanings and scope of older ethnic concepts and structures...in terms of ends, as opposed to means, there is a remarkable continuity between nations and ethnies."[54] At other moments, the nation tends to be confused with the bureaucratic, rational and abstract state, described here as the scientific state. The more the state becomes, as a result of economic necessity, foreign to concrete social realities, the more it correspondingly arouses ethnic resistance and claims (ethnic revival). Despite the unifying action of the national state, the "mythico-symbolic" system, which characterizes the original ethnie or ethnies, remained alive. On the one hand, Anthony Smith tends to underestimate the qualitative difference between the ethnie and the nation, and, so, the capacity of the nation to reinterpret myths, memories, symbols, and values of preexistent ethnies; on the other hand, he tends not to distinguish the nation from the state.

One had to wait for the 1982 work of historian John Breuilly on the birth and development of nationalist movements, in which he underlined "the central and autonomous role of the political to understand nationalism" and recalled that the control of the state was, as a result, the prized goal of nationalist movements before becoming the instrument of the perpetuation of the nation. He rediscovered the inspiration of Max Weber on the essential tie between the nation and the political order, that is to say, the order of power.[55]

Modern political scientists no longer analyze the relationship between the nation and statist institutions, insofar as they privilege relations between ethnies, to which they are sympathetic, and the nation, which they tend to criticize; insofar as they refuse to take into account this political dimension, they no longer distinguish between the politically constituted nation and the nation-community of citizens. In this regard, the goal of objectivity in the social sciences must not contribute to the neglect of the essentially political dimension of the nation. Because the democratic nation has not existed in all countries enjoying a comparable technical and economic development, it seems obvious that the political is not only reducible to or determined by the material conditions of common life.

A Single Idea

It seems proper to denounce the mistaken idea that there are essentially and eternally two ideas of the nation. Analytical thought must not be content to adopt words and arguments stemming from ideological conflicts of the nineteenth century and from conflicts between ethnies and nations, among democratic nations, between democratic nations and politically constituted nations or between nations and empires, by lending them a scholarly and obscure form. Only by confusing the presuppositions of social life, to recall Durkheim's terms, with analytical concepts, can one deduce that there is a dual idea—in the analytical sense of the term—of the nation from the fact that there were effectively two sorts of history of the formation of European nations—"French" and "German" or "Western" and "Eastern"—and two kinds of nationalist ideology. One must avoid the Manichean dualism which always risks invading our reflection.

If one admits the analysis developed in previous chapters and, correspondingly, if one agrees to characterize the democratic nation by its ambition—by definition never fully realized—of creating a political society by transcending concrete roots, particular belongings and loyalties through citizenship, then there cannot be two ideas of the nation, but only one, albeit unequally and imperfectly accomplished, varying from case to case, depending on the political project which is at the origin of national construction.

The nations one has traditionally referred to as of the "American" or the "French" style, when they conformed both to their logic and their proclaimed ideal, were closer to that idea or this ideal-type, since they made political society and citizenship into the organizing principles of common life. Here, it is not a matter of forming a value judgment, which would demonstrate the moral or political superiority of the political nation to the ethnic nation, but of realizing the logical consequences of an analytic definition.

Obviously I do not pretend that the French example constitutes the universal model of the nation. It is only illustrative for historical reasons. Whereas the English nation was born of an internal evolution and from the pragmatic adaptation of the regime to the demands of democracy, the civic nation violently erupted in France as a revolutionary explosion. It therefore received immediate and heightened attention. "France is essentially characterized by the pure and simple affirmation of the individualism of the Enlightenment, as opposed to England which knew how to ally to an individualism some degree of common tradition...and as opposed to Germany which was intensely acculturated around 1800 and which built a culture where, contrary to the English, the individualism of the Enlightenment is generally conceived as an integrated element.... Our traditional French view of things is as clear and simple as it is pure of all compromise with the reality of social life."[56] There one formulated principles of national construction as in no other country, continually evoking in public and scientific life the "republican model," integrative and universalistic. The legitimacy and the sovereignty of the nation; the necessity of submitting particular identities and cultures to its logic; and secularization—were all proclaimed more bombastically than anywhere else; since the Revolution, political and theoretical debate on the nation and its demands has not ceased. England invented in reality the idea of nationhood as a community of free and equal citizens; the French, for their part, perpetually contructed the theory of individual citizenship and of the universality of their political society. They strove to build it in a voluntaristic fashion—which does not mean, as the American scholars cited in the introduction recall, that they were faithful to their own theories. One even wonders if they have not proclaimed these principles more because these latter were never easily applied.

Nationalists and ideologists of an ethnic nation, as in the German fashion, invoked pre-national values and not those values *unique to* or *characteristic of* the nation, the particular form of political organization in the age of democracy. By insisting on preexistent ethnic ties rather than the goal of creating a political society, they neglected what properly characterizes the national project, namely, the effort to overcome concrete belongings and ethnic loyalties, even if it always remains imperfect and even if it cannot fail to be translated into the tension between the ambition of universality and the state's preservation of national differences. Even if the nationalisms of central Europe can be effectively described as ethnic, as much by their characteristics as by the arguments invoked by nationalistic thinkers, it does not follow that there is an ethnic idea—in the analytical sense—of the nation. The ideology of the ethnic nation was a way to justify the failure of the democratic nation in Central Europe. This was moreover, if one abstracts from the evolutionist tendency of his language, the idea of Mauss: "The Slavic and Hellenic East or mixed Europe is entirely populated by young or imperfect nations, or of societies of inferior form to these latter. Western Europe is in on the contrary the empire of nations."[57]

The existence of a single idea of the nation is implicit, it seems to me, in the thought of Louis Dumont, even if he did not formulate it in these terms. He describes "two predominant national ideologies" representing in his own conceptual system the traditional opposition between the "French" nation, which is a "collection of individuals," and the "German," which is a "collective individual"[58] in order to highlight, "even in its dramatic aspect, the difficulty of communication between two ideologies."[59] But what interests Dumont is a strict analysis of the modern *ideology*, as specified even in the title (*L'idéologie allemande*) and the subtitle (*Une perspective anthropologique sur l'idéologie moderne*) of his works. He observes the existence of these two theories: "The ethnic theory of the nation is registered in the major stream of 'modern' political ideas, alongside the elective theory."[60] The German conception has had more influence on other nationalisms: comporting numerous holistic elements, it did not conform to the pure individualist utopia implied by the idea of civic nation. It could be more easily imitated precisely because it was more directly in contact with reality and found itself closest to traditional holism: "Modern civilization witnesses the individualist configuration of which it is the carrier being modified as much as its conquests by the integration of hybrid products."[61]

For Louis Dumont, this hybrid character of the German conception was, in and of itself, pre-national; he grappled with what he called the "systematic coherence" of the idea of nation—in other terms, the logic of the idea of nation—which is to be composed of individuals, but with the exclusion of any hostile component. "The nation is precisely the sort of global society corresponding to the reign of individualism as a value. Not only does it historically accompany it, but the interdependence between the two is imposed such that one can say that the nation is the global society composed of peoples who consider themselves as individuals."[62] The political nation, of which the history of Western democracies supplies examples, is in its principle closer to the ideal-type defined by the principle of the tearing away of the individual by the political from all forms of belongings and ethnic identities, or to recall Louis Dumont's concepts, from all forms of traditional holism.

This is observed today by Germans intellectuals concerned with founding in theory the German democratic nation born in the Federal Republic after the defeat of the Third Reich. In their desire to break radically from an intellectual tradition suspected of having led to Hitlerism, they disqualified any nation, by reducing nation to the ethnic sense of the term, which was to be held responsible for the crimes of Nazism. Habermas proposed a new political form, founded on "constitutional patriotism," by which individuals would be exclusively engaged by principles of *Etat de droit* (see chapter 2). This new patriotism would replace the sentiment of loyalty to the nation as a "community of destiny." From the same perspective, R.M. Lepsius also contrasts the *demos*, carrier of the sole political legitimacy, to the *ethnos*, defined by its historical and cultural properties[63]—which sponsors his contrast between the truly democratic, linked to the *demos*, and the idea that he characterizes as national (that is to say ethnic). But this "postnational" identity that one strives to theorize is not different from the pure form, in the dual analytical and normative sense, of the nation familiarly known as of the "American" or the "French" style. Jean-Marc Ferry underscores that the French republican model is ambiguous, that it does not fully incarnate the civic idea and is composed of ethnic dimensions. But he spoke then of the concrete historical nation, which in reality has never been—and could never be—in conformity with its principle, and not of the idea or the ideology of the civic nation.

These German thinkers reformulate the traditional opposition between the idea of the democratic nation and the *Volk*, between the idea of the civic nation which, contrary to the experience of historical nations, would have eliminated any ethnic dimension and the nation which is known as ethnic. This nation founded on "postnational identity," is it not simply the nation called "civic"—that is to say, the very idea of nationhood? By invoking the *demos* and by calling their vows "constitutional patriotism" so as to found a truly democratic nation, they implicitly recognize that only the "civic" or "political" nation conforms, in its principle, to the idea of nationhood.

Participation in the unique political entity that is the nation is but one moment of a history during which men were progressively integrated into increasingly larger entities. The relation which unites the individual to the group or the social *habitus*, to recall Norbert Elias's concept, was reelaborated by the construction of political nations and the nationalization of the social tie. In Western nations, the moral values according to which the citizen must act were progressively imposed at the expense of clientelism and of the solidarity founded on familial or ethnic ties, even if the logic of this rationality was never—and never can be—fully realized. The national framework is today, on several points, objectively overcome by technical, economic, military, informational, and even political exchanges which unite or oppose men and historical collectivities, some of which are politically constituted nations and others are infranational or supranational. As is commonly observed, today men have become increasingly integrated on a global scale; but haven't the social *habitus,* historical identities, and powerful emotions remained nevertheless closely linked to national belonging?

Yet the movement away from nationhood and toward an integration based on the universal idea of all of humanity seems to require a qualitative change in human nature. "Humanity presents as social unit a curious particularity. In all other levels of integration, the sense of the "we" was developed in relation to the perception of the threat posed by other groups on our own group."[64] Collective belongings have always been affirmed by opposing themselves to others. How might the feeling of belonging to humanity be opposed to the Other? What subjective sentiment can we expect the idea of belonging to humanity to arouse?

Notes

1. C. Tilly in Tilly (ed.), 1975, p. 42.
2. Beaune, 1985.
3. Renan, 1947 (1882), p. 894.
4. Kantorowitz, 1989 (1957), p. 146.
5. Manent, 1987, p. 29.
6. Bibo, 1986 (1946), p. 144.
7. Hagège, 1992, p. 146.
8. Cited in Delannoi-Taguieff (ed.), 1991, p. 318.
9. Weil, 1971, p. 156.
10. Szücs, 1985.
11. Smith, 1986, p. 4.
12. J. Plamenatz in Kamenka, 1976.
13. Dumont, 1991, p. 24.
14. Costa-Lascoux, 1990.
15. Stark, 1988.
16. Schnapper, 1991, pp. 51 and following; Schnapper, 1992; Brubaker, 1992.
17. M. Douglas (*Daedalus,* Autumn 1978), cited by Dumont, 1983, p. 15.
18. This paragraph summarizes, in an inevitably schematic way, the introduction of Alain Renaut in Fichte, 1992 (1806).
19. A. Renaut in Fichte, 1992 (1806), p. 26.
20. Fichte, 1992 (1806), p. 206.
21. A. Renaut in Fichte, 1992 (1806), pp. 41 and 43.
22. J. Roman in Renan, 1992 (1882), p. 24.

23. Lacroix, 1976, p. 241.
24. Expression that Claude Lefort applies to Tocqueville in Wood (trad.), 1991, p. 7.
25. Kohn, 1944.
26. Kedourie, 1960, 1985.
27. Greenfeld, 1992.
28. Girardet, 1966; Winock, 1982.
29. Nora (ed.), 1984–1992.
30. Smith, 1986, p. 2.
31. Kedourie, 1985, p. 74.
32. Hechter, 1975. Berger, 1972.
33. The literature, very abundant, was inaugurated with Glazer-Moynihan, 1963.
34. W. Petersen in Glazer-Moynihan (eds.), 1975, pp. 177–208.
35. Latest example, Hobsbawm, 1990.
36. Tilly (ed.), 1975, p. 6.
37. Latest example, Balibar-Wallerstein, 1988.
38. A.D. Lindsay, 1943, cited by Nisbet, 1974.
39. E. Shils in Geertz (ed.), 1962, p. 21.
40. E. Shils in Geertz (ed.), 1962, p. 22.
41. C. Geertz in Geertz (ed.), 1962, p. 153.
42. C. Geertz in Geertz (ed.), 1962, p. 119.
43. T. Parsons in Glazer-Moynihan (eds.), 1975, p. 59.
44. One finds a good analysis in French of this work by John Crowley in Delannoi-Taguieff (ed.), 1991.
45. K. Deutsch in Deutsch-Folz (eds.), 1963, p. 4.
46. Deutsch, 1966, p. 188.
47. Deutsch, 1966, pp. 7–8.
48. Gellner, 1983, p. 24.
49. Gellner, 1983, p. 37.
50. Gellner, 1983, p. 140.
51. Gellner, 1983, p. 73.
52. Kedourie, 1985 (1960), pp. 147–148.
53. Anderson, 1983, p. 15. Italics added.
54. Smith, 1986, pp. 215–216.
55. Breuilly, 1982.
56. Dumont, 1991, pp. 268 and 270.
57. Mauss, 1969 (1920?), p. 586.
58. Dumont, 1983, pp. 130–131.
59. Dumont, 1991, p. 8.
60. Dumont, 1991, p. 25.
61. Dumont, 1991, p. 30.
62. Dumont, 1983, pp. 20–21.
63. M. R. Lepsius cited by Habermas, 1990, pp. 250 and 259.
64. Elias, 1991 (1986/1987), p. 297.

Conclusion

Democracy against the Nation?

The fact that state institutions and politically constituted nations have been diffused throughout the world does not prove that the civic nation has become the universal form of political organization. I do not intend here to discuss the problems related to the imposition, at least formally, of the Western political order throughout the entire world order, but I would like to conclude with some thoughts on the deterioration of the nation as a political form. This is the case even where it is the product of an internal development, in Western Europe and in North America. Even in the countries which invented the nation, it faces internal contradictions stemming from its own internal logic. The thinkers of the era of nationalisms were fully conscious that "nations are not something eternal. They began, they will end" (Renan). But we are able to see more clearly than they, blessed by our experience of the democratic age, that the decadence of the nation, in both its internal and external dimension, owes its source to its very nature.

The democratic nation is weakened because its sovereignty in the world of politically constituted nations is continually more limited. It is weakened because the political project by which it integrated various populations has been exhausted. National reality has been steadily transformed into a community of work, culture, and the redistribution of wealth. The bond between men becomes less civic than utilitarian or instrumental. Democracy is born under a national form, but the ambition of giving a substantive content to the formal equality of law—embedded in the very values of democratic legitimacy—and the logic of production both risk permanently enfeebling the political project which lay at the foundation of the nation.

Objective Integration and Social Habitus

In 1920, Mauss analyzed the movement toward globalization, or that which he called the "facts of interdependence of modern societies." He noticed the increasing intensity of the "material, intellectual and moral intercourse" between nations and foresaw that "the progress of events goes in the sense of an increasing multiplication of borrowings, exchanges, identifications, even in the detail of moral and material life."[1] More than seventy years after Mauss, one can add nuance to his statements. The increasing intensity of borrowings and exchanges in economic life can not be disputed. In the majority of national societies, the forms of material life, products of the "increasing multiplication" of "borrowings" and "exchanges" at the core of the economic system, become apparently ever closer. The technological culture, even if it retains national specificities, imposes some common norms on the organization of production. Far from explaining the constitution of nations or their maintenance, as one had endeavored to demonstrate under the dual influence of Marxist and development theories, technology and the economy tend, on the contrary, to be universal in nature. However, even if the products, capital, and information are diffused upon all continents, they are far from reaching the different nations equally. National frontiers, which define the different political and economic entities, continue, from case to case, to favor or to frustrate the entry of capital and products. Even information, whose diffusion is technically global, is neither received nor understood in a uniform manner. The movements of peoples collide with political borders which still constitute obstacles, provisional or definite.

The fact remains that independence and external sovereignty, constitutive of the idea of nation, become strictly limited. The United Nations strives to elaborate rules which would bind nation-states and to make recourse to an "international global opinion." In the political and military order, politically constituted nations now act within a system which, as it has become global, constrains the possibilities of the action of each state. No state can escape the necessity of coalitions, nor the pressures, direct or objective, of the most powerful states. The war of 1914 already demonstrated that nation-states no longer possessed the necessary resources to wage modern war: France and Great Britain required the help of the United States to defeat the German empire and its allies. Similarly, one can no longer ensure even internal security without closely collaborating with others: the battle against terrorism, drug dealers, or espionage requires the collaboration between national police forces. All levels, non-statist and transnational actors reduce the role of the nation-state.

Economic independence is equally constrained. The leaders of Western Europe can create money, finance public deficits, and procure resources through inflationary politics only by taking into account the demands fixed by EEC and international economic authorities. Framed by economic legislation and submitted to obligations of an international competitive market, economic life is less and less national. No government can afford to ingore the fact that national economies are integrated in a global system. In 1983, the shifting of the policies of socialists in power in France demonstrated this once again. All European farmers know that their fate depends on decisions made by the European Commission (EC) of Brussels and the negotiations of the General Agreement on Tariffs and Trades (GATT). Also, in many non-Western countries, officials of the International Monetary Fund (IMF), the World Bank, and GATT make major economic decisions. Fundamental decisions made by officials of multinational corporations, in particular to "deterritorialize" their activities, pursue a strictly economic logic. They make use of national legal differences in the domain of social protection, but their decisions escape the control of national governments.

In Western Europe, where nations were born, the construction of the EEC constitutes another challenge to national reality and the national idea. The state, creator of law, is in fact less and less sovereign. Since 1964, one of the most famous judgments of the European Court of Justice established the principle that "the Community constitutes a new juridical order of international law" and that "subjects of the law are not only member states but also nationals." Any citizen of the Community could from now on call on jurisdictional European authorities against his national state. The juridical order of the EC is progressively superimposed on national laws and is superior to them. European High Courts successively recognized "the primacy of the Community law over the law of member States." In France, the Niccolò judgment of the *Conseil d'Etat* in 1989 sanctioned this evolution. Some entire sectors, those of the economy, work, or the protection of human rights, from now on essentially stem from European legislation. Approximately half of the national law is a matter for the field of competence shared between the national state and the Community.

But, even in the midst of this interdependence of modern societies, identities, political and symbolic identifications, and the "moral life" (Mauss) of individuals remain distant from one nation to another. Today, there is a contradiction between the objective integration of men in a virtually global space with their social *habitus*, i.e., their sentiment of collective identity, and also with their political participation which continues to be expressed primarily at the national level.

Inherited from the past, the *habitus* of men, as Elias would suggest, are not necessarily in conformity with their objective integration. The technology has a universalistic dimension, but the national diversity of norms and of values is not reduced by its global diffusion. In Western Europe, the nation as a historical community forged by the centuries, preserves memories, and is still a place for collective identification, despite its political decline, and remains one of the instruments of social cohesion.

The nation remains one of the primary sources of collective identity and of historical continuity. Each nation continues to express itself by certain values and to pride itself on certain activities. The nationality law, which defines citizens, still depends on national sovereignty alone and continues to differentiate countries according to their history and their conception of the national idea. During an age of the weakening of organized religions, the nation remains one of the entities capable of giving meaning to existence. The democratic expression, the sensation of participating in the life of the city, are expressed at the national level. In all countries this is indicated by the differences in rates of electoral participation according to whether it is a local, national or European election. The latter only weakly mobilize the electorate. Western European nations conserve their political tradition: the way it is reflected in concrete forms of democracy—electoral system, forms of parliamentary life and the organization of governmental activity, internal organization and role of political parties. Even for the European elections, the Twelve could not agree to adopt the same method of balloting. Relations with others, foreigners and migrants, are also embedded in a specific tradition. Each tradition is influenced by memories of the birth of the nation and of political legitimacy, colonial empires, wars, and original political projects. In England, for instance, the logic of citizenship is combined with that of minorities: one is both a British citizen *and* a member of a minority group, or, more precisely, citizen *by* virtue of this belonging to a particular community. In France, the logic of citizenship is opposed to that of minorities. To the contrary, Germany maintains the distinction between foreigners and nationals and even refuses to transform the former into German citizens, even when they have been regularly settled for decades. The law of January 1990, which facilitates the naturalization of young foreigners born and educated in Germany, did not fundamentally change the policy.

Nations have remained the actors in international politics, as demonstrated, for instance, by the different reactions of European countries to the Persian Gulf War of 1991. When, a bit later, Slovenians called on Germany while Serbs wanted to make themselves understood to the French according to a diplomatic gambit which furiously evoked memories of 1914, Europe in and of itself did not appear to be an actor in international life. The collective action of the Europeans is always limited by the divergent interests of each nation. Only European nations retain some capacity of political intervention.

Political Project and Productivism: From the Nation to Ethnies?

The political project is also weakened internally by the democratic age's own evolution, whose characteristics in and of themselves pose a challenge to the nation. The social cohesion of civic nations is threatened not only by the "routinization of charisma" (Weber) which was embedded in the original political project, but by the withering of the political character of common life to the advantage of its economic and social dimension. Modern societies are at the same time democratic and productive. But, the very logic of production gives specific forms to relations between men and risks calling into question the civic project.

The legitimacy of modern democracy is founded on the idea that citizens must be able to exercise their rights. It is also founded on the goal of providing, beyond this formal equality, an additional substantive equality. State interventions in the economic, social, and cultural order merely follow the requisite logic of the democratic nation: there is no break or discontinuity between the liberal state and the welfare state. In the name of the rights of the sovereign citizen and of the value of equality for all, the latter undertakes measures intended to guarantee what is believed to be an equitable distribution of resources and the survival of the most impoverished. The politics of the minimum wage alleviates the social consequences of the deterioration of the job market and the weakening of familial and social ties. In all European countries, the national state conforms to the logic of the democratic nation. It strives to foster at least the symbolic participation of all individuals in collective life. But one must distinguish between the principle of the modern state and its effects on the nature of the social bond.

The heightened value placed on the economic and social dimension of collective life—the productivist-hedonist logic which privileges the interest and the pleasure of the individual—tends to undermine the political project constitutive of the idea of the nation. Economic progress and the redistribution of wealth through social welfare serve to increase the objective homogeneity of populations. They render objective inequalities smaller; however, according to the rule formulated by Tocqueville, those remaining are all the more unbearable. Economic activity risks exclusively mobilizing the population, at the expense of public spirit. The increasing of social taxes in all European countries serves only to reflect what one has called the crisis of the welfare state, that is to say, even beyond the financial deficits of the social welfare system, a fundamental reconsideration of social and political integration by redistributive democracy. More and more, social rights appear as the equivalent of political rights and "economic and social citizenship," passes, for some progressive thinkers, for the authentic form of modern citizenship. Strictly political values are rarely invoked in defense of the great Western democracies. More often, defenders refer to their success in creating and diffusing wealth. If the legitimacy of modern democracy is founded on the universality of the rights of citizens and the effects of the welfare state, individuals tend to privilege the latter at the expense of the former. But, material satisfaction is not enough to provide the bond among men required to preserve the political unit. The "contracting parties" are not citizens. In the economic order, what is given to some is taken from others. Economic competition divides men and inflames rivalries among groups that the political project tended to unite. Hegel already perceived that national identity was crumbling when the bourgeois individual became fixated in his socioeconomic particularity at the expense of the political dimension of his existence which reattached him as citizen to the State. Depoliticization remains a constant threat for democratic nations.

The modern welfare state no longer maintains the social bond by rallying populations around a political project, but by intervening in economic life. It acts as entrepreneur when it manages large public services, such as the infrastructure, education, urban development, and some housing; as regulator of the economy when it directs large instruments of economic policy within European and global constraints (budget, taxation, contribution to the fixation of incomes, etc.); as arbitrator, when it manages inequalities and rivalries, when it strives to regulate conflicts between "social partners" by redistributing collective resources. It is less and less sovereign, whereas its role as economic and social regulator steadily increases. Social and fiscal law, the primary instrument of redistribution, remains within the competence of the nation-state in European countries. The development of what one might call modern neocorporatism is linked to the growth of the welfare state.

Conclusion   161

Social politicies foster the creation of redistributive authorities and administrative services at both the national level and primarily the local level; they multiply the number of salaried employees who intervene in the domain of "social" action as well as the groups who are beneficiaries of these interventions. By allocating to various communities or socioeconomic groups the rights to resources, financial funds and even jobs, loans, and various favors, agents of the state and local collectivities entrusted with the tasks of the welfare state have created a logic of clientelism. The welfare state becomes a clientelist state, evidenced in several ways by massive increases of contentiousness, particularly linked to economic activity. In France, by intervening actively in cultural politics, by creating administrative cultural services at the national level and local levels, by acting as buyer and collector, by supporting artists or researchers who benefit directly or indirectly from government subsidies, the state created what can be called a cultural welfare state. In Australia or Canada, two countries which have instituted a general politics of multiculturalism, it also became an ethnic welfare state, organizing the maintenance of "native" cultures, reinvented or reconstituted through the efforts of "ethnic" social workers and specialized intellectuals. Ethnic or cultural communities find themselves enjoying particular advantages. The preeminence of individual rights over group rights, the very principle which lay at the heart of the idea of nation as community-of-citizens, becomes attenuated in favor of collective rights.

This commercial and utilitarian model of social relations extends even to those great national institutions—school, army, magistracy, public services—which were once in charge of instituting national and democratic values but which now operate like any other large-scale industrial concern, neglecting their civic vocation. The mechanisms and symbols of formal democracy—the vote, the organization of debates, and the practice of public life by parties—are called into question by the crisis of party government. The voter hereafter reserves the right to follow his own judgment and to ignore the recommendations of politicians. Public opinion polls, commanded and diffused by mass media, continually risk having more political influence than the votes of citizens. If consensus is no longer organized by the practice and symbols of democracy, if it has become exclusively linked to the material advantages of participation in a collectivity of work and the redistribution of goods, would not this democratic consensus be called into question each time production does not increase? The success of the Lombard league in Northern Italy demonstrates that wealthy regions can cease to be willing to share the fruit of their work with poor provinces, particularly when national solidarity is no longer founded on a common political project and a kindred political culture, and when it instead appears solely founded on material interest. In democratic societies, unemployment represents an ordeal for all and perverts all social ties: unemployed persons lose their dignity; relations among co-workers and within the family, are disrupted. Could societies founded on the values of production withstand a prolonged economic crisis? Could they maintain themselves if they could not afford all members the dignity linked to employment and if they multiplied the number of those whose misery excludes any possibility of their participation in collective life? Once again there is a qualitative difference between political citizenship and what one tends to call "economic and social citizenship."

Evoking a "second French Revolution," Henri Mendras described the French society of the 1980s as a system of production, consumption, and redistribution of material and cultural goods. According to his studies, the French perceived their country as a great economic enterprise based on buying and selling and whose accounts must be in surplus in order for one to live well, thus, legitimating the enterprise.[2] In fact, in a country which prided itself for some time on having invented the modern nation, the nation is characterized less by its political project—even though the very values of the democracy are the object of a unanimous but distant loyalty—than by the specificity of its process of civilization (to recall Norbert Elias's expression) or of its community of culture. Since World War II, great transformations of society had their source in the economy. If the first Revolution invented both public spirit and the priority given to political allegiance over other ties, the "second Revolution" consisted in depreciating the political to the benefit of the economic, social, and cultural community. Electoral debates and campaigns are no longer about moral values or political orientations, but about economic measures. Unemployment obsesses electors and political officials. The crumbling of national institutions is accompanied by a high degree of tolerance toward all behaviors, including those which were for many years judged as deviant, and by a fixation on everyday life and its values. The national feeling has ceased to be "powerfully civic" and has become instead "affective," "almost sentimental."[3] Historians no longer celebrate the person "France," as did Michelet; or its unique destiny, as did Lavisse, but places of common memory—including those of great political conflicts, from the Revolution to Vichysm. The sentimental attachment of the French to the uniqueness of their history and culture has replaced the adhesion of citizens to the French political project.

Until 1989 West Germany constituted a kind of exemplary country of the democratic age. The memory of crimes committed in the name of the unitary state and the separation into two sovereign states had compromised the national idea. Some even deplored that the eventual goal of unifying the two Germanys was inscribed in article 23 of the Fundamental Law, which foresaw the possibility of the adhesion "of other parts of Germany." The experience of West Germany demonstrated that a modern democracy could conduct itself with success without primarily constituting a nation, in the ideal-typical sense analyzed above. It conformed to what Max Weber, in referring to Switzerland, termed an "incomplete nation" or to what one has called a "trading state"[4]: with rights of local collectivities guaranteed by federalism, respect toward the *Etat de droit,* emphasis given to economic activity, discretion of external action until the *Ostpolitik* of the 1970s, and even, for a long time, a reluctance to create an army and to pursue an external policy with a global dimension. In 1983, 20 percent of an age class were conscientious objectors. The abstention of the most prosperous country of Europe from the Persian Gulf war in 1991, in the name of a legalism inherited from the situation imposed on the defeated Germany of 1945, served only to illustrate what stood at the heart of the project of West Germany. Only the building of Europe (of which Germany was along with France the principal instigator) and participation in NATO permitted Germany to maintain an international political project. The new political project was constituted around the double denial of the memory of Nazism and the reality of the Soviet empire: "This double antitotalitarian consensus...determined then the landscape which forged the mentality animating our political culture."[5] This consciousness of itself as an essentially economic nation—which illustrated the role played by the *Deutschmark* as a marker of identity—truly composed "the center around which the political comprehension that the Federal Republic held of itself was elaborated."[6] For fifty years, West Germany was able to be an economic and social democracy, without genuinely being a true nation.

Imposed by the collapse of the communist system and the Soviet empire, the reunification violently called into question this political project. Germany could not remain a trading-state. It became again politically sovereign and the government had to make, in the midst of emergency, a strictly political choice. This choice took into account the many years of common destiny, and included former East Germany in the Federal Republic, thereby reconstituting Germany as a political and economic unit. This course of action imposed the Western political system on the Eastern population and required material sacrifices from the Western population, all in the name of the national idea of a united Germany. The pattern of relations between economic and social actors, between political authorities (federal government and governments of the *Länder*) that were defined in the framework of West Germany had to be reelaborated. Unified Germany could not only be a simple extension of the former West Germany. The crisis of identity that Germany experiences today stems from the fact that not only was the East German political project of building a communist society thrown into question—which is obvious—but also West Germany's goal of being a federal and decentralized, prosperous and egalitarian democracy, which renounced direct intervention in international relations on the global stage.

The very idea of political will was compromised, in Germany as in the entire Western world, by the two great voluntarist adventures which were the Nazi and Communist regimes. In these, one strove to foster among citizens a social bond of a communitarian type. Since World War II, the democratic nations of Europe defined themselves, at least negatively, by their opposition to nazism and communism. The threat of the Soviet army lent them at least a minimum political agenda, that of not becoming a communist country. If, after the collapse of the Soviet empire, they ceased being and defining themselves as political organizations maintaining a specific project, what would be their future? Whereas they were constituted by the breaking down of empires and the transcendence of ethnies, would they not risk becoming ethnies again? That is to say, groups of men united by sentiments of historical community and collective identity and no longer by the strictly civic will to participate in common political life, by overcoming their ethnic peculiarities. Given their intrinsic tendency toward pacifism, they would not survive long if they neglected to cultivate public spirit, which allows passions and wills to be controlled by political practice, regulated at least tendentially, by the constitutional state. Similarly, they would face difficulties if they no longer had the capacity to integrate migrant populations around their political values—immigrants who, attracted by their wealth and their freedom, will continue to arrive, despite the legislative measures by which governors strive to limit or control their entrance. They would further be in danger if they no longer had the will, if not to impose themselves, then at least to defend or prevent a local tyrant from throwing off the balance of power or appropriating the atomic instruments that the collapse of the U.S.S.R. risks dispersing throughout the world. When Holland was only a economic and commercial power without political ambition, it was protected by the British navy. Even the United States no longer wishes to conduct anything but technical and abstract wars, those which avoid the deaths of the boys in uniform. Societies no longer capable of articulating their collective values, even by force if necessary, have always been defeated by the less wealthy but more spirited enemy.

The European formula risks having the unintended effect of contributing to this depolitization of liberal democracies. The peace that it established among European nations demobilized national feelings. Before 1914, the European international system was founded on rivalries between neighboring nations, fostered patriotism, and maintained the integration of each national entity. Any war or threat of war is a factor of integration. Since the end of World War II, the countries of Europe—where nations were born and where wars were, until the twentieth century, a primary instrument of the birth and of the vitality of national pride—have concluded their rivalries by negotiations, compromises, and agreements. Now that—rightly or wrongly—communism no longer appears a danger, the external situation ironically threatens to destroy the proces of national integration, when, moreover, the number of those who are threatened by economic and social exclusion are multiplying. How or by what means can one replace the role of "hereditary enemies" that France, England, Germany, and Russia, according to the time, played for one another?

The EEC, on the other hand, created a Europe of producers, consumers, and merchants. Authorities of Brussels essentially intervene in economic and social life; they strive to act on employment, equality between the sexes, urban renovation and rural development, development and culture. They tend to reinforce powers of regional collectivities, with whom they directly deal, at the expense of national States, and to reawaken the vitality of infra-national identities. The "postnational" citizenship which appeals to those philosophers and jurists who are troubled by any nationalist drift, would moreover, if adopted, work in the direction of depoliticization. It is in the framework of the nation that the legitimacy and practices of democracy were built: the weakening of the nation-state, which is a consequence of the European construction, risks also endangering democracy. The appeal—often awkward and always passionate in France—to "the Republic" by the Left and to "patriotism" and "sovereignty" by the Right, as well as the anxiety which is expressed in all liberal democracies on the failure of the school, where democracy must be taught, reflects an anxiety that the sociologist can analyze on its own terms. In societies which no longer recognize either the legitimacy of the religious principle, or the dynastic principle, the dissolution of the national bond of citizenship in Western Europe risks weakening the social bond even further. Max Weber thought that without the will to power there was no nation. So too, one will not be able to have a Europe without a common political will. Mere participation in the same economic and social system is not sufficient to unite men. Sociologists should be the first to recall that social man is not only *homo œconomicus*, but that he also lives by his passions, values, and will.

The Intrinsic Limits of Rationality

The nation appeared to Max Weber both as a developmental step toward and as exemplary of the rationalization of the world. But he was also aware that the rational disenchantment of the world did not eliminate the irrationality of men. Until the 1960s, sociologists who studied religions and ethnicity asserted that social forms which fell under the logic of the *Gemeinschaft* were destined to disappear, or at very least weaken, as the characteristic rational logic of modern society was diffused. Since the 1970s, the multiplication of ethnic claims, even in the oldest nations of Western Europe, and the dawning of new religious movements and "emotional communities," to recall the Weberian term, born outside of organized churches, has demonstrated the limits of that rationality. Not only is there no incompatibility between certain forms of ethnic and religious passions and modernity, but in fact modernity often provokes religious and ethnic revivals.

I have tried to demonstrate that the universal and rational idea has never been anything more than a dominant principle: at the same time an idea and an ideal of social life. In the democratic age, however, the national order has more difficulty overcoming particular belongings than during the age of the triumphant nation, despite the increasing objective homogeneity of populations. Like religious revival, new ethnic claims are born from the characteristics of democratic societies—their rationality, their abstraction—and contradictions between the ideal of equality that they promise and the inevitably disappointing results they achieve.[7] Egalitarian in its values and rational in its organization

Conclusion 167

of production, modern society cannot help but arouse feelings of dissatisfaction and failure. Modern man, equal to all others, cannot help but compare himself to all others and be disappointed. Democracy proclaims ideals—e.g. the equality of all—which contradict observed realities. It affirms an egalitarian goal beyond merely formal equality, but it cannot eradicate real substantive inequalities from the economic and social order, even if it attempts to limit them. It invokes at the same time the values of equality and authenticity, which come into conflict when one wishes to respect the value of all cultures while at the same time according the equality of opportunity to all individuals. Formally opening all possibilities to all individuals, and hence arousing all social ambitions, democracy cannot help but disappoint many. It gives an absolute value to the individual, but the logic of productivity reduces the value of the individual to his social and professional role within bureaucratic and industrial organizations. The ultimate goal of democracy is the abstract universal of citizenship, whereas one observes everywhere the permanence and vitality of particular belongings, religious or ethnic.

Even more generally, modern society affords no ultimate meaning to existence, or, to recall the Weberian expression, it does not respond to the need of men to possess a system of explanation which justifies worldly imperfections and personal misfortune: a "theodicy of pain and suffering." Founded upon technical and intellectual innovation, upon the invention of new social forms, and hence aimed at the future, modern society and the nation reveal an intrinsically utopian dimension. But, in contrast to religious utopias of the past, it is a matter of a rational utopia, which is built neither on tales from the golden age of the past nor on glimpses of a radically different future. It depreciates the value of the past and promises nothing more for the future than the development and improvement of existing rationality. It cannot act as in the longing for total revolution, rooted in a mythology nourished from the past. It does not give meaning to the collective experience of humanity or to individual destiny. The emptiness of modern societies leaves to each individual the possibility, the charge, the privilege and the anxiety of choosing the significance he himself wishes to give to his own existence.

One wonders if the rationality which presides, at least tendentially, over the organization of collective work and, more generally, over the social order, does not lead individuals to find the meaning of human destiny in non-institutional emotions? The rationality of citizenship no longer arouses collective hopes and enthusiasms. Emotional communities—whether they are based on religious practices, on belonging in an ethnic collectivity, infra- or supranational, on anti-racist militancy or, even more frequently, on the identification with a sports team—answer a fundamental need of man to be recognized as a person. They allow individuals to give meaning to their failures, to supplement the meritocracy and rationality of the world of production and the social world in general. They compensate for the abstraction of political society and of citizenship. All investigations on the underclass show that these groups first claim the dignity and value of democratic legitimacy. The participation of individuals in emotional communities permits them to give meaning to human suffering and to establish direct and affective relations with others. In light of this, the overcoming of particularisms by citizenship can only be made more difficult.

The dreams of "multicultural society" in the 1970s–1980s were aroused less by the requests of immigrated and settled populations in Western European democracies than by the challenges that Europeans themselves, confronted by their political decline, directed toward their national identity. France and England ceased being imperial powers whose decisions influenced the destiny of the world. After the political and moral disaster of World War II, Germans devoted themselves to economic activity. The idea of the multicultural society, by its very ambiguity, permitted one to magically compensate for political decline by invoking other values: namely, the diversity of cultures. It also presented an occasion for symbolically expiating the sins of the past—colonization, the politics of assimilation, or the horrors of World War II. It seemed finally to have found a solution to contradictions arising from the general adherence to the two great values of modernity: that is, individual equality inscribed in the principle of citizenship and the authenticity tied to a particular culture. During the age of the triumphant nation, the national bond was charged with assuring the social tie; the welfare state afterward was conferred the same task. From now on, the "cultural" carried on in the relay. "Cultures," in every meaning of the term—from that of the minister of culture to that of multiculturalist militants—all equal in value—would be charged with resolving the economic or even moral and political crisis. Hereafter the "cultural" would replace obsolete public spirit in uniting men and giving meaning to their existence.

In a more and more technical society, where the management of public affairs is inevitably reserved to specialists, one eagerly invokes the values of local citizenship, whose practice would permit one to respond to the call of "participation" or participatory citizenship, vague but pressing, that individuals formulate. The idea of representation which lay at the origin of the democratic nation is now considered by many to be insufficient: the practice of direct democracy would give satisfaction to the aspirations of a truly active citizenship. But to participate in local management, in which democratization is desirable, is not alone sufficient to unite citizens around a project which establishes a common will; it does not guarantee that citizens would mobilize themselves if need be to defend the political collectivity and values which legitimate it.

In historicizing all concepts and by relativizing all institutions, modern thought—aided by the horrors perpetrated in the twentieth century in the name of political values—had the effect of disenchanting the political, after having already disenchanted the religious. But all power emanates from the sacred. In democratic nations, the organization and acceptance of the institutional expression of the popular will remains the last trace of this "sacred": all accept the results of elections. It is in this way that the sovereignty of citizens is recognized, legitimacy revived, and the political project reaffirmed. But will elections alone suffice to assure the political tie, and hence, social integration? Passions and emotions run over, irrigating the societies of the democratic age as all the others. Churches no longer venture to control sects and charismatic movements and recognize all forms of emotional communities of religious inspiration, in the hope of reintegrating them one day in the ecclesiastic institution. It is by no means certain, then, that the democratic nation may continue to control the inevitable conflicts provoked by the sharing of resources by means of the rational ambition of citizenship. In a commercial democracy, material aspirations by definition know no limits. It is by no means certain that the democratic nation may continue to control the behaviors inspired by feelings of belonging or identification with ethnic communities. There is no guarantee whatsoever that the democratic nation will be able to preserve the social bond.

Europeans witnessed the weakening of the monarchical system in the eighteenth century, which was poorly prepared to respond to the new aspirations of peoples; it may be the case today that the national political form has been similarly exhausted.

Notes

1. Mauss, 1969 (1920?), p. 625.
2. Mendras, 1988.

3. Nora, 1993, III, Vol.3, p. 30.
4. Rosencrance, 1986.
5. Habermas, 1991, p. 240.
6. Habermas, 1991, p. 247.
7. These analyses are developed in Schnapper, 1993.

Works Cited

Anderson, Benedict. 1982. *Imagined Communities: Reflections on the Origin and Spread of Nationalism*. London: Verso.
Armstrong, John. 1983. *Nations before Nationalism*. Chapel Hill: University of North Carolina.
Aron, Raymond. 1962. *Paix et guerre entre les nations*. Paris: Calmann-Lévy.
———. 1967. "Max Weber et la politique de puissance," in *Les étapes de la pensée sociologique*. Paris: Gallimard, coll. Tel.
Badie, Bertrand. 1992. *L'Etat importé: L'occidentalisation de l'ordre politique*. Paris: Fayard.
Balibar, Etienne and Immanuel Wallerstein. 1988. *Race, nation, classes: Les identités ambiguës*. Paris: La Découverte.
Balibar, Etienne. 1992. *Les frontières de la démocratie*. Paris: La Découverte.
Banfield, Edward C. 1958. *The Moral Basis of a Backward Society*, New York: The Free Press.
Barnavi, Elie. [1982] 1988. *Une histoire moderne d'Israël*. Paris: Flammarion/Champs.
Barth, Frederik. 1969. *Ethnic Groups and Boundaries: The Social Organisation of Cultural Difference*. London: Allen and Unwin.
Beaune, Colette. 1985. *Naissance de la nation France*. Paris: Gallimard.
Beetham, David. 1985. *Max Weber and the Theory of Modern Politics*. Cambridge, MA: Polity Press.
Berger, Suzanne. 1972. "Bretons, Basques, Scots and Other European Nations," *Journal of Interdisciplinary History* 3: 167-175.
Bibo, Istvan. [1946] 1986. *Misère des petits Etats d'Europe de l'Est*. Paris: L'Harmattan.
Birnbaum, Pierre and Jean Leca, eds. 1986. *Sur l'individualisme, Théories et méthodes*. Paris: Presses de la Fondation nationale des sciences politiques.
Birnbaum, Pierre, ed. 1991. *Histoire politique des juifs de France*, Paris: Presses de la Fondation nationale des sciences politiques.
Breuilly, John. 1982. *Nationalism and the State*. Manchester: Manchester University Press.
Brubaker, Rogers. 1992. *Citizenship and Nationhood in France and Germany*. Cambridge, MA: Harvard University Press.
Burke, Edmund. [1790] 1989. *Réflexions sur la Révolution de France*, with a preface by Philippe Raynaud. Paris: Hachette/Pluriel.

Connor, Walker. 1978. "A Nation is a Nation, is a State, is an Ethnic Group, is a...," *Ethnic and Racial Studies* 1(4): 377–400.
Costa-Lascoux, Jacqueline. 1990. *De l'immigré au citoyen.* Paris: La Documentation française.
———. 1992. "L'étranger dans la nation," *Raison présente* 106: 79–93.
Delannoi, Gil and Pierre-André Taguieff, eds. 1991. *Théories du nationalisme, Nation, nationalité, ethnicité.* Paris: Kimé.
Devant l'histoire. 1988. *Les documents de la controverse sur la singularité de l'extermination des juifs par le régime nazi,* preface by Luc Ferry and introduction by Joseph Rovan. Paris: Cerf, "Passages."
Deutsch, Karl W. [1953] 1966. *Nationalism and Social Communication: An Inquiry into the Foundation of Nationality.* New York: Wiley.
Deutsch, Karl W. and William J. Foltz, eds. 1963. *Nation-Building,* New York: Atherton Press.
Dumont, Louis. 1983. *Essais sur l'individualisme: Une perspective anthropologique sur l'idéologie moderne.* Paris: Le Seuil.
———. 1991. *L'idéologie allemande: France-Allemagne et retour,* Paris: Gallimard.
Durkheim, Émile. [1899] 1925. *L'éducation morale.* Paris: Alcan.
Eisenstadt, Shmuel N. 1954. *An Absorption of Immigrants.* London: Routledge and Kegan Paul.
Elias, Norbert. [1986] 1991. *La société des individus.* Paris: Fayard.
Ferry, Jean-Marc. 1991. *Les puissances de l'expérience.* Paris: Cerf.
Fichte, Johann Gottlieb. 1992. *Discours à la nation allemande,* with presentation and notes by Alain Renaut. Paris: Imprimerie nationale.
Finley, Moses I. 1985. *L'invention de la politique.* Paris: Flammarion. *Politics in the Ancient World,* Cambridge University Press, 1983.)
———. 1954. "The Ancient Greeks and Their Nation: The Sociological Problem," *The British Journal of Sociology* 5: 253–264.
Furet, François and Mona Ozouf, eds. 1993. *Le siècle de l'avènement républicain.* Paris: Gallimard.
Furnivall, J. S. 1939. *Netherlands India.* Cambridge: Cambridge University Press.
Garrigou, Alain. 1992. *Le vote et la vertu, Comment les Français sont devenus électeurs.* Paris: Presses de Fondation nationale des sciences politiques.
Gauthier, Philippe. 1981. "La citoyenneté en Grèce et à Rome: participation et intégration," *Ktema, civilisations de l'Orient, de la Grèce et de Rome antiques,* no. 6: 176–179.
———. 1979. "Sur le citoyen romain," *Commentaire* 6: 318–323.
Geertz, Clifford, ed. 1963. *Old Societies and New States: The Quest for Modernity in Asia and Africa.* New York: The Free Press.
Gellner, Ernest. 1983. *Nations and Nationalism.* Oxford: Blackwell.
Girardet, Raoul. 1966. *Le nationalisme français, 1871–1914.* Paris: Armand Colin.

Glazer, Nathan and Moynihan, Daniel Patrick. 1963. *Beyond the Melting Pot: The Negroes, Puerto Ricans, Jews, Italians and Irish of New York City.* Cambridge, MA: The MIT Press.
———. 1975. *Ethnicity: Theory and Experience.* Cambridge, MA: Harvard University Press.
Goldenberg, David M., ed. 1990. *Documents in American Jewish History.* Philadelphia: Annenberg Research Institute.
Greenfeld, Liah. 1992. *Nationalism: Five Roads to Modernity.* Cambridge, MA: Harvard University Press.
Grémion, Pierre. 1976. *Le pouvoir périphérique: Bureaucrates et notables dans le système politique français.* Paris: Le Seuil.
Guenée, Bernard. 1971. *L'Occident aux xive a xve siècles: les Etats,* Paris, PUF.
Gueniffey, Patrice. 1993. *Le nombre et la raison: La Révolution française et les élections.* Paris: Ecole des hautes études en sciences sociales.
Habermas, Jürgen. 1985–1990. *Ecrits politiques.* Paris: Cerf.
Hagège, Claude. 1992. *Le souffle de la langue, voies et destins des parlers d'Europe.* Paris: Odile Jacob.
Hansen, Morgens H. 1991. *The Athenian Democracy in the Age of Demosthenes.* Oxford: Blackwell. (French translation, Belles Lettres, 1993.)
Hartz, Louis. 1964. *The Founding of New Societies.* New York: Harcourt, Brace and World Inc. (French translation, Le Seuil, 1968.)
Haupt, Georges, Michael Löwi, and Claudie Weill. 1974. *Les marxistes et la question nationale.* Paris: Maspéro.
Haut Conseil à l'intégration. 1993. *L'intégration à la française.* Paris: UGE, 10/18.
Hechter, Michael. 1975. *Internal Colonialism: The Celtic Fringe in National Development, 1536–1966.* London: Routledge and Kegan Paul.
Hobsbawn, Eric J. 1990. *Nations and Nationalism since 1780: Programme, Myth, Reality.* Cambridge: Cambridge University Press.
Hroch, Miroslav. 1968. *Die Vorkämpfer der nationalen Bewegung bei den kleinen Völkern Europas.* Prague: University Karlova.
Hugger, Paul, dir. 1992. *Les Suisses, Modes de vie, traditions, mentalités.* Lausanne: Payot.
Hume, David. 1972. *Ecrits politiques.* Paris: Vrin.
Ihl, Olivier. 1993. "L'urne électorale, formes et usages d'une technique de vote," *Revue française de science politique,* no. 1: 30–59.
Iribarne, Philippe d'. 1989. *La logique de l'honueur: Gestion des entreprises et traditions nationales.* Paris: Le Seuil.
Kamenka, Eugène, ed. 1976. *Nationalism: The Nature and Evolution of an Idea.* London: Edward Arnold.
Kantorowicz, Ernst. [1957] 1989. *Les Deux Corps du Roi,* Paris, Gallimard.
Kedourie, Elie. 1970. *Nationalism in Asia and Africa.* New York: World Publishers.

Kende, Pierre. 1991. "Quelle alternative à l'Etat-nation," *Esprit*, Oct.: 23–30.
Kohn, Hans. 1944. *The Idea of Nationalism: A Study in Its Origin and Background*. New York: MacMillan.
Lacroix, Bernard. 1976. "La vocation originelle d'Emile Durkheim," *Revue française de sociologie* 17(2): 213–245.
Laqueur, Walter. [1972] 1973. *Histoire du sionisme*. Paris: Calmann-Lévy.
Lévi-Strauss, Claude. 1977. *L'identité*. Paris: Grasset.
Lewis, Bernard. [1961] 1988. *Islam et laïcité*. Paris: Fayard.
Lijphart, Arend. 1968. *The Politics of Accommodation: Pluralism and Democracy in the Netherlands*. Berkeley: University of California Press.
———. 1977. *Democraties in Plural Societies: A Comparative Exploration*. New Haven: Yale University Press.
Lipset, Seymour Martin. 1963. *The First New Nation: The United States in Historical and Comparative Perspective*. New York: Basic Books.
———. 1990. *Continental Divide: The Values and Institutions of the United States and Canada*. New York: Routledge.
Long, Marceau, dir. 1988. *Etre français aujourd'hui et demain*, Rapport présenté au Premier ministre. Paris: Christian Bourgois, 10/18.
Manent, Pierre. 1987. *Histoire intellectuelle du libéralisme, dix leçons*. Paris: Calmann-Lévy.
Mauss, Marcel. 1968–1969. *Oeuvres:* vol. 1, *Les fonctions sociales du sacré* and vol. 3, *Cohésion sociale et divisions de la sociologie*. Paris: Editions de Minuit.
Mendelsohn, Ezra. 1983. *The Jews of East Central Europe between the World Wars*. Bloomington: Indiana University Press.
Mendras, Henri. 1988. *La Seconde Révolution française, 1965–1984*. Paris: Gallimard.
Mommsen, Wolfgang J. 1974. *The Age of Bureaucracy: Perspectives on the Political Sociology of Max Weber*. Oxford: Blackwell.
———. [1959] 1985. *Max Weber et la politique allemande*. Paris: PUF.
Nairn, Tom. 1981. *The Break Up of Britain*. London: Verso.
Nicolet, Claude. 1976. *Le métier de citoyen dans la Rome républicaine*. Paris: Gallimard.
Nisbet, Robert A. [1963] 1984. *La Tradition sociologique*. Paris: PUF.
———. 1974. "Citizenship: Two Traditions," *Social Research* 41(4): 612–637.
Nora, Pierre, dir. 1984–1993. *Les lieux de mémoire*, 8 vols. Paris: Gallimard.
Paugam, Serge. 1993. *La société française et ses pauvres*. Paris: PUF.
Perin, Roberto. 1993. "National Histories and Ethnic History in Canada," *Cahiers de recherche sociologique*, no. 20.
Pirenne, Henri. 1900–1926. *Histoire de Belgique*, 6 vols. Brussels: Henri Lamertin.
Poulter, Sebastian. 1989. "Cultural Pluralism and Its Limits: A Legal Perspective," in *Britain: A Plural Society*. London: Commission for Race Equality.
Renan, Ernest. 1947. *Oeuvres complètes*, vol. 1. Paris: Calmann-Lévy.

———. [1870–1882] 1992. *Qu'est-ce qu'une nation? et autres essais politiques*, with an introduction by Jöel Roman. Paris: Presses Pocket, Agora.
Rosanvallon, Pierre. 1990. *L'Etat en France de 1789 à nos jours*, Paris: Le Seuil.
———. 1992. *Le sacre du citoyen*. Paris: Gallimard.
Rosecrance, Richard. 1986. *The Rise of the Trading States: Commerce and Conquest in the Modern World*. New York: Basic Books.
Rostow, Walt Whitman. 1960. *The Stages of Economic Growth: A Non communist Manifesto*. Cambridge: Cambridge University Press.
Saint-Germain, Charles-Eric de. 1993. "Hegel, l'assimilation et l'exclusion," *Philosophie politique* 3: 45–64.
Schlesinger, Arthur M., Jr. 1991. *The Disuniting of America*. Liana Levi.
Schnapper, Dominique. 1991. *La France de l'intégration, Sociologie de la nation en 1990*. Paris: Gallimard.
———. 1992. *L'Europe des immigrés: Essai sur les politiques d'immigration*. Paris: François Bourin.
———. 1993. "Le sens de l'ethnico-religieux," *Archives des sciences sociales des religions* 81: 149–163.
Seton-Watson, Hugh. 1977. *Nations and States: An Inquiry into the Origins of Nations and the Politics of Nationalism*. London: Methuen.
Shklar, Judith. 1991. *American Citizenship*. Cambridge, MA: Harvard University Press.
Siegfried, André. 1947. *La Suisse, Démocratie témoin*. Neuchâtel: A la Baconnière.
Smith, Anthony D. 1981. *The Ethnic Revival in the Modern World*. Cambridge: Cambridge University Press.
———. 1986. *The Ethnic Origins of Nations*. London: Blackwell.
Stark, Joachim. 1988. "Ethnien, Völker, Minderheiten," *Jahrbuch für Ostdeutsche Volkskunde*, band 31, pp. 1–55.
Szücs, Jenö. [1981] 1986."Sur le concept de nation: Réflexions sur la théorie politique médiévale," *Actes de la Recherche en sciences sociales* 64, Sept. pp. 51–62.
———. 1985. *Les Trois Europe*. Paris: L'Harmattan.
Tilly, Charles, ed. 1975. *The Formation of National States in Western Europe*. Princeton: Princeton University Press.
Tocquevllle, Alexis de. 1991–1992. *Oeuvres*, vols. 1 and 2. Paris: Gallimard, La Pléiade.
Villars, Jean. 1991. "L'Amérique au miroir brisé," *Commentaire*, no. 54 (summer): 425–429.
Wallerstein, Immanuel. 1960. "Ethnicity and National Integration in West Africa," *Cahiers d'Etudes Africaines*, no. 3: 129–139.
Weber, Max. 1947. *La ville*, Paris, Aubier-Montaigne, "Champ urbain," ([1921] 1982). Tübingen: Mohr.
———. 1947. *Wirtschaft und Gesellschaft: Grundriss der verstehenden Soziologie*. Tübingen: Mohr. (French transalation, *Economie et société*,

Paris, Plon, 1971; English translation, *Economy and Society*, edited by Guenther Roth and Claus Wittich, Berkeley, University of California Press, 1978.)

Weil, Eric. 1971. *Essais et conférences*. Paris: Plon.

Wieviorka, Michel, ed. 1992. *Racisme et modernité*. Paris: La Découverte.

Windisch, Uli. 1991. "700 ans, ce n'est qu'un début," in *1991, Regards sur une Suisse jubilaire, 1291–1991*. Geneva: Institut national genevois.

———. 1992. *Les relations quotidiennes entre Romands et Suisses allemands*, 2 vols. Lausanne: Payot.

Winock, Michel. 1982. *Edouard Drumont et Cie, antisémitisme et fascisme en France*. Paris: Le Seuil.

Wood, Gordon S. [1969] 1991. *The Creation of the American Republic, 1776–1787*, with a preface by Claude Lefort. Paris: Belin.

Index of Names

The numbers in italics refer to footnotes.

Anderson (B.), 38, 60, *64*, 83, 145, 147, *154*.
Apter (D.), *13*.
Aristotle, 66, 68, 74, 83, *92*, 115, 141.
Armstrong (J.), 17, 18, *33*, 37.
Aron (R.), *13*, 27, 32, *33*, *93*, *130*.

Badie (B.), *92*.
Balibar (E.), *92*, *154*.
Banfield (E.C.), *93*.
Barnavi (E.), *64*.
Barth (F.), *33*.
Bauer (O.), 58, *64*, 143.
Beaune (C.), *153*.
Beetham (D.), *64*.
Ben Gurion (D.), 62, 103.
Berger (S.), 18, *33*, *154*.
Bergson (H.), 76.
Berlin (I.), *130*, 135.
Besnard (P.), 13.
Beveridge (W. H.), 31.
Bibo (I.), *13*, 42, 49, 56, *64*, *153*.
Birnbaum (P.), *33*, *93*.
Bismarck (O.), 30.
Bonald (L. de), 138.
Breuilly (J.), 148, *154*.
Brubaker (W.R.), *153*.
Burke (E.), 44, 45, 60, *64*, 72, *92*, 138, *171*.

Ceausescu (N.), 60.
Charles I, 45.
Churchill (W.), 32.
Cicero, *92*.
Cobbett (W.), 41.
Comte (A.), 121.
Connor (W.), 18, *33*, 37.
Constant (B.), 65.
Costa Lascoux (J.), 13, 59, *64*, *92*, *153*.
Crowley (J.), *33*, *154*.

Delannoi (G.), *33*, *63*, *130*, *154*.
Deutsch (K.), 38, 145, *154*.
Doubnov (S.), 57.
Douglas (M.), 153.
Dumont (L.), *13*, *64*, 80, *92*, 138, 151, *153*, *154*.
Durkheim (E.), 5, 7, 8, *13*, 31, *34*, 36, *130*, 141, 149.

Eisenstadt (S.N.), *64*, *129*.
Elias (N.), 5, 6, 11, *13*, 61, *64*, 85, *92*, 123, 129, *130*, 152, *154*, 158, 162.
Elizabeth I, 43.
Engels (F.), 143.
Eschine, *92*.

Ferry (J.), 109.
Ferry (J.M.), 59, 61, *64*, 152.
Fichte (J.), 3, 7, 26, *34*, *129*, 139, 140, *153*.
Finley (M.I.), *92*.
Folz (W.J.), *154*.
Furet (F.), *64*, *92*.
Furnivall (J.S.), *92*.
Fustel De Coulanges (N.D.), 66, 136.

Garrigou (A.), *92*.
Gauthier (P.), 13, 68, *92*.
Geertz (C.), 7, *13*, 25, *33*, *34*, 83, *93*, 143, 144, *154*.
Gellner (E.), 23, 26, *34*, 38, 58, 62, *63*, 109, 145, 146, 147, *154*.
Girardet (R.), *154*.
Glazer (N.), *33*, *64*, *154*.
Goldenberg (D. M.), *129*.
Greenfeld (L.), *13*, *63*, *64*, 141, *154*.
Grémion (B.), *130*.
Guenée (B.), *130*.
Gueniffey (P.), *92*.

Habermas (J.), 59, 60, *64*, 152, *170*.
Hagège (C.), *130*.
Hansen (M.), 66, *92*.
Hartz (L.), *64*.
Hassner (P.), 13.
Haupt (G.), *64*.
Hechter (M.), *13*, *154*.
Hegel (G.W.F.), 9, 22, 76, 95, 160.
Herder (J.G.), 129, 138.
Herzl (T.), 55, 62, *64*, 96.
Hitler (A.), 56.
Hobbes (T.), 83.
Hobsbawm (E.J.), *33*, *154*.
Hojda (E.), 60.
Horowitz (D.L.), *33*.
Hroch (M.), *130*.
Hugger (P.), *64*.
Hugo (V.), 81.
Hume (D.), *34*, 44, *64*, 74.

Ihl (O.), *92*.
Iribarne (P. d'), *130*.

Jabotinski (V.), 62.
Jaurès (J.), 125.

Kamenka (E.), *153*.
Kant (I.), 26, 36.
Kantorowicz (E.), *153*.
Kedourie (E.), 38, 141, 146, *154*.
Keller (G.), 21.
Kemal (M.), 102, 103, 111, 114, 115.
Kende (P.), 59, *64*.
Kohn (H.), 137, 141, *154*.
Kossuth (L.), 98.

Lacroix (B.), *154*.
Laqueur (W.), *64*, *130*.
Lavisse (E.), 111, 162.
Leca (J.), 91, *93*.
Lefort (C.), 76, *64*, *154*.
Lepsius (R. M.), 152, *154*.
Lévi-Strauss (C.), 25, *34*, 119.
Lewis (B.), *92*, 118, *129*, *130*.
Lijphart (A.), *92*, *130*.
Lindsay (A. D.), *154*.
Lipset (S.M.), *13*, 38, 41, 46, *63*, *64*, *129*.
Locke (J.), 90.
Long (M.), *130*.

Macaulay (T.B.), 44.

Madison (J.), 47.
Maistre (J. de), 138.
Manent (P.), *13*, *34*, *92*, *153*.
Mannheim (K.), 76.
Martineau (H.), 46, 48.
Marx (K.), 83.
Mauss (M.), 5, 6, 7, 8, 10, 11, *13*, 20, 21, 26, 27, 28, *33*, *34*, 37, 38, 39, 81, *92*, 116, 121, *130*, 140, 151, *154*, 155, 156, 157, *169*.
Mazzini (A. L.), 7, 16.
Meinecke (F.), *133*.
Meir (G.), 103.
Mendelsohn (E.), *92*.
Mendras (H.), 162, *169*.
Michelet (J.), 162.
Mill (J.S.), *92*, 115
Moynihan (D.P.), *33*, *64*, *92*, *154*.
Mommsen (T.), 136.
Mommsen (W.), *13*, 22, *33*.
Montesquieu (C. L. de), 8, 18, 84.

Nairn (T.), *64*.
Nicolet (C.), *92*.
Nisbet (R.), 7, *13*, *154*.
Nora (P.), *154*.

Ozouf (M.), *64*, *92*.

Païssi, 52.
Parsons (T.), 25, *64*, 79, *92*, 144, *154*.
Paugam (S.), 13, *130*.
Perin (R.), *130*.
Pétain (P.), 50.
Petersen (W.), *33*, *154*.
Phillip the Fair, 52, 111.
Phillip of Macedonia, 74.
Pirenne (H.), 52, *64*, 111, 115,
Plamenatz (J.), 137, *153*.
Popper (K.), 15.
Poulter (S.), *130*.

Raynaud (P.), 46, 47, 60, *64*, *92*.
Renaut (A.), 26, *34*, *129*, *153*.
Renan (E.), 3, 7, 9, 20, 23, *33*, 36, 37, 38, 39, 53, *64*, 89, 90, *93*, 100, 132, 136, 139, 140, *153*, 155, 174, 175.
Rex (J.), 78, *92*.
Rokkan (S.), 133.
Roman (J.), *153*.
Roosevelt (F.D.), 48.
Rosanvallon (P.), *13*, *63*, *92*.

Index of Names 179

Rosecrance (R.), *170*.
Rostow (W.W.), 6, 142, 145.
Rousseau (J.J.), 18, 26, 47, 72, 90.

Saddam Hussein, 24.
Saint John de Crèvecœur (J.), 46.
Saint-Simon (H. de), 121.
Saint-Germain (C.-E. de), *129*.
Schlesinger (A.M.), *64*.
Schnapper (A.), 13.
Schnapper (D.), *13, 33, 34, 64, 92, 153, 170*.
Schumpeter (J.), 121.
Seton Watson (H.), 18, *33*, 37.
Shils (E.), *33*, 81, 143, *154*.
Shklar (J.), *13*.
Siegfried (A.), 106, *129*.
Sieyès (E.J.), 3.
Syrkin (N.), 62.
Smith (A.), 7, *13*, 24, 32, *34, 64*, 137, 142, 145, 148, *153, 154*.
Socrates, 67.
Stalin (J.), 97.
Stark (J.), *153*.
Szücz (J.), *13, 33, 64, 153*.

Taguieff (P.A.), *33, 63, 130, 153, 154*.
Tilly (C.), *34*, 143, 144, *153, 154*.

Tito (J.), 18, 82.
Tocqueville (A. de), 3, 47, 48, *64*, 87, *93*, 101, 104, 121, *129, 130*, 141, 160, *154*.
Trevelyan (G.), 125.

Urwin (D.), 133.

Vargas Llosa (M.), 1, 2, 6, 10, *13*, 83, 116.
Vidal-Naquet (P.), 66, *92*.
Vigne (E.), 13.
Villars (J.), *93*.
Voltaire, 8, 84.

Wallerstein (E.), 38, *33, 130, 154*, 175.
Washington (G.), 46, 101.
Weber (M.), 5, 6, 7, 11, 20, 21, 22, 27, 29, 30, *33, 34,* 37, 38, 41, 58, 63, *63,* 70, 71, 88, 91, *92,* 120, 122, 124, *130,* 140, 148, 159, 163, 166, 167, 169.
Weil (E.), 137, *153*.
Wieviorka (M.), 92.
Windisch (U.), 53, *64, 92, 129*.
Winock (M.), *154*.
Wood (G.S.), *64, 154*.

Zangwill (I.), 62.

Index of Places and Themes

The themes are indicated in italics. The pages to which this index refers may treat the theme without containing the exact word designated here.

Abeokuta, 17.
Africa, 30, 113.
Africa, South, 41.
Albanians, 23.
Algeria, 75, 89, 126.
Alsace, 134, 135, 136, 140.
Arabs, 20, 108.
Argentina, 97, 107.
Army (conscription), 35, 49, 50, 87–90, 99, 105, 107, 108, 161–164.
Ashkenazim, 56.
Assimilation (political), 6, 50, 85, 95, 126, 127.
Athens (Athenians, Greek city), 20, 51, 65, 74, 83, 113, 141.
Australia, 41, 78, 97, 161.
Austria, 52, 53, 81.
Austro-Hungary, 21, 58, 122, 133–134. See Habsburg.

Balkans, 23, 123, 137, 146.
Belgium (Belgian people), 52, 53, 81, 89, 99, 100, 109, 111, 115.
Bond, social, 1, 3, 7, 12, 24, 35, 83, 153, 155, 159, 160, 162, 164, 169. See *integration*.
Bosnians, 23.
Bosnia-Herzegovinia, 18.
Boundaries. See territory.
Bourgeoisie (bourgeois), 70, 123, 124, 134.
Brasilia, 114.
Bulgaria, 52.

California, 112.
Cambridge University, 72.
Canada, 41, 42, 97, 99, 107, 112, 161.
Catalonia (Catalans), 32.
Catholics, 37, 102, 115, 133, 147.

Churches, 35, 71, 100–104, 106, 133–134, 166, 169.
Citizen (citizenship), 4, 12, 16, 20, 24, 27–28, 32, 35, 36, 38, 39, 57, 65, 75–77, 82–83, 86, 87, 95, 128.
City (municipal spirit), 53, 66, 70–72, 132–133.
Colonization (colonialism), 1, 2, 50, 84, 90, 120, 121, 126–127, 135, 150, 158.
"*Communities, emotional,*" 166–169.
Conditions, economic and technical, 22, 36, 38, 146, 147, 148, 150, 156, 157, 159.
Congress of Vienna, 30.
Consociative democracies, 53, 81–82, 116–117.
Constraints, 6, 22, 87, 115.
Corsica, 86, 115, 116.
Courtrai, 52, 53, 111.
Croatia (Croats), 23, 98, 115, 133–134.
Czechoslovakia (Czechs), 16, 58, 99, 117, 120.
Culture, 29, 37, 60, 115, 119, 123, 144.

Declaration of the Rights of Man, 3, 59, 60, 61, 127.
Decolonization, 11, 30–31, 46, 85, 120, 126–127, 144.
Democracy, 1, 4, 11, 24, 46, 117, 155–169.
Denmark (Danes), 52.
Difference (right to), 119.
Dignity, 3, 52, 53, 80, 97–100, 116, 117, 118, 127, 128, 146, 162, 168.
Dimension, internal and external, 16, 22, 29–33.
Dominated (groups), 122, 126.

Education, (public schools), 26–27, 42,

49, 75, 99, 105, 108–110, 145, 161, 166.
Educability, 26, 140.
Emblems, 42.
Empires, 2, 126–127, 146, 149, 164.
England (English, Great Britain), 2, 6, 8, 16, 17, 18, 20, 31, 32, 36, 37, 39, 40, 41, 42–46, 50, 71, 72, 73, 78, 84, 87, 101, 102, 113, 118, 123, 124, 131, 132, 133–135, 142, 143, 150, 158, 165, 168.
Equality, 2, 4, 7, 96, 117, 119, 147, 155, 159.
Etat de droit, 59, 60, 61, 80, 152, 163.
Ethnicity, 15, 19, 20, 62, 143, 166.
Ethnies, 7, 9, 12, 16, 17–21, 23, 24, 36, 85, 87, 96, 112, 116, 120, 148, 149, 150, 164.
Ethnic (ethnic communities), 60, 66, 80, 107, 119, 122, 129, 166, 169.
Europe, 41, 47, 120.
Europe, Eastern, 9, 40, 42, 59, 96–99, 123, 131, 135, 137.
Europe, Western, 9, 11, 17, 58, 84, 85, 96, 97, 98, 128, 131, 133–134, 155, 156–157, 166, 168.
European Economic Community (building of Europe), 60, 121, 125, 157, 165.

Flemish, 16, 53, 99, 100, 122, 143.
France (French), 5, 8, 12, 16, 20, 25, 31, 36, 37, 41, 42, 49–52, 77, 87, 100, 105, 107, 109, 113, 115, 118, 122, 132, 133–135, 138, 158, 162–163, 168.

General Will, 72.
Germany, (Germans, West Germany), 12, 17, 22, 30, 31, 32, 36–37, 52, 59, 60, 86, 87, 97, 99–100, 107, 110, 113, 117, 122, 133–135, 138–139, 140, 152, 158, 163–164, 168.
Globalization, 7, 153, 155, 156, 157.
Greece, 51, 113, 115.

Habsburgs, 98, 146. See Austro-Hungary.
Histadrut, 62, 108.
History (teaching of), 40, 52.
Historians (intellectuals, role of), 9, 17, 28, 77, 110–113, 123–125, 132, 136, 141, 147.

Holy Roman Empire, 52, 97, 133.
Homogeneity, cultural, 28, 29, 115–119.
House of Commons, 39, 44, 124.
House of Lords, 44, 45.
Hungary (Hungarians), 17, 23, 98, 133, 137.

Ibos, 17.
Idea (analytical, or theory), 1, 7, 9, 10, 11, 12, 15, 61, 63, 80, 90, 149–153.
Ideas (representations), 39, 49, 61, 152, the two ideas of the nation, 131, 135–140, 149.
Identity, national, 27, 57–58, 85, 129, 152–153, 157.
Ideologies, 9, 10, 120–121, 135–140, 149–151.
Immigrantion (immigrants), 25, 31, 49, 62, 78, 107–108, 126.
Individualism, 3, 72–73, 150–152.
Institutions, 10, 36, 38–41, 51, 63, 65, 112.
Institutions, political, 30, 74, 78, 104–108, 116, 119, 142, 143, 147, 155, 159.
Integration, 16, 20, 24–29, 30, 32–33, 48, 51, 81, 85, 90, 95, 143, 146, 155, 169. see the social bond.
Iran, 21, 24, 58.
Iraq, 58.
Islam (Muslims), 71, 75, 102, 103–104, 118, 134.
Israel, 9, 40, 54–57, 62, 79, 86, 89, 96, 103, 107–108, 110, 113.
Italy (Italians), 36, 90, 122, 133–134, 137, 146, 161.

Japan (Japanese), 31, 87.
Jena, 3, 139.
Jews (Israelis), 19, 20, 37, 58, 78, 122, 132.
Jews, Zionist, 40, 54–57, 62, 96–97, 103–104, 107–108, 125.

King (monarchies of Western Europe), 39, 49, 50, 70, 97, 131–133.
Kosovo, 51.
Kurds, 58.

Language, 29, 36, 37, 53, 58, 59, 62, 67, 81, 105, 113–114, 115, 116, 117, 119, 123, 134, 138, 141, 144, 147.

Index of Places and Themes 183

Latin America, 30, 41.
League of Nations, 21.
Lebanon, 80, 89.
Legitimacy, political, 10, 24, 35, 39, 81, 111, 120, 135, 152.
Liberalism, 128.
Liberty, 2, 4, 8, 45–46.

Markers of identity, 42, 82, 113–114.
Marxism, 6, 7, 123, 124, 125, 128, 143, 145, 156.
Middle Ages, 17, 49, 131, 132, 139.
Mexico, 97.
Mobilization of populations, 12, 60, 61, 78, 89, 91, 112, 125, 126, 142–143, 158.
Multiculturalism, 79, 80, 161, 168, 169.
Myths, national, 43, 46, 47, 48, 49, 105.

Nation (definition), 15–33.
Nation, ethnique, 12, 61, 79, 131, 136, 137, 138, 139, 148, 149, 150, 152.
Nationalism, 8, 15, 23–26, 57, 59, 110, 120, 123, 135, 137, 141–145, 155, 165.
Nationalists, 16, 21, 23, 27, 57, 61, 127, 142.
Nationalities, 17, 57, 90, 123.
Nationality Laws, 42, 50, 86, 87, 105, 107, 138, 158.
Nation state, 28, 59, 97, 132–133, 146.
"Nativism," 48.
Netherlands (Holland), 31, 52, 53, 81–82, 88, 89, 111–112, 117, 135, 165.
Norway, 52.

One Hundred Years War, 58, 132.
Orthodox, 115, 134.
Oxford University, 72.

Palestine, 56–57, 78, 79, 107, 111.
Parliamentarism, 27, 30, 40, 43, 44, 45.
Particularisms, 10, 12, 35, 71, 112, 116, 119, 124–125, 129, 166.
Patriotism, 50, 57, 58, 88, 125, 129, 148.
Patriotism, constitutional, 59, 61, 118, 152.
Pearl Harbor, 87.
People, Chosen, 46, 91, 104.
Perfectibility, 26.
Persian Gulf War, 24, 159, 163.

Poland (Polish), 31, 56, 78, 137, 138.
Polis, 65–68, 83, 96.
Politics (the political, political society, transcendence by the political), 12, 29, 60, 61, 65–91, 98, 117, 149, 150, 157.
Portugal, 31, 52, 135.
Postnational (identity), 60–62, 152.
Productivism, 121, 159–166.
Project, Political, 35, 37–41, 42–57, 95, 116, 119, 126, 148, 155, 156, 159, 160, 163–165, 169.
Protestants, 37, 122, 132, 133.
Protonationalisms, 17, 36, 123.
Prussia, 89, 139.

Quebec, 99, 112.

Race (community of blood), 19, 20, 28, 36, 37, 46, 60, 111, 112, 126, 136, 138, 142.
Rationality, 61, 63, 84, 112, 129, 152, 166–169.
Regions, regionalisms, 116, 123, 133, 134, 142.
Religions, 28, 36, 37, 38, 52, 61, 66, 100–104, 105, 116, 119, 132–133, 156, 166.
Representation (representative democracy, delegation), 47, 72–76.
Revolution, American, 2, 8.
Revolution, French, 2, 3, 12, 49, 57, 72, 105, 108, 139, 150.
Revolution, Glorious (Revolution of 1688), 43, 44, 45.
Rome (Romans), 65, 68–70, 73, 74.
Romanians, 56, 134–135.
Russia (Russians), 56, 58, 79, 89, 138, 165.

Saudi Arabia, 21.
Scotland (Scots), 134, 143, 147.
Secularism, 35, 54, 100–104, 115, 150.
Sephardim, 56.
Serbia (Serbs), 23, 51, 98, 115, 134, 159.
Shoah, 54–56.
Singularity (national), 11, 51, 62, 95–129, 150.
Six Days War, 89.
Slavs, 20, 115.
Slovaks, 16, 98–99.

Slovenians, 23, 159.
Socialization, 26, 112.
Sociology and sociologists (social sciences), 4–9, 10, 11, 12, 26, 62–63, 141–149.
Soviet Union, 57–58, 120, 164–165.
Spain (Spanish), 31, 52, 89, 104, 132–133.
Sparta, 20, 66.
State (state activity), 12, 16, 17, 20–23, 25, 27, 28, 30–32, 36, 38, 49, 50, 51, 63, 82, 84, 86, 87, 90, 95–129, 146, 156.
Sudetes, 138.
Sweden, 52.
Switzerland, 9, 20, 28, 40, 42, 52–54, 81, 82, 86–89, 101, 105–107, 117, 163.
Suffrage, universal (voting, right of voting, elections), 75, 77–78, 81, 91, 99, 124–125, 169.

Technique (advanced society, technical demands), 25, 109, 116, 127, 145–146, 148–149, 156.
Territory (boundaries), 96, 97, 111, 131, 132, 133, 134, 136, 156.
Texas, 97.
Thirty Years War, 30.
Totalitarian regimes, 82, 164.
Tradition (value of), 43, 44, 45, 46.
Treaty of Westphalia, 30.
Turkey (Turks), 9, 30, 31, 102–103, 109, 111, 113, 114.
Tyranny or denunciation of the nation, 1, 2, 6, 10, 83, 85, 87, 116.

Union, Indian, 113.
United Nations, 21, 55, 62, 108, 156.
United States (America), 8, 11, 19, 30, 40, 41, 42, 47–49, 57, 78, 84, 87, 88, 89, 101, 105, 112, 117, 122, 128, 142, 155, 165.
—and blacks, 8, 19, 48, 75, 105, 122, 126.
—and Chinese, 8, 48.
—and Germans, 31.
—and Hungarians, 48.
—and Irish, 19, 48, 78.
—and Italians, 19, 48, 78.
—and Japanese, 8, 48.
—and Jews, 19, 20, 48.
—and Native Americans, 8, 19, 48, 49, 75, 105.
—and "poor whites," 126.
—and Russians, 48.
—and Scandinavians, 48.
—and WASPs, 48, 104.
Universalism (universal), 8, 11, 35, 53, 73, 74, 75, 91, 96, 125, 129, 149–150, 166.

Vietnam War, 88.
Violence, 27, 116.

Wales, 17, 86, 116, 143.
Walloons, 16, 53, 99, 100, 115, 122, 143.
War, 2, 27, 30, 31, 32, 87–90, 120, 121, 165.
War of 1870, 3, 30, 136, 140.
Wars of the Revolution and the Empire, 30, 31, 84, 89.
Washington, D.C., 114.
Welfare state, 4, 31, 41, 75, 124, 128–129, 159–161, 168.
Will to Power (Machtpolitik), 22, 23, 40, 41, 42, 120.
Working class, 124–126.
World War I, 30, 31, 32, 82, 85, 88, 120, 127, 135.
World War II, 31, 32, 54, 55, 62, 88, 120, 124, 127, 168.
Writing, 96, 114.

Xenophobia, 48.

Yishuv, 56, 62, 78–79, 108.
Yorubas, 17–18.
Yugoslavia, 23, 58, 115, 117.

Zionism, see Jewish Zionists.